Praise for
JESUS REVEALED

"A few years ago, science and art came together to accomplish the task of restoring Michelangelo's frescoes on the ceiling of the Sistine Chapel. Until then, the paintings were priceless treasures, and yet we saw so little of their true value. But as the soot from millions of burning candles over hundreds of years was gently cleared away, the world was astounded to discover just how brilliant Michelangelo's palette really was. What we thought was magnificent paled in comparison to the splendor that was revealed. In similar fashion, Mark Roberts gently, painstakingly clears away the 'soot' of misunderstanding that has darkened our vision of Jesus. He helps us rediscover the depth and brilliance and beauty of the original 'Master-piece.' Like the restoration of the Sistine Chapel, *Jesus Revealed* will make you stop and gaze in wonder at the One you thought you knew so well but have only just begun to really see."

—BUDDY OWENS, vice president of Maranatha! Publishing
and general editor of *The NIV Worship Bible*

"At last! A writer with style and knowledge, who can combine deep theological insight with an ability to make sense to the general reader. Dr. Roberts learned his scholarship from Harvard, but his ability to communicate is clearly a product of a decade in the pulpit. In these days of challenges from the Jesus Seminar and other revisionists, Mark Roberts provides a deep well of refreshment for all believers and a rebuttal to bad scholarship on Jesus. This is a book that could only have been written by a man who is both a seminary professor in New Testament and a beloved pastor."

—HUGH HEWITT, host of the nationally syndicated *Hugh Hewitt Show* and of PBS's *Searching for God in America*.

Mark Roberts wants us to know Jesus more clearly. He succeeds tenderly, thoughtfully, and elegantly. His gifts are uncommon: a scholar's mind, a pastor's heart, and a preacher's sense of the vivid illustration. As I read, I took notes, laughed out loud, and wiped a few tears from my eyes. *Jesus Revealed* is a feast for the soul!

—BEN PATTERSON, chaplain, Westmont College,
Santa Barbara, California

Jesus Revealed is power-packed with in-depth scholarship in very impelling communication, personal application to life today, and sparkling with illuminating illustrations. Here is an authentic, biblically sound, life transforming revelation of Jesus. It will stand the test of time as one of the finest books about Jesus as He wants us to know, love, and serve Him today. This book fed my soul, strengthened my courage, and stimulated my mind.

—DR. LLOYD JOHN OGILVIE, former chaplain, U.S. Senate

Jesus

Revealed

JESUS
REVEALED

KNOW HIM BETTER TO LOVE HIM BETTER

MARK D. ROBERTS

WATERBROOK
PRESS

JESUS REVEALED
PUBLISHED BY WATERBROOK PRESS
2375 Telstar Drive, Suite 160
Colorado Springs, Colorado 80920
A division of Random House, Inc.

The author has made every effort to ensure the truthfulness of the stories and anecdotes in this book. In a few instances, names and identifying details have been changed to protect the privacy of the persons involved.

ISBN 1-57856-539-1

Published in association with Yates & Yates, LLP, Literary Agents, Orange, California.

Library of Congress Cataloging-in-Publication Data
Roberts, Mark D.
    Jesus revealed : know him better to love him better / Mark D. Roberts.—1st ed.
        p. cm.
    Includes bibliographical references.
    ISBN 1-57856-539-1
    1. Jesus Christ—Person and offices.   2. Christian life—Presbyterian authors.   I. Title.

BT203 .R63 2002
232—dc21   2002006173

Printed in the United States of America
2004

10 9 8 7 6 5 4 3 2

To my children,
Nathan and Kara,
whose love for Jesus continues to inspire me.
May you know him more clearly,
love him more dearly,
and follow him more nearly,
day by day.

CONTENTS

ACKNOWLEDGMENTS

I want to thank Ron Lee, my editor at WaterBrook, for his partnership in this project from the beginning. I can't imagine a more helpful and enjoyable relationship between a writer and an editor. I also appreciate the encouragement and direction offered by many new friends at WaterBrook.

I would like to thank my literary agents, Yates and Yates, LLP. The expertise of Sealy and Curtis has allowed me to focus on writing while entrusting the other "stuff" to them.

This book began with a series of sermons preached at Irvine Presbyterian Church. I thank my beloved congregation for their support, encouragement, and helpful feedback. I am especially grateful for my partners in learning who join me in the weekly Pastor's Study. Their insights and questions have contributed significantly to my understanding of Jesus and therefore to this book.

Many thanks to my family for their patience during the production of this book. They put up with my preoccupation and graciously gave me the "space" to write. Their love means the world to me. And their love for Jesus has urged me on in this writing project.

Finally, thanks be to God, who has revealed his love and grace through Jesus Christ. To God be the glory.

PREFACE

Seven hundred years ago, a man living in a small village in southern England offered a simple, heartfelt prayer:

> Thanks be to Thee, my Lord Jesus Christ, for all the benefits
> Thou hast given me, for all the pains and insults which Thou
> hast borne for me. O most merciful Redeemer, Friend, and
> Brother, may I know Thee more clearly, love Thee more
> dearly, follow Thee more nearly, day by day. Amen.

This prayer of St. Richard of Chichester has resonated in the hearts of Christians around the world, echoing throughout the centuries, not to mention in the best-known song from the hit musical *Godspell*.

It's easy to understand the enduring popularity of Richard's prayer. His heartfelt plea expresses our own heart's deepest yearnings. We who believe in Jesus, who confess him as Lord and Savior, ache to know him better, to have an intimate relationship with him each day. Moreover, we sense that clearer knowledge of Jesus will lead us to adore him more fervently and to imitate him more faithfully.

Getting to know Jesus is a lifelong process. I was raised by Christian parents who introduced me to Jesus when I was a toddler. I accepted him into my heart at a Billy Graham crusade when I was just six years old. I grew up attending a marvelous Sunday school, where I learned lasting lessons about Jesus and was encouraged to follow him in my daily life. As a graduate student, my desire to know more about him led me to seek a Ph.D. in New Testament. In the last two decades I have taught about Jesus, both in church and in seminary settings. I have been encouraged by my

Christian communities to grow, not only in academic knowledge about Jesus but also in my personal knowledge of him. In worship services I have been helped to love him. My covenant groups have helped me follow him in the trenches of daily discipleship. I am especially grateful for my brothers and sisters at Irvine Presbyterian Church, who continually encourage me to know Jesus more deeply and to speak of him more truthfully.

The more I study Scripture, the more I am surprised when I discover new facets of our Savior's personality and purpose. I have walked with Jesus for decades, yet I have only now begun to know him. Although much popular and so-called scholarly writing about Jesus is filled with poppycock, I continue to find my own perspectives stretched by people of faith who are also outstanding academics. I am especially grateful in this regard for the writings of N. T. Wright and Ben Witherington.[1]

But far beyond the reading I've done, the greatest influence on my personal relationship with Jesus in the last few years has been my children. Their simple but profound faith has inspired me repeatedly. Their questions about Jesus have challenged me not only to know him more clearly but also to communicate about him more accurately. I have dedicated this book to Nathan and Kara because my greatest desire for them is that they know, love, and follow Jesus throughout their lives.

The Jesus we seek to know more clearly is not simply the leading figure of history, one whom we can understand through the careful study of the New Testament. He is also the living Lord who makes himself known today through his Spirit. If we wish to know Jesus personally, and not simply to accumulate knowledge about him, then we must turn to him regularly in prayer and worship, opening our hearts to new experiences of his truth, his love, and his grace.

I have written this book with St. Richard's prayer as my inspiration. I want to help you know Jesus more clearly, love him more dearly, and follow him more nearly, day by day. If this book advances your relationship with Jesus in any of these dimensions, or in all of them, then my time in writing and yours in reading will have been well spent.

CHAPTER I

JESUS REVEALED

A More Accurate, More Intimate Portrait

Jesus seems to be showing up all over the place these days. In Jakarta, Indonesia, Christians by the hundreds claimed to have seen an apparition of Jesus in the water-stained wall of a house. The owner, who happened to be Muslim, did not object to Christians gathering by the dozens to stare at his home. He was not too fond of their midnight prayer vigils, however.[1]

In Stone Mountain, Georgia, Joyce Simpson prayed for a sign from God concerning her participation in her church's choir. Then she saw Jesus on a billboard for Pizza Hut. There, in the midst of spaghetti hanging from a fork, was an image of the Savior, who apparently wanted Joyce to sing in the choir. Her friends agreed that Jesus was really there, though others identified the apparition as country music legend Willie Nelson.[2]

When María Rubio began frying a tortilla for her husband's burrito, she had no idea that Jesus was about to appear. But when she examined the skillet burns on the tortilla, there he was. In the weeks that followed, more than eight thousand people flocked to María's home in Lake Arthur, New Mexico, in order to see this image of Christ. She even left her door unlocked so pilgrims could come in to see the face when María wasn't at home.[3]

LONGING TO SEE JESUS

When I come across stories like these, I confess that my first response is to chuckle. *People will fall for almost anything these days,* I think to myself. But my laughter misses something sublime in the midst of the ridiculous. Most of those who claim to see Jesus on a wall, a billboard, or a tortilla are not jesters seeking to entertain, but Christians who seriously seek to know Jesus. And whether or not their visions tell us anything about Jesus' methods of revealing himself, they speak volumes about the longing in the hearts of many believers. They yearn to see Jesus.

Even if you aren't inclined to look for the face of Jesus on a burrito, can't you nevertheless relate to the passion of those who do? Don't you long to see Jesus more vividly, to know him more immediately? Don't you wish he would reveal himself to you in a way that would transform your life?

I grew up in a strong Christian family and a Bible-teaching church, coming to faith in Jesus when I was a young boy. Nevertheless, in my adolescent years I struggled with doubt. The things I had believed so easily as a child began to grow more uncertain. Yet I wanted to believe in Jesus with all my heart. In times when doubt seemed to be strangling my faith, I cried out for help. "Lord," I prayed, "please show yourself to me. If I could only just see you, then I'd believe for sure." I don't think I really believed I would receive a personal revelation from Jesus, but in my desperation, that's exactly what I wanted.

I never actually saw Jesus, either in a mystical vision or on a billboard. In time, however, he did make himself known to me in a way that put my doubts to rest. But even to this day, I still wish I could see my Lord with greater clarity. With all my heart I echo the prayer of St. Richard, who sought to know Jesus more clearly so that he might love him more dearly and follow him more nearly. That is my daily prayer as well.

Sometimes I envy the simple faith of my children. When my daughter, Kara, was four years old, she was enthralled with Jesus. As Holy Week approached she wanted to hear the story of his death and resurrection over and over again. On Good Friday she was deeply moved by the fact that "Jesus died on the cross for our sins." She looked forward to Easter with great expectation.

On the Saturday evening before Easter, I offered the blessing for our family dinner. "Dear Jesus, thank you for loving us so much. Thank you…"

All of a sudden Kara interrupted me with an indignant voice. "Daddy," she said, "you can't pray to Jesus!"

"Why not, Kara?" I asked.

"Because he's dead! He died on the cross for our sins! You can't pray to him again until tomorrow."

Admittedly, Kara's theology needed a little work. But how I wish that Jesus were as real to me as he was to my young daughter. After almost four decades of being a Christian, and after devoting a substantial part of my life to studying the biblical account of his life, I still yearn to know Jesus with more depth and intimacy. To be completely honest, if I really believed that he could be seen on a tortilla in New Mexico, I'd probably make the trek to see it. As I look forward to heaven, perhaps more than anything else I long to see the face of Jesus.

Can you relate to this longing? Do you share this desire to know Jesus better? I expect that your answer is yes. So then, what should we do?

JESUS AT THE LOCAL BOOKSTORE

Many people who seek to know Jesus better begin their research at the local bookstore. That seems to be a sensible step because there are plenty of books about Jesus. In fact, no person in history has been the subject of more books.

This profusion of books is a mixed blessing, however. Some will actually help you know Jesus more truly and deeply. But a number of books, especially those that fill the shelves of secular bookstores, will steer you wrong, terribly wrong.

Many books about Jesus promise to provide the "real truth" about him, as if no one had ever discovered it before. Yet what they offer is hardly the truth. It is simply a retelling of a familiar and misleading story. It goes something like this: Once upon a time there was a man named Jesus. He did and said some curious things and was put to death for his behavior. His followers didn't let him rest in peace, however. For some reason, probably having to do with some mystical experiences, these believers started attributing all sorts of nonsense to Jesus. They even concluded that he was God in the flesh. But they were mistaken. Jesus was just a man, an unusual man perhaps, a puzzling man to be sure, but in the end, just a man. He certainly had no intention of saving the world or founding a religion or being thought of as divine. All of this came after he was dead, when he wasn't around to set the record straight.

Sometimes the books that recycle this worn-out theory appear to be the result of serious scholarship. This is especially true of the torrent of manuscripts that have come out of the Jesus Seminar, a group of purportedly objective scholars seeking the unbridled truth about Jesus. But a bit of investigation reveals the unbridled truth about the Jesus Seminar itself. It was formed quite intentionally to debunk orthodox Christian belief. The participants were chosen by a process that guaranteed that the results of their deliberations would match the agenda of the group's founder, Robert Funk. Notice what Funk himself has said about Jesus: "We should give Jesus a demotion. It is no longer credible to think of Jesus as divine. Jesus' divinity goes together with the old theistic way of thinking about God."[4] The Jesus Seminar was formed by a person who rejects what Christians believe about Jesus and who openly admits that he intends to knock Jesus down a few pegs.

The Jesus Seminar assumed as gospel truth an idiosyncratic picture of Jesus, envisioning him as a wandering philosopher who said a bunch of perplexing but relatively innocuous things. Anything in the historical records about Jesus that did not fit this picture was discarded as fictional. Not surprisingly, therefore, their "objective" evaluation ended up matching the seminar's predetermined agenda.[5]

Many of these ideas have passed into popular culture, owing largely to the Jesus Seminar's brilliant manipulation of the news media. These ideas have undermined traditional beliefs about Jesus, causing some Christians to doubt or to lose confidence in Jesus himself.[6] Even clergy are not immune. Last year a pastor from my own denomination made headlines by complaining in a public forum, "What's the big deal about Jesus?"[7] He went on to argue for a spirit-centered Christianity that regards Jesus as one among many ways to God rather than as the unique Savior. Once again Jesus gets a demotion.

It would be tempting for me to take potshots at my fellow pastor. After all, shouldn't members of the clergy have already figured out why Jesus is such a big deal? But upon reflection, I believe this pastor needs to be taken seriously. What *is* the big deal about Jesus, really? I'm sure there are many other Christians, both clergy and laity, who find that Jesus is slipping from the place of honor that he once claimed in their lives. They truly want to figure out what the big deal is so they can revive their faith in him. This book seeks to answer this question from several different perspectives. Any single perspective would allow us to see why Jesus is indeed a big deal. Taken together the eleven perspectives in the following chapters will help us see him as the biggest deal of all.

Jesus in Our Own Image

Most Christians I know reject popular theories that relegate Jesus to a lesser status than that given to him in Scripture. They would never intentionally denigrate Jesus. Yet often without meaning to, they end up demoting him by re-creating Jesus in their own image rather than taking seriously the way he is revealed to us.

This happens when we reshape Jesus to fit our own biases. We say we want to be like Jesus, but in reality we also want him to be like us. We want Jesus to be on our side, to endorse our politics, to affirm our lifestyle. I saw this tendency when I was a teaching fellow for a Harvard College course titled "Jesus and the Moral Life." One of my students, a blue-blooded New England preppy, submitted a final paper with the title "Jesus Was a Gentleman." In twenty pages he argued that the Jesus of history followed the code of behavior found in twentieth-century Brahmin Bostonian society. As he read the Gospels, this student couldn't help but project his values onto Jesus. From his perspective, the man who drove the money-changers out of the temple must have kept on repeating, "I beg your pardon, sir," as he politely escorted them to the door. Of course it's a bit of a stretch to find this in the gospel accounts.

We can chuckle at the obvious bias of my student, but he's not alone. Reverend Norman Vincent Peale, a prominent preacher from the last century, once said, "By no stretch of the imagination would Jesus have been a socialist."[8] Former Soviet leader Mikhail Gorbachev disagreed, observing that "Jesus was the first socialist."[9] Lots of people are positive they know what Jesus would be like if he were to join our current society. An opponent of helmet laws for motorcycle riders is certain that he has Jesus in his corner: "If Jesus Christ were alive today—given his status as, among other things, history's most famous Freedom Fighter—He would not be campaigning for mandatory helmet law legislation."[10] A lover of Christian heavy metal rock music proclaims: "If Jesus were alive today, he'd be a Christian Metal Dude!"[11] And it turns out that Reverend Peale knew what Jesus preferred, not only in politics but in sports as well. He once proclaimed from the pulpit: "If Jesus were alive today, he would be at the Super Bowl."[12] (No doubt he'd have seats on the 50-yard line or else be wearing a rainbow wig and holding up a John 3:16 sign.)

These are laughable examples of something we all do to one extent or another. Each one of us puts Jesus in a safe little box where he can be counted on to endorse our personal preferences. But isn't this habit completely harmless? Not when you realize the damage it causes. On the one hand, when we choose to mold Jesus like a lump of gooey clay, we trivialize him, turning him into just one more political partisan, music fan, or Super Bowl spectator. This is a serious problem for those of us who believe that Jesus is anything but trivial.

At the same time, by making Jesus fit our preconceptions, we obscure who he really was and who he really is today. We miss the point of his life and message, not to mention his death and resurrection. Moreover, if we invent a pseudo-Jesus who happens to be just like us, then we completely miss the opportunity to be transformed by the *real* Jesus, to become more like him and to live the life he designed for us. We won't be able to see him more clearly, to love him more dearly, or to follow him more nearly because he will be obscured by the false images we project upon him. Our personal relationship with Jesus will lapse into stagnation as he assumes an increasingly less important place in our lives.

JESUS REVEALED

How can we evaluate the adequacy of our images of Jesus? How can we know him, not as we imagine him to be, but as he really is? The good news is that we are not left to our own devices when it comes to knowing Jesus. He has been revealed to us in a manner that allows us to know him accurately and intimately.

Jesus is revealed to us, first and foremost, in the pages of the Bible. This statement is true on different levels. On a historical plane, almost everything we know about Jesus comes from the New Testament, especially the four Gospels: Matthew, Mark, Luke, and John. Many other ancient sources provide information about Jesus, but almost all of these use the Gospels as their primary sources. So, without presupposing anything about the New Testament other than that it was written by a variety of Christians who lived in the first century A.D., it would be safe to say that Jesus is revealed to us primarily in the Bible, just as Socrates is revealed to us primarily through the writings of Plato.

But Jesus is also revealed to us through the Bible in another sense. As a Christian I believe the Bible is more than simply a human book. Although written by human beings, it is the Word of God. As Paul wrote to Timothy, "All Scripture is inspired by God and is useful to teach us what is true and to make us realize what is wrong in our lives. It straightens us out and teaches us to do what is right" (2 Timothy 3:16). In particular, the Bible teaches us what is true about Jesus. It reveals him to us not merely as a historical person, but as Lord and Savior. Now, that's a revelation that deserves to be taken seriously, don't you think?

Yet God's timeless revelation comes packaged in writings penned in a certain time of history. If we are to understand these writings, and if we are to understand the Jesus they reveal, then we must work hard to grasp the historical meaning and context of the Bible. We need to place Jesus within his own milieu, within the cultural and religious matrix in which he lived. If we fail to do this, we will inevitably project upon Jesus that which we take for granted in our own life experience, thereby misconstruing the meaning of his life and ministry. We won't know who he really was, not to mention who he is today. Remember, Jesus of Nazareth never ate at McDonald's or read a printed word or wore pants or played baseball or voted in an election or switched on a light. In fact, he never actually heard the name "Jesus"—as we pronounce that name—spoken, because nobody in his world spoke English. *Yeshua,* as he was called by his Aramaic-speaking contemporaries, lived in a world that was radically different from our own, linguistically, socially, politically, economically, and religiously.

This book attempts to locate Jesus accurately in his place in history, to see him as a Jewish man from Galilee who lived in the tumultuous world of the first century A.D. It's essential to our understanding that we characterize the place of Jesus not merely with generalizations that one commonly hears, but with specific examples from ancient, primary sources. These help define Jesus' place within history, which then helps us know him more truly and love him more completely.

What Jesus Was Called

There are different ways to approach the identity of Jesus as it is revealed in Scripture. Most writers present an overview of his earthly ministry and message. This is a valuable strategy, but one that has been done already, many times over.[13] In this book we will take a different path, examining the major names and titles of Jesus found within the New Testament. What did his contemporaries call him? What did he call himself? What did the earliest Christians call him?

You can learn a lot about people from what they are called. If you wanted to learn more about me, for example, you could find out plenty by listening to my various titles. In a given week, I am often called "Mark," "Mauk," "Daddy," "Dad," "Honey," "Sir," "Mr. Roberts," "Pastor Mark," "Reverend," "Dr. Roberts," and "Hey, you!" If you took time to unpack the meanings of these titles, you'd get a pretty good idea of who I am—even in the eyes of the disgruntled motorist shaking his fist at me on the way to work.

So it is with the man from Galilee, the one called Jesus (or Yeshua), Rabbi, Prophet, Holy One of God, Son of Man, Messiah (or Christ), Lord, Savior, Son of God, Word of God, and Light of the World. In the chapters that follow, we will unpack the meaning of each of these titles. Each one presents a vivid portrait of some aspect of Jesus' work and identity.

As a pastor and seminary teacher, I have found that even mature Christians often have a cloudy sense of Jesus' identity. To be sure, they know him as their personal Savior and Lord. They confess that he is the Son of God and the Son of Man. But when I ask, for example, what the title "Son of Man" really means, they often don't have too much to say. Some will connect this title with his humanness, others with his role as a figure in the end times. But almost nobody can explain how Jesus uniquely combined Daniel's vision of the Son of Man with Isaiah's prophecies about the Servant of God to describe himself. Shouldn't believers have a better understanding of the title that Jesus preferred to use for himself? Then, if I ask a believer, "What difference does this make in your life?" I face even more perplexity. Many of us don't see a connection between the names and titles of Jesus and our own life of faith.

I'm convinced that it's essential for all Christians to ask and to answer questions like this one. If we don't, we soon find our relationship with Jesus to be limited, even frustrating, precisely because we know him imprecisely and incompletely. When I eventually explain to people what it means that Jesus was the Son of Man and how this identity might influence their relationship with him, they are usually surprised—surprised to learn what something they have affirmed for years really means, surprised to learn how much it can enrich their Christian life.

Those of us who believe in Jesus, especially those of us who have known him for many years, can easily come to the point where we take him for granted. We can lose our ability to be astounded by Jesus, even slipping into nonchalance or boredom. Sometimes, I fear, we are like a boy I saw last summer in King's Canyon National Park, home of some of the largest sequoia redwoods in the world. As I wandered through the redwood grove, I marveled at the strength and sublimity of God's creation.

Then I saw the boy walking along. He appeared to be about fourteen, and he was utterly transfixed—but not by the redwoods. His attention was riveted to his electronic Game Boy. Throughout the several minutes I observed this young man, he never lifted his eyes to look at the trees, not even once. How could a few pixels on a computer screen compare with the majesty of the giant sequoias? I could just imagine what this boy would say in the car on the way home when his father asked, "So how'd you like the trees?" "Oh, they're just big trees, that's all. But I got a new high score on Tetris!"

Exploring the names of Jesus is something like walking through a grove of giant redwoods. As we wander among his titles, we will encounter some of the most breathtaking truths in all creation, truths worthy of our full attention, not to mention our awe. Let me invite you to put down the

"Game Boys" of your life and marvel at who Jesus is, as if you were seeing him for the very first time.

Meeting the Living Jesus

If we are going to meet Jesus as he is revealed to us throughout Scripture, we need to be diligent in our study of the biblical documents. But this does not mean that the process of getting to know Jesus better is merely academic. In fact, learning more about Jesus through careful Bible study can be one of the most moving and transformational experiences in life. The same Spirit who inspired the New Testament writers speaks to us today through the written Word, helping us encounter the living Jesus.

I had just such an encounter several years ago on the Thursday before Easter. I was preparing my Easter sermon, working hard to produce a homiletical masterpiece. (Easter Sunday for a preacher is like Super Bowl Sunday for an NFL player. I wanted to excel in the "big game.") I decided to read through Matthew's account of Holy Week once again, just to refresh my memory. I'd studied this passage dozens of times, but I felt that an additional reading would make my preaching more vivid. As I meditated on this familiar account of Jesus' sacrifice for us, my professional perspective melted into personal passion. The story of Jesus' crucifixion stunned me as if I had never heard it before. Jesus' struggle in the Garden of Gethsemane jumped off the page and into my heart. In Peter's denial of Jesus I saw myself, remembering times when I had been ashamed of my Lord. When Jesus cried out, "My God, my God, why have you forsaken me?" (Matthew 27:46), I realized that he took upon himself that which *I* deserved. He was crucified not just for humanity, but for *me*.

The same Jesus I had received as my Savior more than thirty years earlier met me once again. I was overwhelmed by the wonder of his love for me, by the gravity of his sacrifice, by the immensity of his grace. I was no longer a preacher trying to prepare the perfect sermon, or a New Testament scholar dissecting an ancient text, or a lifelong Christian hurrying through a familiar passage. I was simply a believer who was meeting Jesus all over again.

What I experienced that spring afternoon as I read the gospel of Matthew is common to Christians throughout the ages. As we read the Bible, the Spirit of God opens our hearts to encounter not merely the Jesus of history, but the living Jesus who wants us to know him intimately. Through the combination of Scripture and Spirit, Jesus is revealed to us in ways both old and new. We affirm again what believers have professed about Jesus for centuries. And at the same time, we encounter the vital Lord who seeks to transform us through his love.

As you read this book, I urge you to open your heart to the living Jesus. Allow him to reveal more of himself to you. May his Spirit help you come to know him more clearly, to love him more dearly, and to follow him more nearly, day by day.

CHAPTER 2

THE CHALLENGE
OF NAMING

Unpacking "Jesus"

Like most parents-to-be, James and Karen spent hours debating what to name their baby. They didn't know the gender, so they needed two names. After considerable discussion they settled on a girl's name but remained undecided about what to call a boy baby. James, a meticulous scientist by profession, was unwilling to settle for anything less than the ideal. He considered the sound of the name, its meaning, and its connection to the family. Still, he couldn't decide.

"If we have a boy," he told Karen, "we'll just have to figure out his name after he's born."

Sure enough, Karen gave birth to a much-adored baby boy. When visitors asked what they'd named him, the parents admitted, "We're not sure yet." The hospital authorities insisted on a name for the birth certificate, but James just wasn't ready. He needed to spend more time with his son before deciding what to call him. State law granted parents up to six weeks to name a child, so James wasn't about to rush this decision. Reluctantly the hospital released the unnamed baby to his parents, who simply called him Baby.

Throughout the next six weeks James searched desperately for the name that would capture his son's personality. Karen had long since given up trying to help. On the last day for legal naming, James came home with a triumphant announcement: "I've got it! His name is Wade."

"His name is *what?*" Karen asked.

"Wade. W-A-D-E."

"Okay," Karen responded, "but why Wade?"

"I don't exactly know," James explained. "It just fits him." In the end, the rational scientist got to know his son, and then he simply went with his gut.

The name "Wade" is a bit unusual but certainly not unheard of. In the year 2000, 491 baby boys in America received the name Wade.[1] In terms of popularity, Wade was the 476th most popular name, coming right after Moses and right before Alan. As a name, Wade stood in good company.

But here's the strangest part of the story. As little Wade grew, his name turned out to fit him like a tailor-made suit. Even Karen agreed that their son was the most Wade-ish boy she'd ever known. His determination, creativity, and friendliness all seemed to fit perfectly a boy named Wade. After all of James's angst, he'd found the ideal name, the name that embodied his son's essence.

THE NAMING OF JESUS

Two thousand years ago, a man named Joseph from the Galilean village of Nazareth didn't have the option of spending weeks figuring out what to name the baby his fiancée was carrying. Even before the child was born, an angel appeared in a dream and told Joseph to name the child Jesus.[2] Actually, the angel used the Aramaic version of Jesus. The angel said in Aramaic, "You are to name him *Yeshua*." Then came the divine rationale: "for he will save his people from their sins" (Matthew 1:21).

You can learn a lot about people from their names, especially when God decides on the name. As we reflect on the Aramaic name Yeshua, we can discover a great deal about the cultural context, the religious background, the God-given purpose, and the perplexing identity of the one who bore this name two thousand years ago.

Looking at Jesus within his Jewish culture will help us understand the man whom God named Yeshua. We tend to hear the name Jesus with sacred overtones, but his neighbors in Nazareth wouldn't have shared that perception. Yeshua was a common name, the Aramaic version of the Hebrew name Joshua. In the year 2000, Joshua was the fourth most popular name for newborn boys in the United States, a trend not unlike that in ancient Galilee. Even as parents today name their children after prominent biblical figures, so it was in the first century. For example, among the high priests who served in the Jerusalem temple during the period of Roman domination, "Yeshua" or "Joshua" was the most common name.[3]

The commonness of Jesus' name reminds us that, in many ways, he was a normal Jewish man. Of course he probably lived under the shadow of his apparently scandalous conception. And without question his divine calling set him apart from his fellow Jews during his last years on earth. But for most of his life Jesus lived like any other Jewish male in a small village in Galilee. He was circumcised when he was eight days old. He learned the Torah from his parents and from the rabbis at the local synagogue. There he joined with his fellow Jews in the Kaddish, a prayer asking that God would "establish his kingdom" within the lifetime of those who were gathered for prayer.[4]

Like other boys, Jesus was apprenticed in his father's trade and practiced it until he was summoned to a more unusual vocation. Although a century after Jesus' death some of his imaginative followers made up stories about his childhood, there is no credible evidence that the boy Jesus actually did things such as stretch a piece of wood that Joseph had cut too short or raise his playmate from the dead.[5] In many ways, Jesus was a profoundly ordinary Jewish man.

In conversation with other believers, when I mention that Jesus was, in many ways, an ordinary Jewish man, I often receive two types of reactions, both of them negative. One objection has to do with Jesus' being Jewish; the other is an opposition to the idea of his being in any way ordinary.

JESUS THE JEWISH MAN

Christians often think of Jesus as being a fellow Christian. But Jesus never attended a church service or read the New Testament. He didn't sing "Jesus Loves Me" or go to Vacation Bible School. Jesus was Jewish by heritage and by upbringing, as were nearly all of the earliest Christians. We can't hope to comprehend his life, message, death, resurrection, and multifaceted identity unless we first take seriously his Jewishness.

The story of Jesus' miraculous feeding of the five thousand helps to make this point.[6] The multitudes had followed him into the wilderness to hear him teach. When they became hungry and had almost no food, Jesus produced enough for all to eat, beginning with only five loaves of bread and two fish. After everyone was stuffed, twelve baskets of extra food were collected. For most of my life, I saw this story as an illustration of Jesus' compassion and as a demonstration of his divine power. But these conclusions, however true, miss much of what those who witnessed this miracle would have discerned.

Those who were fed by Jesus would have recalled a time when God supplied their ancestors with supernatural food in the wilderness. God provided manna to feed the Israelites during their exodus from Egypt.[7] Since the Exodus was the chief Old Testament symbol of God's salvation, Jesus' miracle of multiplying the loaves and fish suggested that God was, once again, saving his people from bondage. Furthermore, the parallel between what God did through Moses and then again through Jesus would have suggested that Jesus was the long-awaited "prophet like Moses" promised in Deuteronomy.[8]

Those who ate their fill of Jesus' bread might have remembered prophecies in which God connected his future salvation with his provision of food for his flock.[9] The Lord, as Israel's Good Shepherd, would someday gather his lost sheep and lead them to lush pastures with abundant food.[10]

Or the multitude might have associated Jesus' miracle with the coming messianic banquet, the lavish feast that would accompany God's salvation of Israel.[11] The Old Testament image of salvation as a rich banquet no doubt made the mouths of first-century Jews water with anticipation. Perhaps Jesus was offering not only food for their stomachs but also food for their souls, the very kingdom of God.

When we remember the Jewishness of Jesus and place his actions within the religious context of his day, we discover that one apparently simple miracle is filled with significance we might easily miss if we neglect his religious heritage.

Jesus the Ordinary Man

The second negative reaction to Jesus as an ordinary Jewish man is this: "Jesus most certainly was not *ordinary!*" Many Christians tend to think of Jesus as extraordinary in every possible way. This view gives us a Jesus who never got sick, who never felt pain, who never got tired or felt lonely or needed time to regroup. In short, the "extraordinary" view clings to an image of a Jesus who never really knew what it means to be human. This Jesus never hit his thumb with a hammer in his father's workshop because his aim was perfect. And if he ever did mash a thumb, it didn't hurt. And if it did hurt, then Jesus must have smiled and joyfully thanked God for the privilege of suffering.

I'm not suggesting that Jesus followed his thumb squashing with profane words. But the truly human Jesus surely made mistakes in his workshop, and when those mistakes flattened his body parts, those parts felt real pain, just as they would one day when they were nailed to the cross.

Those who envision an utterly extraordinary Jesus have lost track of what orthodox Christians have affirmed for two millennia. Instead, they are buying into one of the oldest Christian heresies: *docetism*.[12] Docetists claim that Jesus only *seemed* to be human—he only appeared to suffer and to endure temptation. In point of fact, they argue, Jesus was not subject to human experiences like temptation or pain. In one ancient docetic writing, the real, nonphysical Jesus is actually "glad and laughing" while on the cross. His apparent crucifixion was taken seriously only by the unenlightened, who mistook the physical body for the genuine, immaterial Jesus.[13]

The docetic understanding of Jesus is refuted both in Scripture and in classic Christian confessions. Jesus was in fact fully human.[14] He faced temptation just as we do, only without sinning.[15] On the cross, Jesus felt genuine thirst and indescribable pain.[16] As faithful Christians tried to make sense of Jesus' paradoxical nature as both human and divine, they came to confess that he was both "truly God" and "truly man."[17] Without denying the fullness of his deity, we affirm his full humanity as well.

I must confess that I once embraced a docetic view of Jesus. Though I had a wonderful biblical education as a child, emphasis was always placed on Jesus' extraordinary abilities. His human aspects were never denied, but neither were they explored. We never stopped to consider that the same Jesus who healed the sick and walked on water also wept, felt anger, and struggled to obey God's will.[18] Consequently, although I loved and worshiped Jesus in my youth, I always felt as if he were distant from me and untouched by the struggles I faced. When I wrestled with the challenges that plague boys in their teenage years, it never dawned on me that Jesus went through these same struggles. How could it be that the divine Son of God had acne, felt rejected by friends, or struggled with sexual temptation? My docetic theology had created a barrier between Jesus and me. Consequently, I tended not to share with him the very challenges for which I most needed his help. Since I was too ashamed to share them with other people as well, I felt terribly alone.

My transition from a docetic to a more complete view of Jesus began on an intellectual level as I studied the Bible and classic Christian theology. In the Gospels I began to see a Jesus who was both fully God and fully human. I started to take seriously the fact that the divine Word of God had become human in the person of Jesus.[19] Though my theology was being transformed, my heart lagged behind. I knew in my head that Jesus was a complete human being, that he "understands our weaknesses, for he faced all of the same temptations we do, yet he did not sin" (Hebrews 4:15). Nevertheless, I still felt distant from Jesus when I grappled with my own weaknesses. It has taken many years for me to learn to relate to Jesus as one who "will all our sorrows share" and who "knows our every weakness," to quote from Joseph Scriven's beloved hymn.[20]

Accepting the human ordinariness of Jesus, in addition to his divine uniqueness, helps us discover new intimacy with him. When we suffer with a splitting headache, we realize that Jesus actually knows from his own experience how it feels. When we are tempted to sin, we draw strength from the fact that he knew real temptation and nevertheless overcame it. When we mourn the loss of a loved one, we recognize that Jesus once wept as we do. The impervious Jesus of docetism cannot possibly understand our struggles and sorrows. Only the truly human Jesus of Scripture, who was ordinary in many ways, though extraordinary in many others, can know the pain and difficulty that we face in life. This is a Jesus to whom we can draw near with confidence and eagerness.

THE LANGUAGE OF JESUS

The fact that Jesus' contemporaries called him Yeshua, an Aramaic form of the Hebrew name Joshua, reminds us that he spoke Aramaic as his primary language. This was an ancient Semitic language related to Hebrew much as French is related to Spanish. When the Hebrew Scriptures were read in the synagogues of Galilee, they had to be translated into Aramaic for the benefit of many first-century Jewish listeners. Although the New Testament Gospels were written in Greek, several of Jesus' own Aramaic words were preserved in the Greek manuscripts, words such as *mammon, talitha coum,* and *abba.*[21]

The prevalence of Aramaic throughout the world of Jesus was a nagging reminder of a sad history. Hebrew had been the common language of Israel when it was ruled by God before the time of Saul and later by God's anointed regents. But Jewish rebellion against the Lord led to national domination by foreigners. Aramaic became the official language of Galilee when the Northern Kingdom of Israel fell to the Assyrians in the eighth century B.C. It permeated both north and south, including the Southern Kingdom of Judah, after the Babylonians conquered Jerusalem in 586 B.C. Although Aramaic-speaking Jews in Jesus' day would have taken their language for granted most of the time, they surely would have felt a sense of dislocation when they couldn't understand the weekly synagogue reading of their own Scripture in its original Hebrew. Young Jewish men like Jesus had to study Hebrew as a second language so they could read the Torah and discuss its relevance.[22]

In a subtle way, therefore, the Aramaic name Yeshua represents the captivity of the Jewish people. That Jesus was called Yeshua rather than Joshua is rather like when a divorced woman keeps the last name of her former husband for the sake of her children, even though a part of her chafes at this constant reminder of her failed marriage. Yeshua lived among a subjugated people, people who didn't speak the language in which their God had once revealed his own name. While living within the physical boundaries of the Promised Land, they were not fully at home. The words they spoke—and their yearning hearts—remained in exile.[23]

Yet God had not abandoned his Aramaic-speaking people. He would indeed save them from their bondage through a man whose name was a sign both of their need for deliverance and their special covenant relationship with a God who would someday deliver them.

GOD'S FAITHFULNESS TO HIS COVENANT

In the first chapter of Matthew, the angel told Joseph to name Mary's child "Jesus, for he will save his people from their sins" (verse 21). This is an intentional play on words, since the name Yeshua means "Yahweh is salvation." Jesus' Aramaic name embodies the divine name, Yahweh, the name above all names, the name revealed to Moses at the burning bush, the name that represents God's mercy and love for his covenant people.[24]

Even though Jews in the time of Jesus had been squashed under the thumb of Rome, they still trusted in the hand of Yahweh. They alone among all peoples knew God's special name. They were still the people of his covenant. True, they had dishonored their Lord so thoroughly that they had been overthrown by foreign rulers.[25] But the Jews knew that God hadn't abandoned them forever. They yearned for the day when Yahweh would finally fulfill his promise spoken centuries earlier by Jeremiah:

> "The day will come," says Yahweh, "when I will make a new
> covenant with the people of Israel and Judah. This covenant
> will not be like the one I made with their ancestors when I took
> them by the hand and brought them out of the land of Egypt.
> They broke that covenant, though I loved them as a husband
> loves his wife," says Yahweh.
>
> "But this is the new covenant I will make with the people
> of Israel on that day," says Yahweh. "I will put my laws in their
> minds, and I will write them on their hearts. I will be their
> God, and they will be my people. And they will not need to
> teach their neighbors, nor will they need to teach their family,
> saying, 'You should know Yahweh.' For everyone, from the least
> to the greatest, will already know me," says Yahweh. "And I will
> forgive their wickedness and will never again remember their
> sins." (31:31-34)[26]

Yahweh had not forgotten his covenant people. At just the right time, he would forgive the sins that led to their exile, make a new covenant with them, and reestablish his rule over them. The name Yeshua symbolized Israel's faith in Yahweh and their hope for his future salvation. Ironically, this name that came packaged in the Aramaic language of the Exile served as a vivid reminder of God's faithfulness. The God of Yeshua would never forget his people, even as a nursing mother cannot forget her own beloved child.[27]

THE FULL MEANING OF SALVATION

Prophetic passages such as Jeremiah 31:31-34 no doubt echoed in Joseph's mind when he heard the angel say, "[Y]ou are to name him Jesus, for he will save his people from their sins" (Matthew 1:21). Even before Jesus was born, God had made known the destiny of his Son. The baby born in Bethlehem would save his people from their sins.

When we Christians hear this promise, we immediately think of our own personal salvation, the salvation from sin and eternal death that Jesus earned for us by his death and resurrection. Our response is borne out in Scripture but remains incomplete. It misses the most immediate sense of the angel's revelation to Joseph. Before we explore the truth that Jesus died to save us from sin and its sorry implications,[28] it's important to grasp what the angel was saying. What did Joseph understand when he heard the promise that Jesus "will save his people from their sins"?

The fact that the angel's statement is not, on the most obvious level, about personal salvation can be seen in the wording of the statement itself. The angel said Jesus would save not everybody, not the Gentiles, not sinners, not even individual Jews, but "his people" from their sins. The salvation promised through Jesus was directed first at the covenant people of Yahweh, the nation of Israel. The fact that Gentiles would ultimately be included within God's covenant people was known to the Lord, of course, but it's not revealed here. The angel says that Jesus came to save "his people" first and foremost.

And what would this salvation entail? If you had asked Joseph after he awoke from his dream, he would have given the same answer that any faithful first-century Jew in Galilee would have offered. When the Lord saves his people, he will forgive the sins of the nation of Israel that led to bondage to foreign rulers. He will gather his people scattered throughout the world. He will renew his covenant with them. He will rebuild the nation of Israel and will once again rule over his people as their God.[29]

If this notion of corporate, national salvation sounds foreign to us, it's because we are twenty-first-century Christians, not first-century Jews. Throughout the writings of the Hebrew prophets, salvation is regularly associated with forgiveness of national sins and restoration of God's kingdom. The promise of an afterlife in God's presence, safe from the fires of hell, is a minor theme in the Jewish symphony of salvation. The major theme, accompanied with blaring trumpets and joyful singing, is national deliverance and blessing under God's gracious rule.[30]

We have already examined the passage from Jeremiah 31 in which God promised a new covenant and the forgiveness of sins. Now let's look at some of the verses from that chapter that establish the context for this promise:

> "In that day," says the LORD, "I will be the God of all the families of Israel, and they will be my people. I will care for the survivors as they travel through the wilderness. I will again come to give rest to the people of Israel."
>
> Long ago the LORD said to Israel: "I have loved you, my people, with an everlasting love. With unfailing love I have drawn you to myself. *I will rebuild you,* my virgin Israel. You will again be happy and dance merrily with tambourines....
>
> Now this is what the LORD says: "Sing with joy for Israel! Shout for the greatest of nations! Shout out with praise and joy: *'Save your people, O LORD, the remnant of Israel!'* For I will bring them from the north and from the distant corners of the earth.

I will not forget the blind and lame, the expectant mothers and women about to give birth. A great company will return! Tears of joy will stream down their faces, and I will lead them home with great care. They will walk beside quiet streams and not stumble. For I am Israel's father, and Ephraim is my oldest child." (verses 1-4,7-9, emphasis added)

In this same context, God promised to forgive Israel's sins. The divine forgiveness of Jeremiah 31, therefore, relates not to the heavenly salvation of individual Jews but to the gathering of God's exiled people and the restoration of divine rule in Israel. According to Joseph's angelic revelation, God's gathering and restoration will happen through Jesus.[31]

When the angel promised Joseph that Jesus would save his people from their sins, he meant that Jesus was coming to fulfill the deepest hopes of the Jewish people. Beginning with his earthly ministry and culminating in the future at a time known only to God, Jesus was going to accomplish that which Jeremiah and the rest of the prophets had promised hundreds of years earlier. Whatever his impact on human existence in the afterlife, Jesus was coming to change forever the nature of human life on earth, beginning with God's covenant people.

Let me repeat that I'm not denying that Jesus died for the sins we commit as individuals. On the cross he paid the price for our personal sins, a fact for which I am eternally grateful. But I *am* suggesting that his death—not to mention his life—was part of a divine plan that was much broader than most of us imagine, even as that plan was much broader than most Jews in the first century imagined. Today we tend to overlook the earthly dimension of salvation for the oppressed nation of Israel, while first-century Jews usually overlooked their need to be saved from their personal sins. It's important for us to recognize that God was indeed acting through Jesus to address the expressed yearnings of the Jewish people. But, as we'll see later, God also was up to something far deeper, far wider, far more inclusive, and far more magnificent: the salvation of all humankind from sin and the restoration of his universal kingdom.

THE SURPRISE OF JESUS

As I read the gospel account of Joseph's encounter with the angel, I try to stand in his shoes or, perhaps more accurately, to sleep in his pajamas. When I do I am overwhelmed with surprise. Consider Joseph's multiple surprises. Initially, there was the unhappy shock of Mary's pregnancy. Then there was the unexpected angelic visitation. And then the angel's news— such news! Mary had *not* been unfaithful to Joseph but was pregnant by the very power of God's Spirit. Her child would save his people from their sins. God wanted Joseph to redirect his life in a dramatic fashion by scuttling his plans to break his engagement to Mary and proceeding with the marriage. By implication he would become the earthly father of the national savior. Now, that's a prodigious collection of emotional bombshells, don't you think?

Right from the start Joseph's experience of Jesus was filled with surprises. I am convinced that ours will be also, if we have an open, genuine, growing relationship with him. Of course there's the initial amazement of grace, the surprise that comes when we realize that Jesus died for us when we were not only sinners but God's enemies.[32] But as we live in fellowship with Jesus, we can expect a life full of surprises.

If you're a relatively new Christian, what I've just said probably makes perfect sense. But if you've known Jesus for years, even decades, you may not be convinced. Perhaps your heart yearns to be surprised by Jesus, but your experience doesn't match your yearning. Maybe, if you're really honest, you've even become a little bored with Jesus. He feels rather like an old slipper, comfortable, familiar, but hardly astonishing. "Is it possible," you may wonder, "to be surprised by someone I've known for so long, someone I seem to know so well?" Yes, I believe that it is possible, and not only possible but essential, and not only essential but delightful.

You may have had the experience of learning something startling about someone you thought you knew fairly well. This happened to me fifteen years ago.

I knew my father very well. He and I spent countless hours together during my childhood, playing Candy Land on the living room floor when I was small, pulling weeds in the garden, and watching the UCLA basketball team decimate its foes. When my adolescence put some distance between us, my dad and I still managed to remain on friendly terms. During the last years of his life, the fact that my father had terminal cancer provoked both of us to open our hearts more fully to each other. On the day of his death, I knew my father better than I ever had before.

Even in his last months, when he became more communicative, my father was not what you would call chatty. I was the one who talked too much in school, who made speeches, and who pursued a vocation that involved speaking to groups of people. My dad, on the other hand, was an unusually attentive listener, but a reticent speaker. Only once had I seen him address a large group at church, and then I spent most of the time cringing because I imagined how uncomfortable he must have felt. So you can imagine my surprise when, at my father's memorial service, his friends from work described him as outgoing, talkative, always quick with a joke or a word of encouragement.

My shock was compounded as my family and I began to sort through my father's belongings. Tucked away in his dresser, next to his collection of Cross pens, was a stack of certificates, prizes for public speaking! Dumbfounded, I asked my mother if she knew anything about these awards. She explained that during the last few years of his life, my father had joined Toastmasters International, a group devoted to public speaking. Even she, however, was not aware that he had won so many prizes for his oratory.

I was astounded. My dad, the one who seemed to have a hard time getting the words out, was a decorated public speaker. The man I thought I knew so well turned out to have interests and abilities I'd never imagined.

As I came to know my father more completely, I was thoroughly surprised and delighted.

That's how it is when we come to know Jesus more completely. Even those who know him very well find that there's always much more to learn, and the learning process brings plenty of surprises. Some of these discoveries will delight us, while others will force us to let go of cherished but false images in order to make room for Jesus as he really is. Surprise is not the main point, of course, but an emotion that accompanies the life-transforming process of getting to know Jesus more truly and completely.

I'll have to wait for heaven before I can hear my dad using his significant oratorical skills. I wish I'd been aware of his Toastmasters awards before he died so I could have congratulated him. I wish I'd known more of my dad in this life. Similarly, I want to know more about Jesus before I finally meet him face to face. The good news for us is that, through careful study of God's written Word, Jesus will indeed be revealed to us more clearly. As this happens, we will be surprised not only by the Jesus of history but also by the living Jesus who meets us right where we are.

As you read this book, you may be surprised to learn the true historical meaning behind titles you've applied to Jesus for years. You may even be startled to realize that what you thought a certain title meant is not what Scripture actually teaches. You may be shocked to discover new things about a Friend you thought you knew so well, but who far exceeds your expectations of him. You may be astonished to experience how the multi-faceted identity of Jesus alters your relationship with him today. I hope and pray that you will be surprised and delighted by the joy of a deeper relationship with the living Jesus as you come to know more accurately who he is.

CHAPTER 3

THE PARADIGM-
SHATTERING TEACHER

Jesus the Rabbi

The expression "paradigm shift" has become ensconced in popular culture. Whenever a business leader or a psychological guru or a politician thinks we need to change the way we think about something, we're told we need a "paradigm shift."

When I was in college this was *the* hot phrase. In class after class we debated the relevance of "paradigm shift" to everything from physics to English literature. The book that gave birth to the expression, Thomas Kuhn's *The Structure of Scientific Revolutions,* was assigned in more of my classes than any other textbook.[1] My fellow students and I dissected Kuhn's writing like medical students left alone with a cadaver. We cited lots of authorities to prove that our own interpretations were definitive. For all of our efforts, however, I'm not sure we ever agreed on a truly authoritative reading of Kuhn's text. Nobody could say for certain what a paradigm shift really was.

In my junior year of college, something changed all of this. Kuhn, who at the time was a professor at Princeton, showed up for dinner in my dormitory. After years of wondering what he really meant by "paradigm shift," I found myself sitting next to the man himself. Here was the trump card for my arguments, none other than the world's leading authority on the authoritative meaning of "paradigm shift."

When I asked Dr. Kuhn what this disputed phrase meant, he didn't cite other authorities. He didn't even refer to his book. He simply told me, in fairly straightforward language, what a paradigm shift was. That was that. I had the authoritative interpretation, right from the horse's mouth, if you will.

A "paradigm shift," according to Kuhn, is a major change in theory, behavior, and worldview. It occurs in science and in other domains of life when experiments or experiences don't fit the existing or "normal" paradigm. At first, a conceptual "crisis" occurs, but out of this crisis a new paradigm emerges, one that better accords with reality. This whole process Kuhn calls a "revolution."

Not only did Thomas Kuhn coin the phrase "paradigm shift," but he also created one. His work profoundly altered the way we understand science in particular and human experience in general. The concept of "paradigm shift" helps us to better understand the ministry of Jesus even as it provides a way to examine our own image of Jesus.

Almost all of us, I believe, need a paradigm shift in our knowledge of Jesus. We have in our minds an image of Jesus that, though derived partly from the Bible, doesn't adequately fit the sum total of biblical evidence. Have you ever had the experience of reading a gospel story about Jesus and finding yourself terribly uncomfortable with what Jesus is doing or saying? I have. It's common to most Christians. When this happens we often tend to ignore that which offends us because it doesn't fit our existing paradigm of Jesus. Or maybe we attempt to make the story fit our paradigm, even though we end up twisting it out of shape in the process. If we really seek to know not the Jesus of our own creation but the Jesus of history and Scripture, then we must accept the fact that our own paradigms are insufficient and begin the search for a more adequate paradigm.

This isn't always a pleasant experience, believe me. In writing this book I have been confronted with Jesus in a way that has sometimes been quite unsettling. I have wrestled with certain biblical texts as never before. In the process I found that my own paradigm of Jesus needed a major overhaul, if not a complete shift. It would have been far easier and less painful to reject what didn't fit my existing paradigm and remain satisfied with what felt so familiar. But that's not the kind of relationship I want with Jesus. Moreover, rejecting the parts of Jesus' ministry that don't suit my fancy would be completely contrary to his role as my Rabbi.

JESUS THE UNUSUAL RABBI

If you find your paradigm to be inadequate when you take a closer look at Jesus, don't worry. You're not alone. Jesus has been exploding paradigms ever since he first ministered in the hills and along the seashore of Galilee. Two thousand years ago he caused a revolution centered in a paradigm shift. His revolution was not scientific, political, or even religious in the narrow sense. Rather, the revolution of Jesus had to do with God and his presence among us. It all began when the Rabbi from Nazareth started acting in a way that didn't fit the common rabbinic paradigm of his day.

Jesus entered the synagogues and taught from the Law and the Prophets, but in doing so he forced his contemporaries to completely rethink what it meant for someone to be a teacher of God's truth. From a distance Jesus appeared to be just one more Jewish rabbi, a teacher worthy of respect and admiration. Yet upon closer inspection, it became clear that his unexpected approach threatened the reigning paradigm of normal Jewish pedagogy. The oddness of Jesus led to a crisis, a crisis that demanded a paradigm shift in the hearts of those who chose to acknowledge him as their teacher, their mentor, their rabbi.

To understand how Jesus forced a paradigm shift, you must first know something about the "normal" rabbi in the early first century A.D. The word *rabbi* was a term of respect used for lay religious teachers and others worthy of high regard. Literally it meant "great one." The use of "rabbi" as a title for a Jewish clergyman came years later. When people referred to Jesus as Rabbi, as they often did, they weren't calling him anything like "Reverend," but something more akin to "Master" or "Teacher" or "Chief."[2]

Jesus had much in common with other teaching rabbis in his day. Like them, he was not a priest—a person who had to be a direct descendant of Moses' brother Aaron—but a layperson. Like other rabbis Jesus used the local gathering places, called synagogues, as principal settings for his instructional efforts. Like his peers he expected his students to live in close proximity to him, learning both his message and his way of life. These disciples were expected to believe his teaching, obey his commands, and imitate his example. Like other rabbis Jesus spoke about God and about how the covenant people should live in relationship to the Almighty. He was conversant in the oral traditions of Jewish religion and was an expert in the Hebrew Bible. But despite his qualifications as a first-century rabbi, the similarities between Jesus and a typical rabbi of his day actually help accentuate his uniqueness.

Jesus Taught with Unexpected Authority

While Jesus shared many common rabbinic traits, he never hesitated to reject the practices of other teachers. Ordinary rabbis expended great effort in passing on the traditions of earlier sages. They believed that God had revealed two kinds of law to Moses on Mount Sinai, the written Law, inscribed in the first five books of the Hebrew Bible, and the oral law, which had not been written down. This oral law, apart from which one could not correctly interpret the written Law, had supposedly been passed down from Moses to Joshua to the elders and prophets and on down to the first-century rabbis.[3] A teacher's top priority was to preserve and to pass along the oral tradition, being sure to cite past authorities in the process. So, for example, when he taught, a rabbi would say:

Joshua ben Perachiah and Nittai the Arbelite received the tradition from the rabbis before them. Joshua ben Perachiah said, "Procure for yourself a rabbi, and acquire for yourself a fellow learner, and judge all people in the scale of merit."[4]

The hearers would receive not only the oral tradition but also the sources of the tradition as it had been passed down. A teacher who quoted Rabbi Joshua was to be believed not on the basis of his own wisdom, nor because Rabbi Joshua was wise, but because they both stood in the chain of tradition that extended back to Moses, and therefore to God himself.

The oral tradition concerned itself with far more than rightly understanding the major topics of the written Law. Sometimes the content of rabbinic teaching focused on the miniscule details of ceremonial observance. For example, when considering how much water a man needed to make his hands ceremonially clean, Jewish teachers said:

If one poured cleansing water over only one of his hands with one rinsing, his hand becomes clean; but if he poured water over both his hands with an amount suitable for one hand only, Rabbi Meir declares his hands to be unclean, unless he poured over them at least a half-cup. If a portion of the offering for the priest fell into the water after a man had poured a half-cup of water in a single rinsing over his hands, it remains clean. Rabbi Jose declares it unclean.[5]

This portion of rabbinic teaching cites the earlier rabbis, even showing disagreement among them. The detail provided in this interpretation allowed those who applied the oral tradition correctly to feel confident of their ceremonial cleanliness and thus their acceptability to God.

Jesus never taught like this, however. With his departure from the oral tradition and any reliance on the interpretations of earlier rabbis, Jesus introduced a paradigm shift. He spoke with an authority that was independent of all other teachers. He did not base his teaching upon a daisy chain that linked him to Moses. Rather, Jesus spoke simply and confidently. He didn't bother with the "what-ifs" so common among other Jewish teachers. Nor did he document his sources with oral footnotes. No wonder that the people who heard him "were amazed at his teaching, for he taught as one who had real authority—quite unlike the teachers of religious law" (Mark 1:22). If for years you had heard teachers drone on about the precise amount of water needed to cleanse your hands, you'd sit up and take notice of one who announced, "The time is fulfilled, and the kingdom of God has come near; repent, and believe in the good news" (Mark 1:15, NRSV).

The direct and confident authority of Jesus reminds me of my encounter long ago with Thomas Kuhn. When talking about what he meant by "paradigm shift," Kuhn didn't have to cite sources because the authoritative interpretation was his to make. He taught with authority, not as the teachers in contemporary academia. Likewise, when teaching about the kingdom of God, Jesus didn't have to cite human sources because he spoke with the very authority of God. Thus Jesus the Rabbi taught in a completely anomalous way, much to the delight of the crowds and the chagrin of competing rabbis.

Jesus Chose His Own Disciples

Another common rabbinic practice rejected by Jesus had to do with the process by which teachers gained disciples. Remember the instruction cited earlier, given by Rabbi Joshua ben Perachiah: "Procure for yourself a rabbi." Similarly, Rabbi Gamaliel, the mentor of the apostle Paul, once said, "Provide yourself a teacher, and relieve yourself of doubt, and accustom yourself not to tithe by guesswork."[6] Rabbi Joshua and Rabbi Gamaliel agreed that it was the duty of the disciple to find a teacher. This was common practice in the time of Jesus among both Jews and Gentiles throughout the Roman world. If you wanted to be taught by some famous philosopher, you asked to become one of his students.

Jesus reversed the order completely. Rather than waiting to be approached by potential disciples, he sought them out. "Come, be my disciples," he beckoned to a couple of Galilean fishermen, "and I will show you how to fish for people" (Mark 1:17). Even though his invitation did not fit the established rabbinic paradigm, the two men "left their nets at once and went with him" (Mark 1:18). Notice carefully: They left their nets immediately. So compelling was Jesus' authority that people chose straightaway to change their lives completely in order to be his disciples. From that moment onward the disciples would live with Jesus, sharing in his teaching, his homelessness, his persecution, and his ministry of the kingdom of God.[7] Nothing would ever be the same again.

Without a doubt, Jesus was a paradigm misfit. The imminence of God's kingdom propelled him to seek out those disciples whom God had destined for divine purposes. Those who received the call of Jesus confronted a watershed choice: either dismiss him as some strange rabbi who just couldn't get it right, or embrace an altogether new paradigm of how God was raising up disciples for the kingdom. Some chose to leave everything and follow him. Many others clung to the security of their familiar paradigms, declining the call of Jesus, the anomalous rabbi.[8]

RESPONDING TO JESUS THE RABBI

So, then, how should we respond to Jesus the Rabbi? What should we do with one who teaches with divine authority and who doesn't wait for us to approach him, but who summons us to follow him right now?

Even as Jesus rattled first-century paradigms, so he disturbs those in the twenty-first century. The very activities that startled the contemporaries of Jesus should shock us as well. If we pay close attention, if we take him seriously, we will find ourselves in a position very much like that of those two Galilean fishermen. We can respond positively to the compelling authority of Jesus, adopt a radically different paradigm for life, and embark upon a journey from which we can never return home unchanged. Or we can decide to say "no thank you" and go about our business as usual. What we cannot do, if we take Jesus the Rabbi on his own terms, is make him conform to our own values and the norms of our culture. We cannot say "yes" to Jesus, yet continue to live more or less as we were living prior to our encounter with him.

In the context of twenty-first-century Western culture, Jesus confronts our paradigms in three significant ways. He challenges our belief about religious choice; he confounds our understanding of vocation; and he confronts our assumptions about authority. If we shift from the accepted paradigms to embrace the way of Jesus the Rabbi, we will experience a radical change in our lives in each of these areas.

The New Paradigm of Choice

Americans prize religious freedom, and rightly so. It's one of the great blessings of living in the United States. The fact that our government doesn't dictate our religious belief allows us to choose what we will believe and how we wish to express our faith.

Given our political context, it's easy for American Christians to assume that religious freedom applies also to our relationship with God. According to our paradigm of religion, we who believe in God do so because we have freely chosen this path. After having some spiritual experiences and examining the biblical data, we chose to believe in Jesus, and that's that.

But then we must consider the call of Jesus, who summons us to follow him today even as he once called several Galilean fishermen. Jesus' initiative in choosing his first disciples illustrates God's choice of us, upsetting our paradigm of personal religious choice. We don't choose so much as we are chosen. Consider the implications of New Testament passages such as this one:

> Long ago, even before he made the world, God loved us and
> chose us in Christ to be holy and without fault in his eyes. His
> unchanging plan has always been to adopt us into his own
> family by bringing us to himself through Jesus Christ. And
> this gave him great pleasure. (Ephesians 1:4-5)

Though many aspects of God's choice and our response remain a mystery, this much is clear: If you are a Christian, then you have been chosen and called by God, just as the disciples of Jesus were chosen and called by him. You have been selected for relationship with God and for partnership in the work of his kingdom. Of course, as a Christian, you have chosen to say yes to the divine call, but the "first chooser" was God himself.

Christians respond in various ways to the idea that God's choice of us takes precedence over our choice of him. Those who are particularly fond of the American ideal of religious freedom sometimes recoil at the thought. It is humbling, after all, to realize that our relationship with God depends more on him than it does on us. In our own self-reliant way, we'd much prefer to take responsibility for it. Other Christians worry that emphasizing God's choice in the matter turns us into mere puppets. Although this might appear to be true on the surface, it fails to do justice to the full balance of biblical teaching. Though God chose us before the foundation of the world, we are still responsible for our decision to respond to his call.

The fact that you and I have been called to be disciples of Christ can be both humbling and honoring. I'm reminded of an experience I had in my third year of graduate school. I received a call from Harvey Cox, the most famous (some would say infamous) professor at Harvard Divinity School. As a doctoral student at Harvard, I knew about Professor Cox but had never met him. I couldn't fathom why he was calling me.

"Mark," he began, "I've heard many positive things about you, and I have a job I'd like you to do."

So far so good, I thought, though I couldn't imagine how he'd heard anything about me, positive or negative.

"I'm planning to teach a new course next year. I'm calling it 'Jesus and the Moral Life.' I want to examine the historical records about Jesus and then consider various ways Jesus informs ethical choices today. I would like you to be my head teaching fellow. You would help me design the course. You could share in the lecturing, if you wish. You would also lead discussion sections for the students. Are you interested?"

Of course I was—and much more than merely interested. I was honored that Professor Cox had asked me, and I was thrilled by the chance to teach a subject so dear to my heart. When I hung up the phone, my heart was soaring.

Sometimes I wish Jesus would call us on the phone. Imagine how it would feel to hear him say, "I have chosen you to be one of my disciples—to spend time with me and to share in my work. Are you willing?" It would be the greatest thrill in life, a watershed moment after which we'd never be the same. Unfortunately, Jesus doesn't call us on the phone. But he does call us to be his disciples through the Holy Spirit. This call is just as real, just as exciting, and just as transformational. Jesus the Rabbi wants you to be one of his disciples. How will you respond to his call?

The Call to a Radical New Vision

Jesus called Simon and Andrew to leave behind their vocation as fishermen and to become "fishers of men" instead (Mark 1:17, KJV). Choosing to follow Jesus meant a complete change of life, including career, location, and lifestyle.

Jesus still calls some people to leave their careers and to follow him into a completely different line of work. Consider the case of my friend Paul, a man who had a very profitable high-tech career until he heard the call of Jesus to become a church planter in South Africa. Or take the example of Jan, a member of my church who has been a kindergarten teacher for twenty-five years. She recently heard the call of Jesus to leave the security of her career for a challenging new ministry caring for victims of sexual abuse. Her positive response to this call led her to move to another state. Even as Jesus once did on the shores of the Sea of Galilee, he still calls men and women to leave everything behind in order to follow him.

Most of us, however, won't receive a summons to abandon our work, our homes, and our friends. Rather, Jesus calls us to be his disciples right where we live and work. We follow our Rabbi not by adopting a radically different career, but by adopting a radically different perspective on our current career. We realize that we are working not simply to make money or to be successful, but for the sake of God's kingdom. God seeks to permeate our workplaces with his presence, using us as the means of his infiltration.

My friend Jack was a professor of business administration at a major university. He believed that God had placed him there for the primary purpose of sharing the good news of Jesus with students, faculty, and staff of the university. Dozens of people came to believe in Jesus as a result of Jack's effort.

Then there's the case of Jon and Jennifer, a couple of archetypal entrepreneurs. Using lots of creativity and hard work, they've built their business from a tiny operation that began in their garage to a major company that occupies 200,000 square feet and employs more than three hundred people.

Yet, unlike most American start-ups, Jon and Jennifer's company is, more than anything else, a tool of God's kingdom. They reject the common separation of the secular from the sacred as they offer their business to the Lord each day in prayer. They seek God's will for their professional endeavors just as they seek it for their family life. Moreover, they employ Christian values in the workplace and use their financial blessings to advance the work of Christ. Not only are they actively involved in church work, but they also have invested their time and their treasure to see the kingdom of God make an impact on China. During a Christmas vacation, Jon and Jennifer, along with their two daughters, traveled to China to open a new orphanage. On Christmas Eve, they welcomed dozens of abandoned children into a new home. For those Chinese orphans, there was finally room at the inn.

If you have put your faith in Jesus, then be assured that he has chosen you to be his disciple. Your discipleship might take you across the globe. More likely, it will leave you where you are geographically but give you a radically new vision for why you are there. Your mission, should you choose to accept it, is to proclaim, to demonstrate, and to extend God's kingdom in the place where God has placed you. That's part of what it means to be a disciple of Rabbi Jesus.

The Sole Authority

If you're old enough to remember the slogan "Question Authority," you know that originally it had a countercultural meaning. It was an audacious call to buck the power structure, but now the phrase just seems quaint. We don't have to question authority anymore because we don't have a singular authority to question. Our postmodern world is filled with lots of opinions and suggestions, but few real authorities. Or to look at it another way, each of us has become our own authority.

Take dieting, for example. If you go to your local bookstore, you'll find dozens of books that promise to help you lose weight. Each book purports to be written by an authority. Yet when you look inside, you find that all of these books disagree on the best way to lose weight. Some tell you to cut down on fat. Others claim that you actually need fat in your diet if you want to lose weight. Some authorities prefer high-carb diets. Others urge you to severely limit your intake of carbohydrates. And so it goes.

Then there's the case of pets and children and allergies. Popular wisdom used to affirm the benefit of having pets at home. But then the medical experts spoke. Pets, they claimed, exposed children to unacceptable levels of dirt, dust, and animal hair. Having pets increased the incidence of allergies and asthma. Parents were urged to get rid of their dogs and cats and to keep their houses exceptionally clean. Now the experts have spoken again. Recent studies found that "kids exposed to animals seemed to be better off" when it came to lowering their chances of developing allergies and asthma. The latest theory holds that "Americans grow up too clean, that a lack of environmental contaminants means immune systems over-react when they encounter allergy-inducing substances."[9] Go figure!

With so many competing authorities, we come to the point where we trust none. We consider claims to speak with authority as either honest mistakes or cynical efforts to manipulate us. The only authority you ought to trust, contemporary culture tells you, is yourself. You must be the measure of all things. This is the common paradigm of authority in our day.

This individualistic paradigm pervades American religious sentiments as well. Throughout most of the world and most of human history, religious doctrines and values have been passed on through religious communities. But even this practice has been rejected in our day. In a survey, 80 percent of Americans agreed that "an individual should arrive at his or her own religious beliefs independent of any churches or synagogues."[10] Not only do we claim the right to choose what we believe, but we also want to make that choice in a vacuum, without influence from recognized religious leaders and communities.

So then, what ought we to do with Jesus the Rabbi who teaches with the very authority of God? Jesus did not say, nor does he say today, "Hey, I've got some nifty ideas here. Maybe you'll want to borrow a few of them as you formulate your worldview." Rather, he proclaims the kingdom of God and calls for a total response, a response both of belief and of action.[11] Saying yes to Jesus requires giving up our self-centered paradigm of authority and shifting our trust to him as our ultimate authority, even when we'd rather not.

Everyone who attempts to follow Jesus soon confronts the uncomfortable challenge of his authority. When someone has hurt me and I want to wallow in unforgiveness, I stumble over the words of Jesus: "If you forgive those who sin against you, your heavenly Father will forgive you. But if you refuse to forgive others, your Father will not forgive your sins" (Matthew 6:14-15). In my hurt I must decide who is the chief authority in my life. In situations like this, choosing to respect Jesus as my Rabbi doesn't come easily, I must confess.

Several years ago a young woman I'll call Jill came to my office in search of pastoral counseling. Although she was a member of another church, she felt too ashamed to share her struggle with her own pastor. She was newly married to a fine Christian man. Just about everything in their relationship was wonderful, with one giant exception: Her husband had no interest in sexual intimacy, and he didn't seem to know why. This was devastating to Jill, who couldn't help but take it as personal rejection. She was angry with God for playing what seemed to be a dirty trick on her. She had tried so hard to honor his directives for sexual purity and had not been sexually intimate with a man before marriage. Then, after years of hopeful anticipation, her sexual relationship with her husband was nonexistent, and Jill was deeply hurt.

As a biblically informed Christian, Jill knew that God intended her bond with her husband to be indissoluble.[12] She came to me not so much for direction as for moral support and prayer. During the next several years, Jill and her husband struggled with what seemed at times to be an unsolvable problem. They sought counseling together. They argued. They forgave. They wept together. Yet healing came very slowly, if at all. Jill began to fear that she might go through life not only without sexual intimacy but without children. Her anger and hurt became compounded by fear.

Many advisors in Jill's life told her to get out of the marriage. At times she was sorely tempted. But she clung to Jesus and to his teaching about marriage. When most other authorities said, "Get divorced and get on with your life," Jill embraced Jesus as her sole authority. When her heart was broken with hurt, she sought to forgive her husband, not because she wanted to, but because Jesus instructed her to.

Throughout several painful years, Jill followed Jesus without any assurance that her marriage would be mended. In time her prayers began to be answered. Her husband opened his heart to Jill and to the Lord. His deep-seated fears of sexual intimacy began to be healed. Slowly, tenderly, Jill's marriage was brought to wholeness. Today, she and her husband are blessed not only with children but with a rock-solid relationship built on the foundation of Jesus' authority. Jill's submission to Jesus the Rabbi proved to be right, not only in principle but also in the results it produced.

We may not always enjoy the fruits of our submission this side of heaven, as Jill did, but if we call Jesus our Rabbi, then we ought to submit to him no matter what.

The Joy of Submitting

The whole idea of submitting to authority can sound harsh, even dehumanizing. Surely there are times when it isn't fun to respond to authority, like when you see those dreaded flashing lights in your rearview mirror and realize that you're about to encounter a police officer who, no doubt, will exercise authority that will affect both your pride and your bank account. Of course there are times when people in power abuse their authority to the detriment of their underlings. But there are many situations when following a rightful authority is quite pleasant and leads to a delightful result.

When I was in high school I joined the track team. Among the events in which I had marginal success was the high jump. When I first began trying to clear the bar, I could manage only about five feet, not nearly enough to score points for my team. But over time I improved enough to help the team, eventually clearing six feet. My modest success could not be attributed primarily to natural ability or even to hard work. Rather, the main reason was that I was very well coached. My regular coach was wise, to be sure. But every now and then a recent graduate of my high school dropped by to offer his advice. He'd watch me make some pathetic attempt to clear the bar and then would say something like, "Mark, why don't you move your rear marker about six inches back and try again?" How did I respond to his advice? With gratitude and eagerness! Why? Because my walk-on coach was Dwight Stones, the American recordholder in the high jump at that time, who, for several years, was the best high jumper in the world. I was more than happy to let Dwight be the absolute authority over my high jumping because he knew what he was talking about. He had proven it beyond any doubt. Moreover, I knew he wanted to help me excel in the sport.

To accept Jesus as our ultimate authority does not turn us into mindless robots who can't help but obey. Rather, we seek his direction as we make thousands upon thousands of choices throughout our lives. Jesus is not like the boss who micromanages every aspect of an employee's performance. Instead, he lays out the broad principles of God's kingdom, allowing us to apply those principles in the nitty-gritty details of daily life. To help us in the process of moral discernment, God provides additional guidance through Scripture, through the Holy Spirit, and through the community of disciples.

I accepted the authority of Dwight Stones because he deserved it. How much more ought we to accept the authority of Jesus! As we'll see, Jesus is not merely an authoritative rabbi but the one through whom life itself came into being. Jesus is the very embodiment of divine truth. There could be no better authority on how to live than the one who created life and who wants us to experience the fullness of life, both now and forever.[13]

In a very practical way, accepting Jesus as your Rabbi will involve a paradigm shift in the way you live each day. As you awake your first thought will be, *Lord, what would you like to teach me today? How can I serve you? How can I take part in the ministry of your kingdom?* Then, dozens of times throughout the day, you'll offer yourself to Jesus. You'll offer him your opportunities and challenges, your desires and fears. It will become a top priority for you to study the teaching of Jesus as it is embodied in the whole of Scripture.

Over the years, seeking and following Jesus' guidance will become more intuitive, more familiar, and more delightful. You'll realize that Jesus has always wanted the best for you and that his guidance is unsurpassed. You'll know that the popular paradigm of unbridled self-reliance is filled with flaws, and you'll shift your trust to Jesus the Rabbi. More than anything else in life, you'll want to follow him, to obey his Word. In the process you'll discover the truth of the Rabbi's statement that the words he spoke are intended for us to experience the fullness of joy.[14]

May you know the daily joy of following the Teacher who speaks not as the rabbis do, but with full, absolute, flawless, and gracious authority.

CHAPTER 4

MESSENGER OF THE KINGDOM OF GOD

Jesus the Prophet

In the days when Rome dominated Judea, a Jewish man named Jesus arrived in Jerusalem during a major feast. Entering the sacred temple, he began to announce God's judgment upon Jerusalem, suggesting even that the temple itself would soon be destroyed. This prophet's boldness antagonized the Jewish leaders, who tried to silence this troublesome voice. In desperation they brought him before the Roman governor, who had Jesus flogged and then attempted to interrogate him. But the prophet remained strangely silent.

You might think that you know this story, but you probably don't. I'm not referring to Jesus of Nazareth here, but to Jesus the son of Ananias. This Jesus prophesied in Jerusalem around thirty years after the Jesus we know, beginning in A.D. 62. His story appears in the writings of the first-century Jewish historian Josephus, an invaluable source of information about Judaism in the time of Jesus.[1]

When I first read the story of Jesus, son of Ananias, I was astounded. I had spent many years studying the New Testament in its historical context, but I never ran into this figure until I was doing research for this book. When I read this story, I was struck once again by the richness of the world of Jesus of Nazareth and how knowledge of that world helps us understand who he really was.

If you're like me you get excited when you discover new things that help you see Jesus more clearly. Our pulses quicken with both the joy of discovery and the potential implications of what we have found. In this chapter we'll examine some of the most significant data for understanding Jesus. The ideas surrounding Jesus the Prophet demand and deserve considerable effort. You may even want to have your Bible close at hand so you can check my references and read them in context. I promise that whatever you invest in seeking to know Jesus better will be returned to you tenfold. This isn't a credit to my writing, but to the one about whom I am writing.

THE PROPHET FROM NAZARETH

The historian Josephus chronicled the failed careers of numerous self-proclaimed prophets in the first century A.D. These men frequently appeared in Judea, promising that God was about to do something momentous. The popular prophets tapped a gusher of hope in the hearts of the Jewish people, hope that Roman rule would soon be banished and God's kingdom restored. But many prophets failed the biblical test of a true prophet because historical events did not fulfill their hopeful words.[2]

Jesus of Nazareth certainly looked and sounded like one of the Jewish prophets of his era. According to the Gospels, that's exactly how many of his contemporaries viewed him—as a prophet.[3] When Jesus miraculously produced food for the crowds, they didn't respond excitedly with "Hey, here's a free lunch!" but with "Surely, he is the Prophet we have been expecting!" (John 6:14). The multitude that celebrated Jesus' triumphal entry into Jerusalem identified him as "the prophet from Nazareth in Galilee" (Matthew 21:11).

Some of the people, however, recognized that Jesus stood apart from the ordinary strain of Hebrew prophets. They knew him to be the special prophet promised in the Old Testament. To them, Jesus represented the new Elijah, the one whom Malachi had predicted would prepare Israel for the long-awaited coming of the Lord.[4] Others saw Jesus as a prophet like Moses, one who spoke with God face to face and did amazing wonders, just as Moses had done.[5] Some of these people even wanted to force Jesus to become their king, but he declined.[6] While each of these interpretations granted Jesus high honor, none of them constituted a complete understanding of his prophetic role.

Jesus did accept the designation of prophet, at least implicitly.[7] Some of his closest followers regarded him as a prophet.[8] They did so for good reason, because in manifold ways the ministry and message of Jesus were continuous with the Old Testament prophets. Like Elijah, Isaiah, Jeremiah, and the rest, Jesus delivered God's Word with authority.[9]

Like his Old Testament archetypes, Jesus communicated his message both through words and symbolic actions.[10] Like the prophets before him, Jesus backed up his words with mighty works, such as controlling the weather, healing the sick, and raising the dead.[11] The similarities between Jesus and the Hebrew prophets supported his claim that he had come not to abolish their words but to fulfill them.[12]

The message Jesus preached also resounded with prophetic language and themes. Even as the prophets spoke of the future, so did Jesus.[13] But prophesying entailed far more than making predictions. It was proclaiming God's word, God's will, and God's call. Like the prophets of old, Jesus challenged the people of Israel to repent, to turn from their sinful ways, and to live according to God's rule and righteousness.[14] Moreover, like the Old Testament prophets, Jesus emphasized the kingdom of God.[15]

GOD'S COMING KINGDOM

In various ways, Israel had always professed God's kingdom. Isaiah, for example, announced that "the LORD is our judge, our lawgiver, and our king. He will care for us and save us" (Isaiah 33:22). Through Malachi, God stated bluntly, "I am a great king…and my name is feared among the nations!" (Malachi 1:14). The celebration of God's kingship also is found in the psalms that guided Jewish worship. Take Psalm 145, for example:

> All of your works will thank you, LORD,
>> and your faithful followers will bless you.
> They will talk together about the glory of your kingdom;
>> they will celebrate examples of your power.
> They will tell about your mighty deeds
>> and about the majesty and glory of your reign.
> For your kingdom is an everlasting kingdom.
>> You rule generation after generation. (verses 10-13)

These confident affirmations of God's glorious kingdom stood in stark contrast to Jewish experience, however. If God was king, why were the people of God subject to centuries of foreign domination? If God's kingdom was everlasting, why were the Jews ruled by the kingdoms of Assyria, Babylon, Persia, Macedonia, Egypt, Seleucia, and Rome? The answer from the leading prophets was incisive but chilling. Israel had rebelled against the Lord so ferociously and consistently that he gave them over to foreign rulers, just as he had promised when he established his covenant with them in the time of Moses.[16] Although God remained king over all the earth,[17] his people languished under pagan dictators as a direct result of their sin. Rather than living together in God's realm, they were scattered throughout the world.

Through the Old Testament prophets, however, God promised that one day he would save his people, gathering them from the many places they had been dispersed, rebuilding their nation, and reestablishing his kingdom over them:

> Sing, O daughter of Zion; shout aloud, O Israel! Be glad and
> rejoice with all your heart, O daughter of Jerusalem! For the

LORD will remove his hand of judgment and will disperse the armies of your enemy. *And the LORD himself, the King of Israel, will live among you!... "He is a mighty savior.* He will rejoice over you with great gladness. With his love, he will calm all your fears. He will exult over you by singing a happy song." (Zephaniah 3:14-17, emphasis added)

To this stirring promise the Lord himself added a personal word:

> I will gather you who mourn for the appointed festivals; you will be disgraced no more. And I will deal severely with all who have oppressed you. *I will save the weak and helpless ones; I will bring together those who were chased away.* I will give glory and renown to my former exiles, who have been mocked and shamed. *On that day I will gather you together and bring you home again.* (Zephaniah 3:18-20, emphasis added)

When God returns to reign over Israel, it will be a day of rejoicing, a demonstration to the whole world of God's saving power:

> How beautiful on the mountains are the feet of those who bring *good news of peace and salvation, the news that the God of Israel reigns!* The watchmen shout and sing with joy, for before their very eyes they see *the LORD bringing his people home to Jerusalem.* Let the ruins of Jerusalem break into joyful song, for the LORD has comforted his people. He has redeemed Jerusalem. The LORD will demonstrate his holy power before the eyes of all the nations. *The ends of the earth will see the salvation of our God.* (Isaiah 52:7-10, emphasis added)[18]

It isn't hard to imagine how the hearts of first-century Jews must have been stirred by these promises. Every Roman battalion, every burdensome tax, and every coin bearing Caesar's image served as a reminder of Jewish captivity and fueled their longing for the restoration of God's kingdom. If the prophets were to be believed, the day would come when Israel would finally throw off the yoke of her oppressors.

We find pervasive evidence of this longing throughout first-century Jewish life. Some activists expressed their yearning for God's kingdom by leading armed revolts against Rome. Inevitably they surrendered, giving up their armies, their nationalistic hopes, and usually their lives. Josephus relates the story of one self-proclaimed prophet, an unnamed Jewish man from Egypt. He promised to lead an armed rebellion against the Roman garrison in Jerusalem, beginning with what he believed would be the miraculous demolition of the city walls. Thirty thousand people followed this insurrectionist to the Mount of Olives outside the city, where they experienced not the tumbling of the Jerusalem walls but an ambush by Roman troops. Many followers of the Egyptian were killed, while he escaped into a life of safe obscurity.[19]

Experiences like this one kept most Jews from outright defiance of Rome until the fateful years of A.D. 66–70, when the Jewish people dared to wage war against their far superior opponent. Their valiant effort ended, predictably, with the slaughter of thousands, the destruction of Jerusalem, and the obliteration of the temple. Prior to the Jewish War, those Jews who were careful enough to avoid antagonizing the Romans nonetheless yearned for God's kingdom. Weekly synagogue services in the time of Jesus included the following prayer: "May God establish his kingdom in your lifetime and in your days and in the lifetime of all the house of Israel, even speedily and at a near time."[20]

Similarly, every faithful Jew prayed the Eighteen Benedictions over and over again. Two of these benedictions stated:

> Blow the great horn for our liberation, and lift a banner to
> gather our exiles. Blessed art Thou, O Lord, who gatherest the
> dispersed of Thy people Israel!

Restore our judges as at the first, and our counselors at the
beginning; and reign Thou over us, Thou alone. Blessed art
Thou, O Lord, who lovest judgment![21]

The prophetic promises of God's coming kingdom sprang from the lips
and beat in the hearts of Jews in the time of Jesus. It comes as no surprise,
therefore, that his preaching created quite a stir.

Before we examine the prophetic dimensions of Jesus' ministry, we
should pause for a moment to put ourselves in the shoes of his Jewish contemporaries. It's so easy to read about their yearning for the kingdom without letting it touch our hearts. We get the point but miss the passion.

I have never personally known anything like what the first-century Jews
felt, but I have seen something like it. I think back to the massive demonstrations that preceded the end of Communist domination of Eastern
Europe. Throughout East Germany, Hungary, and Czechoslovakia, hundreds of thousands of people gathered to protest and to pray, their hearts
and lips crying out for freedom. Before long the governments that had
oppressed them fell beneath the power of the corporate will of the people.

I will never forget the outpouring of joy when Germans destroyed the
Berlin Wall, which had for so long divided their leading city, their nation,
and their hearts. With tears streaming down their faces, they took apart
that wall bit by bit. Their joyful abandon helped me grasp, if only in part,
what their yearning for freedom must have been like during decades of
Communist oppression.

As we consider the prophetic ministry of Jesus, perhaps these images
will keep our hearts and our minds open to the incredible good news of
God's salvation that Jesus proclaimed and enacted.

The Prophet of God's Kingdom

Like the Old Testament prophets, Jesus focused his message on the coming
of God's earthly reign: "The time is fulfilled, and the kingdom of God

has come near; repent, and believe in the good news" (Mark 1:15, NRSV). When we hear this announcement against the backdrop of Jewish hope, it's easy to understand why Jesus drew such crowds. They would have understood him as saying that the time foretold by the prophets had arrived and that the kingdom of God was near, probably to be experienced within their own lifetime. In their view God would soon throw the Romans out of the Promised Land, gather his scattered people, and rule over reunited Israel once again through a human king from David's lineage. With these expectations in mind, they hailed Jesus as a prophet of the kingdom.

But what did Jesus mean when he spoke of the kingdom of God? The answer is not as simple as it seems. Perhaps nothing in the teaching of Jesus has been more consistently misunderstood than his proclamation of the kingdom. Therefore, as I attempt to explain what Jesus meant, I will also note what he did *not* mean. If we want to know Jesus, we must understand his proclamation of the kingdom of God.

Gordon Fee, professor of New Testament studies at Regent College, said, "You cannot know anything about Jesus, anything, if you miss the kingdom of God.... You are zero on Jesus if you don't understand this term. I'm sorry to say it that strongly, but this is the great failure of evangelical Christianity. We have had Jesus without the kingdom of God, and therefore have literally done Jesus in."[22] Since we don't want to be "zero on Jesus," we must focus our minds on discovering the meaning of the kingdom of God.

In broadest terms the kingdom of God is God's reign over creation, especially the earth.[23] It is God's sovereignty, God's authority, God's dominion. When Jesus proclaimed, "The Kingdom of God is near!" (Mark 1:15), he meant that God's power was at hand and that God was beginning to assert his rule on earth in a new way. As the King who was exercising his rightful authority, God would reign over individuals and families, religious traditions and social mores, demonic powers and political institutions. The Lord would establish his righteousness and justice, aligning all things according to his rule.

The Kingdom Is More than Internal

Some people have limited Jesus' promise of the kingdom to an offer of internal communion with God. This view has been popular among liberal Protestants in the last two centuries and among New Agers in the last two decades. It resonates with the assumption that religion is, after all, simply a matter of the heart.

But limiting the kingdom of God to internal experience completely misses the breadth of Jesus' vision of the kingdom. When Jews in the first century, including Jesus himself, prayed for God's kingdom to come, they were seeking a major change in the world, not just in their hearts. They were asking for a new social, political, and economic order that would be part and parcel of their new experience of God.[24]

The mistaken equation of the kingdom with internal experience alone is often based on something Jesus said to the Pharisees. In response to their question about when the kingdom would come, Jesus answered,

> The kingdom of God does not come with your careful obser-
> vation, nor will people say, "Here it is," or "There it is," because
> the kingdom of God is *within you.* (Luke 17:20-21, NIV,
> emphasis added)

When we pay close attention to this statement, however, we find that the reference to the kingdom being "within you" is a misleading translation. The original Greek of this passage should be translated "the kingdom of God is *among* you."[25] Jesus was not telling the Pharisees, those whom he often accused of resisting God, that the kingdom of God was actually hidden somewhere in their hearts. Instead, he was saying, "The kingdom of God is in your midst right now—because I am here." Jesus was implying that in his words and deeds, the reign of God had already invaded the earth. To be sure, it would touch the human spirit, so that one who began to live in God's kingdom would have inner communion with the King. But the kingdom of God would also transform human institutions, cultures, nations, and, ultimately, the whole creation.[26]

The Kingdom Is More than Heaven

The earthly dimension of the kingdom of God does not, of course, limit God's sovereignty to terra firma. God rules over earth and heaven.[27] But the kingdom of God is not what many Christians call "heaven." Jesus' announcement, "The kingdom of God is near," didn't mean "You can now go to heaven after you die." This common but mistaken paraphrase is fueled by the fact that the New Testament sometimes uses the phrase "kingdom of heaven" (literally, the "kingdom of the heavens") rather than "kingdom of God."[28] This phrase does not, however, locate the kingdom of God in the sky or limit it to some postmortem reality. Rather, "the kingdom of the heavens" was a common Jewish figure of speech that referred reverently to God, much as my grandmother used to exclaim "Good heavens!" rather than "Good God!" Furthermore, when Jesus told Pontius Pilate that "my Kingdom is not of this world," he was not denying its earthly dimension, but its earthly origin.[29] Literally, Jesus said, "My kingdom is not *from* this world" (John 18:36, NRSV, emphasis added). His authority came not from anything on earth, but from God alone.

Perhaps the clearest indication we have of the earthly relevance of God's kingdom comes from the prayer of Jesus that we call the Lord's Prayer. Jesus taught his followers to pray, "Thy kingdom come, Thy will be done *in earth,* as it is in heaven" (Matthew 6:10, KJV, emphasis added). Here Jesus employs a common poetic or liturgical form, where one phrase is parallel to and expanded by the next. "Thy kingdom come" is elaborated by "Thy will be done in earth, as it is in heaven." When God's kingdom comes, therefore, it will be experienced on earth as in heaven. The will of God will reign over human affairs as it now rules over heavenly matters.

The Kingdom Is "Already, but Not Yet"

This apparently straightforward petition from the Lord's Prayer raises the irksome question of the timetable for God's kingdom. We ask for his kingdom to come, but will it come soon or in some distant future? Is the kingdom of God a present or a future reality—or somehow both at once?

At times Christians have used the language of the kingdom to refer only to the age to come. Though the kingdom of God has a decidedly future dimension, we must not limit it to the future. Throughout his ministry, Jesus proclaimed the kingdom as both a future and a present reality. Some of his sayings appear to support the equation of the kingdom of God with a future reign. For example, at the last meal before his death, Jesus said: "I solemnly declare that I will not drink wine again until that day when I drink it new in the Kingdom of God" (Mark 14:25).[30] But Jesus also spoke of the kingdom as something to be experienced in the present: "[I]f I am casting out demons by the power of God, then the Kingdom of God has arrived among you" (Luke 11:20). The core of Jesus' message was the good news that the kingdom of God had drawn near.[31] In some sense, it was already present in the villages and on the hillsides of Galilee where Jesus taught, ministered, and performed miracles. Yet in another sense, it was still coming. Theologians describe this paradox by speaking of the kingdom as being "already, but not yet."

This notion of "already, but not yetness" seems odd at first, but it is actually quite common in our experience. When my wife and I were expecting our first baby, we were thrilled. We had waited a long time to get pregnant, and the imminent birth of our first child filled our lives. We found out the baby's sex and chose to name him Nathan. We decorated his room and filled it with the required paraphernalia. We took classes on how to feed, bathe, and diaper a baby. In many ways, Linda and I were already acting and feeling like parents. But we weren't quite there yet. We were "already, but not yet parents," living in the reality of the future while still awaiting it.

Our experience was similar to that of the early followers of Jesus, who experienced the presence of the kingdom of God in many ways, in works of power and words of love. As Jesus taught, the kingdom was already present, but not yet fully present. There was still much more to come.

Jesus often used parables to announce and to illustrate the kingdom of God. One of these parables helps to explain the present and future dimensions of God's reign.

Jesus asked, "How can I describe the Kingdom of God? What story should I use to illustrate it? It is like a tiny mustard seed. Though this is one of the smallest of seeds, it grows to become one of the largest of plants, with long branches where birds can come and find shelter." (Mark 4:30-32)

In the ministry of Jesus, the kingdom of God had truly arrived, but only as an apparently insignificant seed. It was not yet the all-encompassing, world-transforming kingdom promised by the prophets.[32] In due time, the fullness of the kingdom would come, even as a tiny mustard seed becomes an impressive plant. But during the earthly life of Jesus, the kingdom had only begun to show its final shape and could be easily overlooked by those who were expecting a fully grown mustard bush from the outset.

EVIDENCE FOR THE KINGDOM

We have seen that the kingdom of God is God's reign upon the earth. It is not limited to the internal realm of your heart or to the spiritual realm of life after death. It is something that comes in the future, and yet it is present in the moment wherever Jesus is present. If you find the intricacies of Jesus' preaching of the kingdom a bit puzzling, you're not alone. Even John the Baptist, who had so confidently prepared the way for Jesus' ministry, began to have doubts about whether Jesus was the one who was bringing the kingdom of God. At one point he sent his disciples to ask Jesus, "Are you the one who was to come, or should we expect someone else?" (Matthew 11:3, NIV). John, like so many of his fellow Jews, had been expecting the kingdom of God to look like an impressive mustard plant, not just a tiny seed.

Jesus' response to John's disciples is illuminating. He told them to report to John what they had observed: "[T]he blind see, the lame walk, the lepers are cured, the deaf hear, the dead are raised to life, and the Good News is being preached to the poor" (Matthew 11:5). Jesus was saying, "Look at what God is doing through me, and you'll know that the kingdom of God is at hand."

Jesus' mighty works were an essential aspect of his kingdom proclamation. If he had announced the reign of God without compelling demonstrations, the crowds would have quickly dismissed him as one more false prophet. Yet because he performed works of power, they linked him with the prophets of old, who backed up and symbolized their words with wondrous deeds. Moreover, the healings Jesus performed also fulfilled prophetic promises concerning what would happen when God came to save Israel. Isaiah had long ago prophesied:

> Say to those who are afraid, "Be strong, and do not fear, for
> your God is coming to destroy your enemies. He is coming to
> save you." And when he comes, he will open the eyes of the
> blind and unstop the ears of the deaf. The lame will leap like
> a deer, and those who cannot speak will shout and sing!
> (Isaiah 35:4-6)[33]

How similar this is to what Jesus passed along to John the Baptist: "[T]he blind see, the lame walk, the lepers are cured, the deaf hear..." (Matthew 11:5). In Jesus, God had come to save his people. His kingdom had arrived and could be experienced in healings and other works of power.

POLITICS OF THE KINGDOM

One of Jesus' mighty works involved feeding thousands of people from one sack lunch. When the crowd had finished eating the food mysteriously produced by Jesus, they exclaimed, "Surely, he is the Prophet we have been expecting!" (John 6:14). Then they began to take what they considered to be the next logical step and to crown Jesus as their king. He declined the coronation and took off into the hills for some solitude.[34]

This story illustrates something we might easily overlook: the inseparable connection in the minds of first-century Jews between the kingdom of God and earthly politics. When Jesus fed the multitudes, not only did they enjoy a free lunch as beneficiaries of God's power, but they also assumed that this power should take political forms. Because Jesus worked wonders, he was not just the long-awaited prophet. He was also the one through whom God's kingdom would be reestablished in Israel. Given so many prophetic passages that spoke of God's coming reign in plainly political terms, not to mention Jewish prayers that sought divine government in Jerusalem, Jews in the day of Jesus simply assumed that the kingdom of God would be a political one.[35] It would involve kicking the Romans out of the land and reconstituting the government of Israel under the rule of God and, perhaps, his anointed king.

But Jesus refused to be identified as Israel's new earthly king. When the crowds hailed him with palm branches on his triumphal entry into Jerusalem, they expected him to expunge Roman rule from the holy city. Yet he upset their apple cart by assaulting not the Antonian Fortress with its Roman soldiers, but the sacred temple with its vendors who supported the sacrificial system. The fact that the crowds in Jerusalem went from celebrating Jesus' arrival in the city to calling for his crucifixion in only four days probably reflects their disappointment over his failure to inaugurate the political kingdom they were anticipating.

Though Jesus proclaimed the kingdom of God, at times he seemed to accept Roman rule with puzzling equanimity.[36] Moreover, he called his compatriots to reject armed rebellion, to turn the other cheek, and to love their enemies rather than to attack them.[37] He warned that those who used the sword to oppose Rome would be killed by Roman swords.[38] Jesus' refusal to link the kingdom of God with violent revolution must have frustrated and confused those who placed their hopes in him. He seemed oddly tolerant of their enemy.

THE ENEMY OF THE KINGDOM

First-century Jews had a clearly defined enemy: Rome, with its onerous taxation, military domination, and pagan religion. So why was Jesus so tolerant of this godless imperial force? His refusal to attack this enemy rested not simply on his commitment to turning the other cheek,[39] but on his identification of the true enemy of the kingdom of God, an opponent much bigger than the Roman Empire.

Jesus' very first mighty work in the gospel of Mark unmasks his true opponent. One day, as he was teaching in a synagogue in the Galilean town of Capernaum, he was rudely interrupted by a man with an evil spirit: "Why are you bothering us, Jesus of Nazareth? Have you come to destroy us?" (Mark 1:24). Ordering the demon to be silent, Jesus promptly commanded the spirit to leave the man. Jesus' action revealed that the evil spirit had been correct. Jesus had come to destroy him and his evil cohort.[40] The kingdom of God was at war with the kingdom of evil, the kingdom of Satan.

Stories like this one appear frequently throughout the Gospels. Even Jesus' opponents admitted that he cast out demons, though they accused him of doing so by the authority of Satan.[41] Jesus denied their accusation, connecting his exorcisms with the kingdom of God: "[I]f I am casting out demons by the power of God, then the Kingdom of God has arrived among you" (Luke 11:20). The ministry of Jesus demonstrated that God's kingdom did indeed have an enemy, Satan and his minions.[42] Jesus expelled demons as a demonstration of the presence and the dominant power of the reign of God. As with his other mighty works, in casting out demons, Jesus enacted what he preached.

As I write this chapter, America is still reeling from the terrorist attacks on the World Trade Center and the Pentagon. In response, our military is bombing Afghanistan as a first step to eradicating the master terrorist, Osama bin Laden. Two months ago, the average American had never heard of this man. Now he is hated and feared by almost every American. It's not uncommon for him to be called an "evildoer" or even "the evil one."

Though we surely recognize the evil of terrorism, as followers of Jesus we must remember that human enemies are not the ultimate enemy. The ministry of Jesus illustrates the principle articulated by Paul in one of his letters:

> For we are not fighting against people made of flesh and
> blood, but against the evil rulers and authorities of the unseen
> world, against those mighty powers of darkness who rule this
> world, and against wicked spirits in the heavenly realms.
> (Ephesians 6:12)

So, though we rightly confront the human dimension of evil, we are not fooled into reducing evil to human activity alone. Even if the world's military powers were to find a way to rid the planet of terrorism, evil would not suddenly disappear. Injustice, poverty, child abuse, materialism, pride, and a host of other evils would still thrive. Thus, we who follow Jesus will seek to confront evil, not just in its most obvious forms, but in every form it takes. Moreover, we will wage our war on evil not primarily with military might or human cleverness, but with the power of God, which alone defeats evil. We will be people of prayer, truth, and the good news of God's kingdom inaugurated in Jesus.

FROM SELF-RULE TO THE RULE OF GOD

How do we as Christians, living almost two thousand years after Jesus preached the kingdom of God, respond to his message? How should we react to the Prophet who proclaimed that God's power had invaded the earth and who backed up his proclamation with mighty works?

Jesus called for a distinct response from all who heard his message: "[T]he kingdom of God has come near; *repent, and believe in the good news*" (Mark 1:15, NRSV, emphasis added). Those who heard the prophetic words of Jesus were to believe them, to accept the good news that God's kingdom had drawn near. But intellectual affirmation wasn't enough. Jesus also demanded repentance. He called for a complete change of mind, heart, and life. Repentance was not merely feeling sorry for one's sins and trying to do better next time. Jesus expected a total reconfiguration of one's life based upon the good news that God had begun to reign.[43] Repentance involved turning away from everything that competed with God's authority and devoting oneself completely to God as King.

Although we find ourselves in quite a different place from that of Jesus' first audience, his call to repentance hits us squarely between the eyes. Even those of us who have been following Jesus for years need to go deeper in the lifelong process of turning from our own agendas and submitting to the supreme agenda of God. We need to believe the good news that God has begun to reign through Jesus, and we need to live accordingly in every facet of our lives. We need to turn away from our godlessness and to turn toward God as our King, to adopt a radically different way of life in which we "seek first the kingdom of God and his righteousness" (Matthew 6:33, author's paraphrase).

What does true repentance look like? If we took seriously the call of Jesus, what difference would it make in our lives? The story of the encounter between Jesus and Zacchaeus provides a vivid illustration. Zacchaeus was a rich Jewish tax collector and therefore a traitor to his people. Up until his encounter with Jesus, Zacchaeus had profited from his collusion with the Romans. Zacchaeus, you might say, was serving the kingdoms of Rome and materialism. But when Jesus came to town, the short tax collector climbed a tree so he could spy upon this famous Prophet. When Jesus noticed the man in the tree, he invited himself to Zacchaeus's home for dinner. Right there on the spot, Zacchaeus repented, promising to give half of his wealth to the poor and to pay back four times the amount of taxes he had overcharged. In dramatic fashion this man's heart had been transformed by his encounter with Jesus, and not just his heart, but his way of living, especially his business practices. Jesus commented, "Salvation has come to this home today" (Luke 19:9). He might well have said, "This man has repented and come to believe the good news. He is now seeking first the kingdom of God and his righteousness."

May I ask you a couple of personal questions? What kingdoms vie for your submission? What kingdoms do you seek even more than you seek the kingdom of God? We all struggle with competing kingdoms, those institutions or values or worldviews that order our lives and shape our hearts. Perhaps you serve the kingdom of success, striving first to accomplish your chosen career goals and to attain suitable recognition. Perhaps you've been lured by the kingdom of materialism, devoting your time and talent to accumulating stuff. Maybe your kingdom revolves around your children and your commitment to their achievement and advancement. Maybe your primary kingdom is religiosity or alcohol or drugs or music or sexual gratification or self-expression or security. What do you seek first of all? What is your number one kingdom?

As Jesus preached two thousand years ago, so he says to us today: "The kingdom of God is at hand. Repent and believe this good news" (Mark 1:15, author's paraphrase). He invites you to turn from all opposing kingdoms and to seek God's reign above all. He urges you to live in a radically different way from the world around you, to be transformed in mind, heart, and lifestyle.

One of the most well-known modern examples of repentance is Charles Colson. As a hatchet man for President Richard Nixon, Colson was infamous for his ruthlessness and his disregard for ethics. He once said that he would trample his own grandmother to get Nixon elected. But Colson cut too many corners, including legal ones. Caught in the web of Watergate, he ended up pleading guilty and serving time in prison.

But, as he so often does, Jesus used a time of suffering to eternal advantage. Inspired by the simple testimony of a friend, Chuck Colson began to consider the claim of Jesus upon his life. Finally he accepted the good news and committed his life to Jesus. During his stint in prison, Colson was upheld by his faith and by the support of his new Christian family. But prison presented not merely a challenge to be endured but also a vocation to be embraced. God used Colson's experience behind bars to call him to a new focus for his life, ministering to people in prison and to their families. One of the country's most notorious sinners became one of the kingdom's most faithful servants. Moreover, God has used Colson to speak prophetically to our nation through his speaking and writing, not to mention his example of personal integrity and Christian commitment.[44]

Notice that Chuck Colson's repentance included far more than feeling sorry for his sins and making a private confession of faith in Jesus. It was a profound turning away from his former way of life and turning to God and the lifestyle of the kingdom.

Moreover, the case of Chuck Colson illustrates a necessary implication of our repentance. As we leave our sinful ways behind and begin to seek first the kingdom of God, we become spokespersons for the kingdom. Jesus enlists us as his colleagues in his prophetic mission. We are called to proclaim the good news of God's kingdom and to do the works of the kingdom so that people around us might also believe the good news and turn their lives around.

Throughout the world, Christians are announcing and enacting the kingdom of God. This happens in word and deed when we feed the hungry or set up tutoring programs for inner-city children. Around the globe today, followers of Jesus are bringing the message of the kingdom to the sick, who are being healed by the same power with which Jesus once cured lepers and opened blind eyes.

I have watched with gratitude when members of my church have turned away from the materialism that infects our culture and begin to invest in the ministry of the kingdom. I think of a man named Gabby who became involved in a ministry to disadvantaged young people in our area. In the process his heart was set afire. At first he served as a lay minister while continuing to work in a lucrative management position. But, in time, Gabby decided to leave behind his comfortable career and to take a job with an inner-city ministry that cares for the material and spiritual needs of the poor. Though his new position came with a much lower salary, Gabby knew that Jesus was leading him to make this financial sacrifice.

For Gabby, leaving behind the ways of the world to follow Jesus was not a burden, but a joy. The ministry of the kingdom is giving new meaning to his life, and it is contagious as he shares with the rest of us his passion for serving the poor. Through Gabby I am reminded that repentance is costly, but it is also a source of countless riches or, as Jesus said, "treasures in heaven" (Matthew 6:20).

In a world filled with self-absorbed, self-promoting egoists, our singular commitment to the kingdom of God will be revolutionary. Our repentance, our turning away from self-rule to the rule of God, will seem crazy to some, yet strangely attractive to others. Those who yearn to live for something more than their fleeting pleasures will receive the message of the kingdom with open hearts and will be drawn through us to meet Jesus, the Prophet of God's kingdom.

Today, just as it was two thousand years ago, the kingdom of God is at hand.

CHAPTER 5

HOLINESS INSIDE OUT

Jesus the Holy One of God

As we entered the crowded common room where student groups at Harvard University frequently gathered, my friend Doug and I stuck out like two sore thumbs. For one thing, we were the only males in the room without yarmulkes on our heads. What would you expect from a couple of Gentiles who were crashing the Sabbath evening meeting of the Harvard Hillel Society, the Jewish students' organization on campus?

As Doug and I stood there, an elegant, bearded man with a fancy yarmulke approached us with a pastoral smile. "Shabbat shalom," he said, extending his hand. "Are you gentlemen here for the lecture?"

"Yes," we answered hopefully.

"Well, we're glad to have you," the man continued. "We'll be starting in a few moments with our Sabbath prayers. They'll be in Hebrew, but here are a couple of booklets with translations. Please feel welcome here." Gratefully, Doug and I took the booklets and quickly found some seats.

We weren't there primarily to experience Jewish worship, but to hear a lecture by one of our philosophy professors, Hillary Putnam. Professor Putnam, a logician known for his Marxist atheism, would be addressing "The Probability of the Existence of God." As a couple of Christian philosophy majors, Doug and I were curious to hear what he actually thought about God.

After about twenty minutes of Hebrew songs and prayers, the leader of the Hillel Society introduced Dr. Putnam. Those of us who were expecting some compelling rationale for positing God's existence—or even his nonexistence—were sorely disappointed. Right from the start Professor Putnam droned on about obscure issues in the philosophy of science, focusing his critique on the views of Karl Popper, a leading advocate of a particular theory of scientific knowledge. My initial excitement drained away as I struggled to keep my eyes open.

All of a sudden a jarring outburst started my adrenaline racing. A man in the front row, sitting just six feet from Professor Putnam, shouted at the top of his lungs: "FALSE! YOU KNOW NOTHING ABOUT KARL POPPER. EVERYTHING YOU HAVE SAID TONIGHT IS A TISSUE OF LIES!" The man's veins bulged and his angry face turned blood red as he screamed his objection. Then, in the stunned silence that followed, every eye focused on Hillary Putnam. How would this august Harvard intellectual respond to such a rude interruption? As it turned out, he addressed his critic politely but firmly, explaining that Karl Popper was a close friend and that never in twenty years of dialogue had he ever been accused of misrepresenting Popper's philosophy. Then the professor returned to his lecture, concluding that the probability of God's existence is 50 percent. It must have been a relief to the Lord to finally have this settled, don't you think?

THE PERPLEXING HOLY MAN

I doubt that Professor Putnam realized it, but his experience at this Sabbath gathering was quite similar to something that happened to Jesus. As a guest lecturer in a synagogue at Capernaum, Jesus was impressing the crowds with his teaching when, all of a sudden, a man interrupted him by shouting: "What have you to do with us, Jesus of Nazareth? Have you come to destroy us? I know who you are, the Holy One of God" (Mark 1:24, NRSV). But unlike Hillary Putnam, Jesus didn't disagree with his questioner. Instead, he spoke not to the human being, but to the evil spirit that had spoken through the man, commanding the spirit to come out. When the demon left, those assembled marveled at the authority of Jesus, who, by the way, did not weigh in on the probability of God's existence.

As a general rule, I wouldn't recommend that you base your understanding of Jesus on the words of an evil spirit. But, ironically, what the demon shouted at Jesus was true. In Jesus, the kingdom of God had dawned, shining its piercing light into the earth's darkness. He was, indeed, the Holy One of God who had come to destroy Satan, his works, and his minions.[1] If you're concerned that it was a demon that pronounced the title "Holy One of God," don't worry. This title appears elsewhere in the New Testament, flowing from the lips of a much more reliable source, none other than the apostle Peter.[2]

The title "holy man" was used by Jews to label someone who possessed unusual spiritual aptitude. The prophet Elisha qualified for the designation "holy man."[3] In postbiblical Jewish writings, the title was applied to Moses and to those who were martyred for their Jewish convictions.[4] In the time of Jesus, Herod feared John the Baptist because he considered him to be a "holy man."[5] The term "holy man" continues to be used in rabbinic literature as a label for Jewish men who lived exemplary and often miracle-filled lives.

In many ways Jesus' life was both exemplary and miraculous. He certainly would have been considered a holy man, just like his predecessor, John the Baptist. But Jesus fulfilled the job description for a holy man rather oddly. The Jews of that era, and especially those who opposed Jesus, would have been perplexed by his iconoclastic behavior. In some ways he perfectly fit the holy man mold; in other ways he shattered the mold completely.

Like other so-called holy men in his day, Jesus seemed to have a direct line to God. One of his Galilean contemporaries, Rabbi Hanina Ben-Dosa, was a wise teacher who healed the sick and whose prayers led to dramatic miracles. Yet, in stark contrast to this famous holy man, Jesus did things that seemed utterly *unholy,* such as hanging out with reviled tax collectors and other notorious sinners. That's not what holy men were supposed to do. In fact, it was the polar opposite of religiously orthodox holiness, according to the teachings of the religious elite of Jesus' day. So when Jesus was having dinner at the house of Levi the tax collector, along with others who were known to be notorious sinners, some Pharisees cried out, "Why does he eat with such scum?" (Mark 2:16). Jesus the holy man got it all wrong, from the Pharisaic vantage point. Holy men don't violate the Pharisaic oral traditions by defiling themselves at meals shared with flagrant sinners and those who consorted with the Roman oppressors. Under no circumstances would a holy man do the things Jesus was known for. Rather than exemplifying the common Jewish notion of holiness, Jesus was turning holiness inside out.

The Deeper Meaning of Table Fellowship

To make sense of the Pharisaic ire and confusion over Jesus' dining chez Levi, we need to know how the Pharisees understood holiness. They took the call of God in Leviticus with utmost seriousness: "Be holy because I, the LORD your God, am holy" (19:2, NIV). God's holiness consisted in his being set apart from the profane world with its imperfection and evil. The people of Israel were holy because God had set them apart from all other peoples of the earth for himself and for his purposes. They were to express their holiness by obeying God's revealed law.

Yet for the Pharisees, holiness meant more than following the perfect law of God and avoiding the sinful practices of their pagan neighbors. Holiness also meant separating themselves from these neighbors, and even from some of their fellow Jews. The Pharisees, whose name probably means "the separated ones," kept their distance both from Gentiles and from Jews who applied the ceremonial law less stringently than they did. The Pharisees referred to these Jews with the derogatory expression "the people of the land," which could be paraphrased as "outsiders" or "those not like us." Though these Jews lived in the Promised Land, the "people of the land" were not members of the elite Pharisaic brotherhood. Those within this inner circle went to great lengths to be sure that they were not tainted by fellowship with those they considered moral and religious slackers.

The Pharisees would never share a meal with "the people of the land" for two reasons. First, although they were not priests, the Pharisees, for the most part, applied to their dinner tables the legal standards for ritual purity that were employed by priests in the temple. Thus, meal sharing with non-Pharisees would corrupt their own purity. It would render them unfit for relationship with God, or so they believed. Second, the Pharisees, like peoples throughout the Mediterranean world, viewed table fellowship as a deeply intimate and symbolically powerful event. Sharing a meal with someone was never a casual activity with a mere acquaintance. First-century Jews didn't "do lunch." Rather, as they shared food together, they united their lives, their hearts, and their friendship. They became like family. The choice to engage in table fellowship with someone was, therefore, a powerful gesture of mutual acceptance.

It's hard for us to understand the symbolic meaning of table fellowship among first-century Jews. Only once in my life have I experienced something roughly similar. In the late 1970s in my college dormitory, which was populated primarily by Anglos, there was also a fairly large population of African American students. Whites and blacks studied together, played intramural sports together, and often became friends. But when it came to eating, segregation prevailed. The black students sat in one section of the dining hall. White students sat elsewhere. The racist implications of our dining practices bothered my roommate Henry, our African American friend Michael, and me. So one day when Michael invited us to join him for lunch, we gladly accepted. We knew that we weren't simply enjoying a sandwich together, but making an intentional statement about the need for racial reconciliation in our dorm. Our statement was heard loud and clear by both white and black students, many of whom looked at us first with surprise and then with disdain. We had broken the rules of mealtime fellowship. Our actions suggested that racial segregation in the cafeteria was wrong. Many of our friends felt angry, not only because we had flaunted the unspoken code of the cafeteria but also because they sensed in our behavior an implicit critique of their own practices.

Similarly, when Jesus dined at Levi's house, the Pharisees expressed consternation and scorn. This supposed holy man was allowing himself to become ceremonially unclean by eating with "the people of the land" and, even worse, the infamous sinners among them. Levi was, after all, a tax collector who had sold out to the Romans in order to make a bundle of money at the expense of his own people. No doubt his dinner party was filled with other "notorious sinners" just like him.[6] Yet Jesus entered into fellowship with such people. It would be rather like Billy Graham throwing a party and inviting a bunch of people who were widely known for their enthusiastic support of Osama bin Laden and his band of terrorists.

Moreover, Jesus' presence at Levi's table broadcast his acceptance of people who, from the Pharisaic point of view, ought to be despised and avoided at all costs. The holy followers of a holy God should never defile themselves by dining with anyone whose behavior flaunted the Jewish law and thereby undermined the Jewish nation. When Jesus gladly reclined at table with these sinners, it suggested to his opponents that Jesus was joining them in their dissolute living. Perhaps he also was a "glutton and a drunkard," since he hung out with such rabble (Matthew 11:19). Moreover, Jesus' eating with commoners and sinners presented a silent condemnation of the Pharisees. If this holy one of God shared meals with sinners, it implied that the Pharisaic pattern of exclusion was inconsistent with true holiness.

Turning Holiness Inside Out

What was Jesus thinking? If he wanted to establish that he was in fact the holy one of God, why did he compromise his ceremonial purity and his reputation as a holy man? Notice carefully his answer to the Pharisees' question. When asked, "Why does he eat with such scum?" (Mark 2:16), Jesus responded, "Healthy people don't need a doctor—sick people do. I have come to call sinners, not those who think they are already good enough" (Mark 2:17). Jesus was advocating a new understanding of holiness and establishing a new standard, one that flew in the face of accepted norms. The kingdom of God would not be populated with those who trusted in their own righteousness, but with sinners who put their faith in the mercy of God.[7] Ironically, Jesus also offered the kingdom of God to the Pharisees because they, too, were sinners. He joined them for dinner just as he did with tax collectors.[8] And when Nicodemus, a leader among the Pharisees, came to Jesus with his questions, Jesus willingly entered into dialogue with him.[9] But sadly, most of the Pharisees were blinded by their own conceptions of righteousness and were, therefore, unable to enter the kingdom.

Though Jesus had fellowship with sinners, he did not thereby endorse their sinfulness. In a passage in the gospel of Luke, Jesus explained that he came to call sinners "to repentance" (Luke 5:32, NIV). He did not reject the Old Testament call to godlike holiness. Rather, he recovered the original sense of biblical holiness, rejecting the Pharisaic obsession with ritual and external purity and instead defining true holiness as a matter of the heart and the actions that flow from it. God had called his people to love him, not primarily with outward observances, but with "all your heart, all your soul, and all your strength" (Deuteronomy 6:5).

In Mark 7, for example, the Pharisees were distressed because the disciples of Jesus didn't wash their hands in the manner prescribed by the rabbinic oral tradition. A section of rabbinic teaching actually specified the precise amount of water required for ritual hand washing. These teachings were ignored by Jesus and his retinue. In fact, Jesus refuted the oral tradition and its hand-washing ordinances altogether. A lack of cleanliness, he explained, was not a matter of externals, what a person eats or touches, but internals, the content of the heart and the expression of the heart in action:

> For from within, out of a person's heart, come evil thoughts,
> sexual immorality, theft, murder, adultery, greed, wickedness,
> deceit, eagerness for lustful pleasure, envy, slander, pride, and
> foolishness. All these vile things come from within; they are
> what defile you and make you unacceptable to God.
> (verses 21-23)

If, therefore, the heart of Levi the tax collector had motivated him to be greedy or deceitful, then he was truly unholy and needed to repent. Likewise, if the hearts of the Pharisees were full of slander or pride, then they also fell short of God's holiness and needed to turn to God and away from their sin.

Jesus turned holiness inside out, rejecting the Pharisees' preoccupation with outer appearance and focusing instead on the inner dimension of the heart. Jesus' version of holiness was *inside out* because he knew that whatever lies inside our hearts will be expressed in our behavior. If my heart is full of sexual immorality, then I will engage in sexually immoral behavior. If my heart is greedy, then I will seek to accumulate wealth for my personal benefit. The unholiness of my heart will reveal itself in the unholiness of my actions.

Jesus upheld God's standards, denouncing sin and calling people to live holy lives. Yet contrary to what was expected, Jesus was willing to share intimate fellowship with unholy people of all stripes, including tax collectors and Pharisees. Thus he demonstrated that the kingdom of God was available to all. The presence of the kingdom called forth repentance from all people, a completely new way of thinking and living, a rejection of false standards for external purity, and a commitment to internal purity expressed through transformed living. For "the people of the land" who had been excluded by Pharisaic notions of holiness, the gospel of the kingdom was good news indeed. They had a place in God's realm after all. They were not just "outsiders" or "moral slackers," but the chosen people of God.

For those who prided themselves on their exemplary spirituality, however, the message of Jesus challenged the core of their religious identity. The supposed good news of the kingdom must have sounded to the Pharisees like bad news indeed. But for all who acknowledged their sinfulness—including tax collectors and scribes, prostitutes and Pharisees—the gospel of the kingdom was the best news of all.

The Good News for Us

What difference might it make for us that Jesus was the Holy One of God who turned holiness inside out? I want to reflect on two dimensions, one that offers good news for us and another that presents a stirring challenge.

First, the fact that Jesus entered into deep fellowship with sinners is tremendous news because we, too, are sinners. Even as the Holy One of God hung out with unholy people, so he hangs out with you and me. Scripture is abundantly clear that "all have sinned and fall short of the glory of God" (Romans 3:23, NIV). That "all" includes both social outcasts and religious leaders, both the poor and the wealthy, both you and me.

Jesus does not demand that we have pure hearts and perfect lives before he enters into relationship with us. If he did, we'd be out of luck, completely and eternally. Rather, Jesus draws near to us while we are thoroughly unholy.[10] He cleanses our hearts and fills us with the Holy Spirit. The transformation of heart and life comes not by our efforts, but through the effort of God at work in and among us.

Moreover, when we who know Jesus fail to live according to his standards, he does not separate himself from us as the Pharisees would demand. He never dismisses us as scorned "people of the land." Rather, he continues to call us to holiness, to reform our hearts, and to help us live as holy people.

As a pastor I often hear people's deepest secrets, their hidden sins. They come to me to share their marital unfaithfulness, their professional dishonesty, or their parental failings. By the time they speak with me, they're far beyond rationalization and denial. They are broken by their sin and disobedience and have come to me because they yearn for help and healing.

In many cases, I am the first person to hear their confessions. When they are finally able to admit what they have done, the dam breaks. Shame, horror, and despair pour out, often with lots of tears. "How could I have made such a mess of my life?" they wonder. "How can things ever be right again?" And then they get to the core question, the deepest of all their fears: "Can God ever forgive me for what I've done?"

For this question there is a simple answer, simple yet profound and transformational: "Yes, God can forgive you, through Jesus Christ. If we confess our sins to him, 'he is faithful and just to forgive us and to cleanse us from every wrong' (1 John 1:9)." What astoundingly good news this is for all of us! The Holy One of God took on our unholiness so that we might be made holy. He draws near to us when we are mired in sin so that we might be forgiven, freed, and empowered to live holy lives. The Holy One is not just a friend of saints but of sinners like you and me.

> *Jesus! what a friend for sinners!*
> *Jesus! lover of my soul;*
> *Friends may fail me, foes assail me,*
> *He, my Savior, makes me whole.*
>
> *Hallelujah! what a Savior! Hallelujah! what a friend!*
> *Saving, helping, keeping, loving, He is with me to the end.*[11]

THE CHALLENGE FOR US

The holiness of Jesus offers not only good news but also a vigorous challenge. Even as he communicated a new vision of holiness to Israel, so we are to communicate this vision to our world. We are to pass on the message of Jesus and to live in the mode of Jesus. We are called to imitate Jesus by entering into relationship with unholy people and also calling them to holiness.

Keeping these two activities together isn't easy. Christians often emphasize one and neglect the other. For example, some of us abandon the message of biblical holiness, replacing it with an articulation of the world's values. We can label materialism as "divine blessing," racism as "a good joke," gossip as "godly concern," and sexual immorality as "freedom in Christ." We do so for a variety of reasons. Maybe we're tired of always being different. Maybe we don't want to hurt people's feelings by suggesting that their behavior is wrong. Maybe we're afraid of being accused of bigotry by a culture that blesses any belief, other than a belief in transcendent, absolute moral values. Like Jesus, we continue in relationship with sinners, but, unlike Jesus, we don't bother to call them to a new way of living.

Conversely, some Christians continue to uphold biblical holiness in their words, but they adopt a Pharisaic version of holiness in their works. We denounce sin as we withdraw from sinners. We advocate holiness as we separate ourselves from people we consider to be unholy. Usually we define unholiness in a self-serving way, denouncing that over which we claim mastery while excusing the sin that masters our own hearts. Another's sexual immorality is an abomination to the man who has been happily married for twenty years, but whose heart is mired in pride over his faithfulness. We are selective about the unholiness we choose to denounce. Coarse language, despicable. Greed, no problem.

As we seek to imitate Jesus, the Holy One of God, we will struggle to speak clearly and consistently about holiness of heart and life and, at the same time, to open our hearts and lives to those who don't embrace biblical holiness. We must avoid the tendency to resolve the tension in Jesus' model of holiness in a way that panders to our personal preferences, favoring either moral relativism or legalistic separatism.

Holiness and Homosexuality

Perhaps no issue in our day requires the inside-out holiness of Jesus more than the issue of homosexuality. The reason? Few, if any, issues lead Christians into an imbalanced imitation of Jesus more readily than this one.

On the one hand, some Christians believe that loving fellowship with gay and lesbian people requires the abandonment of biblical standards for sexual holiness. They agree with "dining with sinners," but they don't take the next step of calling those sinners to repentance and righteous living. Several years ago I spoke in a church that affirmed homosexual behavior as a legitimate lifestyle option. To their credit this congregation wanted to hear from "the other side." I spent an hour laying out the biblical vision for sexuality. Simply put, sex is a good gift from God, which, like all of his gifts, must be used within certain parameters. Scripture calls us to sexual faithfulness within heterosexual marriage and to abstinence outside of marriage. From this point of view, both straight and gay people should not engage in sexual intimacy outside of marriage. There is no double standard based on sexual orientation.

When I finished my presentation, it was obvious that I had failed to convince my audience. They didn't question my interpretation of Scripture. Rather, they couldn't accept the direct application of biblical principles to gay and lesbian people. "Sexuality is a complex thing," one man said. "Who am I to judge others and the choices they make?" A woman added, "I have friends whose children are gay. They have experienced too much pain already. How could I add to their hurt by saying that their children are wrong?" Another woman raised a fairly common objection to what I had said: "Jesus never talked about homosexuality. How can we condemn what Jesus never even mentioned? Shouldn't we just try to love people as Jesus did?"

"Yes, of course we should imitate the love of Jesus," I responded. "But it isn't loving to approve of someone's behavior if that behavior violates God's requirements for us. So we're back to the question of whether Jesus' silence concerning homosexuality can be understood as some sort of endorsement."

If Jesus addressed homosexuality in any of his teachings, it wasn't recorded. But it stretches the imagination past the breaking point to take Jesus' silence as an implicit endorsement of homosexual behavior. He also never specifically addressed rape, child molestation, or pornography, but Christians today have no trouble believing that Jesus stands in opposition to those evils. And Jesus addressed homosexuality indirectly when he cited related evils that issue from our hearts, specifically sexual immorality.[12] What fell within that category? In keeping with biblical counsel elsewhere, Jesus surely considered sex outside of marriage to be inconsistent with God's will. There's not an iota of evidence to the contrary. Although he related to prostitutes in a way that scandalized his legalistic opponents, Jesus never said to these women: "Who am I to criticize your professional activity as long as it's between consenting adults?" It's much more likely that Jesus said to prostitutes what he once said to the woman who was caught in adultery, "Neither do I condemn you. Go now and leave your life of sin" (John 8:11, NIV).[13]

When it comes to sexuality, our job is not to make up new judgments consistent with our culture, but to apply God's judgments as revealed in Scripture. We must do so humbly, but clearly. We must freely acknowledge our own sinfulness in the process, but without minimizing the wrongness of sin. If mentioning biblical standards causes pain to those who don't live by those standards, then we have no choice but to cause pain. Of course, if the pain comes from our self-righteousness, our rudeness, or our lack of love, then we have failed to imitate Jesus, the Friend of sinners.

This suggests a further challenge for Christians who seek to imitate the holiness of Jesus. Many who rightly uphold biblical standards for sexuality have cut themselves off from people who don't affirm these standards, especially if they happen to be gay or lesbian people. A woman in my congregation once confided that two of her children were living with their lovers outside of marriage. Her son lived with his girlfriend, her daughter with *her* girlfriend. The mother recognized that both relationships were inconsistent with God's will, but she had a much harder time relating to her lesbian daughter than to her "normal" son. In fact, she had almost completely severed her relationship with her daughter while she continued to be fairly close to her son and his girlfriend. How could this woman demonstrate the love of Christ to a daughter she refused to remain in contact with? We need to follow Jesus completely in his example of holiness, reaching out to unholy people without being dominated by our personal biases.

When I was one of the pastors at Hollywood Presbyterian Church, our senior pastor, Lloyd Ogilvie, believed that we should start a ministry to people suffering with AIDS, most of whom in the Hollywood area were gay men. A ministry proposal was presented to the board of elders, and it elicited heated debate. The proposal clearly articulated the biblical view of sexual behavior but called the church to reach out to suffering people with the love of Christ. One elder who opposed the plan objected: "How can we care for these people without implying that we approve of homosexuality? How can we possibly be in league with those kind of people?" Sounds familiar, doesn't it? A lot like "How can Jesus eat with such scum?"[14] In the end the elders voted overwhelmingly to follow the challenging, risky example of Jesus and start a ministry to people with AIDS.

If one objects that Jesus was simply eating with sinners and not entering into serious relationships with them, this objection misses the meaning of table fellowship in the first century. By sharing a meal with outcasts, people whose unholiness was obvious and well practiced, the Holy One of God entered into their cultural exclusion. He allowed himself to become ceremonially unclean, in clear violation of the rabbinic tradition. His reputation as a holy man was tarnished. His proclamation of the kingdom of God was called into question by his demonstration that God welcomed both ordinary folk and even sinners into his realm.

If Jesus had lived in a world like ours, one in which the issue of homosexuality is a significant matter of public debate, there is no question that he would have identified same-gender sexual activity as contrary to God's holiness. Yet there is also no question that Jesus would have entered into intentional, intimate fellowship with these people. His behavior would have troubled the religious elite, even as many Christians today become upset when other Christians reach out with love to gay and lesbian people.

If we are to imitate Jesus, then we must stand firmly for biblical holiness while embracing unholy people, even as we have been embraced by God in our own unholiness. Though we must judge all things according to

God's revealed Word, we must also avoid self-exalting judgmentalism. As soon as we take pride in the fact that "we are not like *those* people," then we have blessed the unholy pride in our hearts, and we need to repent.

At the same time we must acknowledge a legitimate concern among many Christians. You do put your reputation at risk when you pursue genuine relationships with "sinners." You risk your reputation among other Christians, who might misunderstand these friendships. And you might be tempted to relax your own standards in an attempt to befriend those who don't share the same biblical standards of morality.

Will we sometimes struggle to articulate holiness while loving unholy people? No question about it. Do we still need to take the risk? Absolutely.

Jesus' peculiar version of holiness—that it includes getting involved in the lives of the unholy—got him into trouble with the religious authorities. In fact, it was ultimately a major reason for his execution. Yet if we are to imitate Jesus, the Holy One of God, then we can't escape the messiness of living in an unholy world even as we try not to conform to the standards of that world.

Fifteen years ago I watched my mother struggle with the challenge of being holy as Jesus is holy. Her challenge began during an excruciating season in the life of my family when my father was dying slowly and painfully of cancer. His failing health laid a heavy burden on my mother. A friend of my sister learned what we were going through and offered to live in my parents' home. Rick was a loving man who cheered up my mother and father with his humor and excellent cooking. He helped care for my father in many ways. Rick also happened to be gay. He was not a Christian, so he didn't see anything wrong with his lifestyle.

When Rick moved in, my mother made clear what she believed about sex outside of marriage. She asked him to respect her values in her home, which Rick was glad to do. During the months of his stay, he and my mother had many discussions about the most important things in life. They talked about family, love, God, sex, and dozens of other subjects.

Over time Rick became like a member of our family. He shared our holiday celebrations and our long vigils at my dad's bedside. To put it in biblical terms, Rick became a full member of our table fellowship.

Shortly after my father died, Rick discovered that he was HIV positive. In those days medical treatment was less advanced, so he quickly developed full-blown AIDS. During that painful time Rick continued to be a part of our family, sharing our life as we shared his.

I'm sure there were some who wondered about Rick's presence in our family. My mother was a highly regarded leader in the church, a woman of exemplary Christian maturity. Perhaps some people questioned her openness to Rick. Though my mother sometimes struggled over how to relate to him, she never abandoned her commitment to being holy as Jesus was holy. She continued to open her heart to Rick in his time of suffering, even as he had opened his heart to us when my dad was dying.

Rick eventually moved home to Canada to spend his last few months with his family. During that period my mother visited him. Once again they talked about what it means to be a Christian. Through much suffering Rick had come to realize his need for God. He finally put his trust in Jesus. Rick's own imminent death, a tragic loss for those of us who loved him, would be his eternal gain. He is with the Lord today, largely because my mother imitated the challenging holiness of Jesus.

In our effort to imitate Jesus in his holiness, we won't always get it right. But we must continually seek to be holy, even as Jesus is holy. We must find a way to stand for God's truth and to reach out with God's love. True holiness flows out of transformed hearts into transformed lives. Truly holy people unabashedly proclaim God's standards and unhesitatingly welcome those who fail to meet them, embracing "sinners" in love and introducing them to the Holy One of God—the one who came to invite sinners like us into the kingdom of God.

The Holy One of God turned holiness inside out. He calls us to do the same.

CHAPTER 6

ROYAL REGENT AND SUFFERING SERVANT

Jesus the Son of Man

"Look! Up in the sky! It's a bird. It's a plane. It's...Superman!"

Those magic words quickened my pulse when I was eight years old. I loved watching *The Adventures of Superman,* starring George Reeves as the Man of Steel. My heart pounded as my TV hero raced faster than a speeding bullet, overpowered locomotives, and leaped over tall buildings in a single bound. He only appeared to be an ordinary mortal. But Superman had powers that vastly exceeded human capacities, a fact I sadly recognized when my attempt to don a towel as a cape and fly around the living room ended with an inglorious thud.

But Superman wasn't invulnerable. Kryptonite, the mineral remains of his home planet, Krypton, could weaken or even kill the Man of Steel. Then there was the whole problem of his secret identity. Superman couldn't just walk around in form-fitting tights all day. No, he had to masquerade as Clark Kent, mild-mannered reporter for the *Daily Planet.* You would have thought he could have cooked up a more sophisticated disguise. But the best Superman could do was to hide behind some thick glasses and a business

81

suit. From my youthful perspective, Clark Kent still looked exactly like Superman. Yet, amazingly, his friends were completely fooled, never once seeing through his thin disguise.

The inability of Clark Kent's closest associates to recognize him as the Man of Steel illustrates the power of expectation to shape perception. Since Lois Lane and Jimmy Olsen saw Clark as nothing more than a mere mortal, they couldn't see him as anything else, no matter how much he looked exactly like Superman. We are just like Lois and Jimmy. In fact, all human beings perceive reality in light of their past experiences and current convictions. These produce expectations that both help and hinder us. They help us see truth that would otherwise remain hidden, but they often lead us to miss that which should be obvious. When our experience clashes with our expectations, we are sometimes unable to see what's right in front of our nose. Almost always we're surprised and confused.

THE CONFUSING SON OF MAN

Jesus generally confused those who encountered him. We have seen how he repeatedly confounded the expectations of his contemporaries. He was the anomalous Rabbi who demanded a paradigm shift. He was the Prophet who proclaimed the kingdom of God, yet failed to foment rebellion against the tyranny of Rome. He was the Holy One of God who shared life with unholy sinners.

We observe a similar phenomenon when it comes to Jesus' identity as the Son of Man, the one title he preferred for himself. More than seventy times in the Gospels, Jesus used the phrase "Son of Man." In contrast, the title "Son of God" issued from his lips only twice, and he never called himself "Messiah" or "Christ."[1] When others called him Messiah, Jesus quickly redirected their thinking by referring to himself as the Son of Man.[2]

Given how often Jesus used the expression "Son of Man," we might suppose that his hearers would have grasped his meaning. But we would be wrong. In the final hours of his ministry, Jesus said, "The time has come for the Son of Man to enter into his glory.… And when I am lifted up on the cross, I will draw everyone to myself" (John 12:23,32). The crowd was perplexed, asking: "How can you say that the Son of Man must be lifted up? Who is this Son of Man?" (John 12:34, NRSV). Even after repeatedly hearing Jesus speak about himself as the Son of Man, the people still weren't sure what in the world he was talking about. Even more surprisingly, Jesus' closest followers failed to comprehend his mission as the Son of Man. Peter, James, and John joined the crowds in their puzzlement.[3]

ENGAGING THE PUZZLING JESUS

Have you ever felt like the puzzled people who fill the pages of the Gospels? Have you ever been perplexed, perhaps even frustrated, in your attempt to know Jesus better? I have, many times.

At first glance Jesus doesn't seem that elusive. He is simple enough to be known by a child who faithfully sings, "Jesus loves me, this I know, for the Bible tells me so." And yet, Jesus confounds the most brilliant theologians. After twenty centuries of microscopic analysis, he continues to be the subject of more study than any person who ever lived. But for all of this effort, scholars still haven't completely figured him out.

As I have studied his bewildering use of the title "Son of Man," I have become convinced that Jesus chose this self-designation, in part, to confound people's expectations. He could have laid everything out with crystal clarity for his disciples, if not for the people at large. Yet, as we'll see, Jesus intentionally chose a rather obscure title for himself and then used it in shockingly unexpected ways. Talk about creating confusion!

I do not believe, however, that Jesus was merely being difficult. Rather, by calling himself "Son of Man," he was inviting people into personal engagement with him. He didn't lay out his mission in a way that might end up in a *Jesus for Dummies* book, something one could study from a safe distance. Rather, he revealed himself in a way that drew people close to him and demanded their intimate involvement with him. For first-century Jews to grasp Jesus' identity as the Son of Man, they had to seek him with open hearts. Those who took the risky step of engaging Jesus were richly rewarded. Those who didn't missed out on the most wonderful of God's gifts.

Many times I have cried out, "Lord, I just don't get you. I don't get who you are and what you're doing in my life. Why won't you make yourself clear to me?" In these seasons of uncertainty, my heart longs to know Jesus better, yet that longing goes unfulfilled...for a while. But then, in his gracious time and manner, the Lord makes himself known to me all over again. At those times, I know him more truly than before. False and inadequate images of Jesus are pruned away from my heart so that truer and more complete images might grow in their place. Perplexity turns out to be a necessary component of the process of knowing Jesus better.

As we look more closely at Jesus' identity as the Son of Man, you may feel a bit flummoxed. Don't worry; it's part of the process. If you feel bewildered, you will identify closely with most of the Jews in Jesus' own day, who found him more confusing than clear, more obscure than obvious.

EXPECTATIONS FOR THE SON OF MAN

One of the chief causes of Jewish confusion was the gap between their expectations for the Son of Man and Jesus' innovative use of this title. The Hebrew expression *son of man* literally means "human being" or "mortal." Ninety-three times in the book of Ezekiel, for example, God addressed the prophet as "son of man," emphasizing his mere humanness in contrast to God's divine power.[4] However, that is only one of the meanings.

The Son of Man in Daniel

In the book of Daniel, the biblical expression "son of man" takes on a new connotation.[5] One night Daniel had a terrifying dream about the future of human history. In his dream, he saw four dreadful beasts who will rule over the earth and devour people through political oppression. But in the dream, in the midst of the beasts, God appeared as the "Ancient One" who existed even before time itself (Daniel 7:9, NRSV). He sat upon his throne in the presence of his heavenly court, judging the four beasts and taking away their power. Then, unexpectedly, a new figure appeared:

> As I watched in the night visions,
> I saw *one like a human being*
>   coming with the clouds of heaven.
> And he came to the Ancient One
>   and was presented before him.
> To him was given dominion
>   and glory and kingship,
> that all peoples, nations, and languages
>   should serve him.
> His dominion is an everlasting dominion
>   that shall not pass away,
> and his kingship is one
>   that shall never be destroyed.
>   (Daniel 7:13-14, NRSV, emphasis added)

In the original language of Daniel, the phrase "one like a human being" reads literally "one like a *son of man*." This human figure rises from the earth into the sky so that he might appear in God's presence, where he receives the kingdom of God. His dominion is unlike any human reign because it "is an everlasting dominion that shall not pass away" (Daniel 7:14, NRSV).

While still dreaming, Daniel approached one of the divine attendants, asking for the interpretation of the dream. He learned that the four beasts represent four kingdoms that shall dominate the earth. But when the Ancient One finally executes judgment upon the four beasts, the saints of God will be exonerated. In fact,

The kingship and dominion
> and the greatness of the kingdoms under the whole heaven
> shall be given to the people of the holy ones of the Most
>> High;
their kingdom shall be an everlasting kingdom,
> and all dominions shall serve and obey them.
>> (Daniel 7:27, NRSV)

The divine attendant explains that the "one like a son of man" in verse 13 represents the faithful people of God who, like the Son of Man, receive an everlasting kingdom from God.

Along with other Jewish prophets, Daniel foresaw a time when God will intervene in history, righting wrongs, punishing the wicked, and rewarding the saints. God's saving activity is centered in *the restoration of God's kingdom,* a kingdom that will include the whole earth and will last forever. Daniel's vision adds something not found in the other Prophets, however. Here, "one like a son of man" receives an everlasting kingdom and is served by all peoples on earth. This "human being," who represents the faithful people of God, joins the Ancient One in the heavenly court, ruling with divine authority and receiving divine glory.

The Son of Man in First-Century Expectation

In the first century A.D., Daniel's vision of the Son of Man did not dominate Jewish expectations for the future. There is little evidence that most Jews in the time of Jesus regularly hoped for the coming of a redeemer thought of as the Son of Man. Yet, when they did utilize this rather obscure title, they added layers of meaning to Daniel's vision. In one first-century writing, a being called "the Son of Man" appears alongside God to execute judgment upon sinners:

> This Son of Man whom you have seen is the One who would
> remove the kings and the mighty ones from their comfortable

seats and the strong ones from their thrones. He shall loosen
the reins of the strong and crush the teeth of the sinners.... The
faces of the strong will be slapped and be filled with shame and
gloom. Their dwelling places and their beds will be worms.[6]

Accordingly, the righteous Jews who have suffered will be rewarded for
their sacrificial faithfulness. They will worship the Lord in the presence of
the Son of Man, while this divine agent pours out wrath upon the kings
of the earth.[7] In this apocryphal vision, the Son of Man not only receives
the benefits of divine judgment, as in Daniel 7, but also exercises this judgment himself.

Another Jewish text from the first century A.D. goes even further in
granting superhuman powers to the Son of Man. In this document a person named Ezra has a dream that begins with a wind-tossed sea.

And I looked, and behold, this wind made something like the
figure of a man come up out of the heart of the sea. And I
looked, and behold, that man flew with the clouds of heaven;
and wherever he turned his face to look, everything under
his gaze trembled, and whenever his voice issued from his
mouth, all who heard his voice melted as wax melts when
it feels the fire.[8]

When multitudes of humanity wage war against this human figure, he
sends forth a stream of fire from his mouth that completely consumes his
enemies. Thereafter, he gathers the faithful remnant of God's people to
dwell together in peace.[9] In Ezra's vision, the Son of Man has become not
merely a human figure who ascends to heaven to receive divine glory, but a
Superman who flies in the heavens and metes out divine judgment with
fire from his mouth. Those Jews who hoped for the coming of this super
Son of Man yearned to hear words similar to those that once thrilled my
boyish heart: "Look! Up in the sky! It's the Son of Man!"

So, although the Son of Man did not play a major role in Jewish hopes for the future, he did make cameo appearances, as seen in these apocryphal writings. In all of these, the Son of Man participates in God's final victory in which the wicked rulers are condemned, the righteous are redeemed, and the kingdom of God is established on earth.

JESUS AS THE SON OF MAN

In some of his sayings, Jesus reflected the Jewish vision of a glorious Son of Man who appears at the climax of history to execute divine judgment:

> But when the Son of Man comes in his glory, and all the angels
> with him, then he will sit upon his glorious throne. All the
> nations will be gathered in his presence, and he will separate
> them as a shepherd separates the sheep from the goats.
> (Matthew 25:31-32)

> And then at last, the sign of the coming of the Son of Man will
> appear in the heavens, and there will be deep mourning among
> all the nations of the earth. And they will see the Son of Man
> arrive on the clouds of heaven with power and great glory.
> (Matthew 24:30)

Jesus may not have envisioned the Son of Man flying in the sky and spewing fire from his mouth, but heavenly fireworks do figure in his future: "For as the lightning lights up the entire sky, so it will be when the Son of Man comes" (Matthew 24:27).

If these were the only things Jesus had said about the Son of Man, we would conclude that he, like Daniel and other Jewish visionaries, prophesied the future coming of a superhuman being who shared God's glory and authority. We would probably not, however, interpret Jesus' statements about the Son of Man as referring to himself. Yet in other passages from the

Gospels, Jesus quite clearly used the title "Son of Man" where he might just as well have said "I." For example, when a man promised to follow Jesus wherever he went, Jesus responded: "Foxes have holes, and birds of the air have nests; but the Son of Man has nowhere to lay his head" (Matthew 8:19-20, NRSV). Or when Jesus wanted to know what people thought of him, he asked his disciples, "Who do people say that the Son of Man is?" (Matthew 16:13).

As I read these passages I'm reminded of Arthur Fonzarelli from the classic television hit *Happy Days*. "Fonzie," as he was called by his friends, rarely used the first person singular pronoun. If he was dragging some poor soul into the men's restroom of Arnold's Drive-In to straighten the kid out, Fonzie would never say, "I'm takin' you to my office." Rather, he'd say, "The Fonz is takin' you to his office." Like a judge who speaks of himself as "the court," Arthur Fonzarelli always referred to himself as "The Fonz." His peculiar language gave him an aura of intrigue and authority. Likewise with Jesus. When he referred to himself as "the Son of Man," Jesus drew the attention of his listeners, making them wonder just what sort of man he was. He implied that, among other things, he shared the very authority of God.[10]

The Suffering Son of Man

Jesus inspired the greatest wonderment—and puzzlement—by predicting that, as the Son of Man, he would suffer, even to the point of death. These predictions perplexed all who heard him, including his closest disciples. For Jews inspired by Daniel's vision, the Son of Man would exercise divine power and share in divine glory. He would reward others who had suffered, but the Son of Man himself would never suffer. That would be inconsistent with his supernatural character and his superlative authority. According to Jesus, however, suffering lay at the heart of his vocation as Son of Man. It's no wonder that his words confused his listeners.

In one of the most dramatic scenes in the gospel of Mark, Jesus asked his disciples who they thought he was. "You are the Messiah," answered

Peter boldly (Mark 8:29). But then Jesus began to teach them that he, as the Son of Man, "must undergo great suffering, and be rejected by the elders, the chief priests, and the scribes, and be killed, and after three days rise again" (Mark 8:31, NRSV). This revelation horrified Peter, who actually rebuked his master. Jesus responded with a stunning rebuke of his own: "Get away from me, Satan! You are seeing things merely from a human point of view, not from God's" (Mark 8:33).

Those of us who look at this incident with the clarity of hindsight might find it easy to scoff at Peter's foolish audacity. But if we recall Daniel's vision, not to mention the development of this vision in later Jewish speculation, then we can begin to understand why Peter responded as he did. Everything Peter believed up to that moment identified the Son of Man as the victor, not the victim. He was to be glorified, not crucified. He was to judge the Gentiles, not to die under their judgment. Jesus was turning the image of the Son of Man completely upside down, and Peter intended to save his master from such folly.

If you're having trouble standing in Peter's shoes, imagine the following scene. A presidential candidate has just been elected by a landslide. He steps to the podium to give the traditional acceptance speech. But rather than proclaiming victory and thanking his supporters, he says, "In light of this election, I will now be going to prison, and then to the electric chair." It isn't hard to imagine how quickly the candidate's chief advisors would whisk him away from the television cameras and try to talk some sense into him. That's what Peter was doing with Jesus. "The Son of Man suffering and dying, Lord? Surely, you're mistaken. That can't be right."[11]

The Son of Man as God's Servant

Jesus' other closest followers, James and John, shared Peter's confusion. When Jesus again predicted his imminent suffering, these two disciples couldn't let go of their picture of his future triumph. They asked Jesus, "In your glorious Kingdom, we want to sit in places of honor next to you…one at your right and the other at your left" (Mark 10:37). It's as if they were saying, "All of this bizarre talk of suffering aside, we know that you'll soon be enthroned as the Son of Man, and we want to get a piece of your glory for ourselves." Jesus responded by explaining that they really didn't know what they were asking. If, indeed, James and John sought to share in his work as the Son of Man, then they first had to share in his suffering.

When the rest of the disciples realized what the two had asked, they became angry, presumably because they wanted to protect their own share of glory. Jesus reproved the whole group:

> [W]hoever wishes to become great among you must be your
> servant, and whoever wishes to be first among you must be
> slave of all. For the Son of Man came not to be served but to
> serve, and to give his life a ransom for many. (Mark 10:43-45,
> NRSV)

The disciples expected Jesus to be the luminescent Son of Man, the one who would be served by all peoples, as prophesied in Daniel 7. Jesus, on the contrary, saw his initial mission as Son of Man as rendering service, not receiving it, even serving to the point of giving up his very life for the sake of others.

Nothing in the disciples' background had prepared them for this astounding claim. Nowhere in Jewish thought prior to Jesus was the Son of Man envisioned as a servant who surrenders his own life for others. Where in the world did Jesus get this idea? Was it a brand-new thought, a novel bit of special revelation? Or was Jesus bringing together familiar Old Testament concepts in some startling, unprecedented combination?

The latter option appears to be correct. Jesus was framing his mission as the Son of Man by combining Daniel's fantastic dreams with Isaiah's poignant portrait of the suffering Servant of God, something that had not been done before in Jewish thinking. In the so-called Servant Songs found in chapters 42–53 of Isaiah, God speaks of his chosen servant, the one in whom his soul delights: "I have put my Spirit upon him. He will reveal justice to the nations" (Isaiah 42:1). Beyond reestablishing the kingdom of God in Israel, the Servant will extend God's salvation "to the ends of the earth" (Isaiah 49:6).

In chapter 52, Isaiah's description of the Servant seems at first to fulfill Jewish expectations for the one who will inaugurate God's reign: "See, my servant will prosper; he will be highly exalted" (verse 13). But then the prophet's picture of the Servant takes a staggering turn. Many are "astonished" at his features because his appearance was "marred...beyond human semblance" (verse 14, NRSV). Not only does he lack any sign of glory, but he is so battered and disfigured that people hide their eyes.[12] The Servant's shocking suffering is not in vain, however, because he agonizes for the sake of others:

> Surely he has borne *our* infirmities
>   and carried *our* diseases;
> yet we accounted him stricken,
>   struck down by God, and afflicted.
> But he was wounded for *our* transgressions,
>   crushed for *our* iniquities;
> upon him was *the punishment that made us whole,*
>   and by his bruises *we are healed.* (Isaiah 53:4-5, NRSV,
>   emphasis added)

God's Servant even "poured out himself to death," giving up his life as "an offering for sin" (Isaiah 53:10-12, NRSV).

Jesus appropriated these images when speaking of himself as the Son of Man who "came not to be served but to serve, and to give his life a ransom for many" (Mark 10:45, NRSV). Through the ransom paid by his suffering and death, he would set many free from their captivity, just like God's Servant who took upon himself "the punishment that made us whole" (Isaiah 53:5, NRSV). As the Servant "poured out himself to death" for the sake of others, Jesus would soon "pour out" his blood "for many for the forgiveness of sins" (Matthew 26:28, NRSV).[13]

Jesus interwove the unsettling picture of the Servant of God in Isaiah with Daniel's mysterious vision of the Son of Man. In this extraordinary tapestry, he combined Jewish hopes for God's glorious salvation with divine promises of the Servant's vicarious suffering. The Son of Man will be glorified, Jesus said, but not as you have expected, at least not at first. He will be lifted up, as you have hoped, but not initially into the heavens. Rather, the Son of Man as Servant of God will be lifted up on the cross, and, paradoxically, from there he will draw the whole world to himself.[14] He will be glorified through a most inglorious death. Yet his sacrifice will be the source of life for others, the ultimate act of servanthood, the ransom for many.

OUR RESPONSE TO THE SON OF MAN

How should we respond to Jesus the Son of Man? Many Christians answer this question by focusing on the coming glorious appearance of Jesus as the Son of Man, his Second Coming, as it's often called. Without question, he did speak of a time in the future when he, as Son of Man, would come in glory and sit upon his glorious throne.[15] But Jesus did not encourage us to invest countless hours trying to figure out when this would happen. In fact, he admitted that he didn't even have this information.[16] So, though we live in hope of Jesus' triumphant return, we should not respond to Jesus the Son of Man by trying to solve the puzzle of when this will happen. We're to live as if it will happen soon, whether "soon" actually means tomorrow or a thousand years from now.

Jesus made it very clear how we are to respond to him. When it comes to our response to Jesus the Son of Man, servanthood is the key:

> [W]hoever wishes to become great among you must be your
> servant, and whoever wishes to be first among you must be

slave of all. For the Son of Man came not to be served but to serve, and to give his life a ransom for many. (Mark 10:43-45, NRSV)

Hearing Jesus say this, we might be tempted to rush ahead too quickly in focusing on his call to servanthood. Our service is crucial, of course, and we'll look at it more closely in a few moments. But before we consider how we might serve others, we must first take to heart how Jesus has served us. As Son of Man, he gave his life as a ransom for many, including you and me. Our response must begin right here.

The Greek word translated here as "ransom" signified something that bought freedom—freedom of an oppressed people from foreign rulers, freedom of a slave from ownership by a master, freedom of a prisoner from iron shackles. Jesus came as Son of Man to offer multiple freedoms. To the demonized he gave freedom from evil spirits. To the sick he provided freedom from illness. To the Israelites he tendered freedom from self-defeating violence.[17] To all people, including you and me, Jesus offers freedom from the most repressive bondage of all: the bondage to sin and death.

Those of us who are Christians, especially if we have been believers for a long time, can easily miss the wonder of this gift of freedom. We can take it for granted as yesterday's news. We can even become nonchalant over what that gift cost Jesus, namely, his own life. Jesus, the Son of Man and Servant of God, was wounded for our transgressions so that we might be forgiven. He was bruised so that we might be healed. He was broken so that we might become whole. He died so that we might live forever.

The Cost of Sacrifice

When I think of costly sacrifices for the sake of another, I am reminded of a couple from my church, Tom and Terry. For years, Tom suffered with kidney problems, enduring all kinds of painful treatments that were only temporarily effective. More than once he was close to death. Finally the doctors determined that the only thing that would save Tom's life would be a kidney transplant. That's easier said than done, of course, because it's hard to find a donor match whose kidney can be safely transplanted into another person. Even when a match is found, the potential donor often chooses not to endure the suffering of surgery, not to mention the permanent loss of a vital organ.

Amazingly, Tom's wife, Terry, turned out to be a perfect match. If she were willing, she could give one of her kidneys to her husband. Terry's willingness was never in question. In fact, there might never have been a more willing donor. Her love for her husband was so great that she was thrilled to help him, and help him she did. Literally, Terry was bruised so that Tom might be healed.

How would you feel if someone made such a sacrifice for you? Grateful? No doubt. Honored? Absolutely. Humbled? Completely. Loved? Perhaps as much as anyone has ever felt loved by another person.

As you imagine Tom's feelings, now multiply them by a hundred, or even a thousand. That's how you and I would feel if we could ever grasp the magnitude of Jesus' sacrifice for us. Not only did he put aside his heavenly glory for us, he also took our sin, our brokenness, our lostness, our hopelessness, and even our death upon himself.

Take time to let this reality sink into your heart. If necessary, put this book down and reflect on it. Let the wonder of this good news permeate your soul. Jesus came as Son of Man, not to be served, but to serve you and to give his life as a ransom for you. What words can express the wonder of this sacrifice? Perhaps Charles Wesley put it best:

> And can it be that I should gain
> An interest in the Savior's blood?
> Died He for me, who caused His pain?
> For me, who Him to death pursued?
> Amazing love! how can it be
> That Thou, my God, shouldst die for me?

He left his Father's throne above,
So free, so infinite His grace!
Emptied himself of all but love,
And bled for Adam's helpless race!
'Tis mercy all, immense and free,
For, O my God, it found out me.

Long my imprisoned spirit lay
Fast bound in sin and nature's night.
Thine eye diffused a quick'ning ray,
I woke—the dungeon flamed with light;
My chains fell off, my heart was free,
I rose, went forth, and followed Thee.[18]

Serving in Imitation of Jesus

Wesley's marvelous hymn gets the order right. At first we marvel over the amazing love of God revealed in Jesus as we are transformed by God's mercy and set free by his grace. And then, as a free response to this grace, we rise, go forth, and follow Jesus along the path of servanthood. Rather than seeking our own greatness, we become servants, just like the Son of Man who came not to be served but to serve. Rather than striving to be number one, we give our lives away for the sake of others, just as Jesus did.

I find it easy to pay lip service to the call of Jesus to servanthood, but, honestly, I'm not all that keen on actually serving. When one of my children wakes up in the middle of the night with a stomachache, my first thought is not, *Great! What a marvelous opportunity to serve one I love!* but *I wonder if Linda will get up first.* When a friend needs some help moving furniture, I don't find it natural to offer my back—that so easily gets tweaked—as a living sacrifice. True servanthood usually involves hard work. Jesus-like servanthood rarely earns accolades or other worldly compensations. Sure, Mother Teresa became world famous. But who can name any other woman in her religious order? They serve in obscurity. If we are to imitate Jesus as the serving Son of Man, then we must be willing to give of ourselves even if nobody besides Jesus ever knows or cares.

My friend Toni is a leader in the home-building ministry Habitat for Humanity. Several years ago she was responsible for a major project in the Atlanta area. It was a particularly demanding undertaking because the goal was to build several homes in a very short time period. Hundreds of volunteers worked from sunup way past sundown in order to finish the project. Even former President Jimmy Carter lent a hand, as he often does with Habitat for Humanity. Yet, for all of their valiant efforts, the volunteers were beginning to fall behind schedule.

Late one night Toni received a call from one of the watchmen. "You'd better hurry down to the project," he said. "Something odd is happening."

Throwing on her clothes, she rushed down to the site, nervous about what she might find. When she arrived, she noticed that one of the partially built homes was lit from the inside. Someone was in there. As Toni approached the structure, she noticed a couple of men standing outside. She recognized them as ones she had seen earlier in the day.

"Is he in there?" Toni asked the men.

"Yes," was their clipped answer.

Upon entering, Toni found President Carter diligently working on bathroom plumbing.

"Why are you here so late, Mr. President?" she asked. "It's the middle of the night, for goodness sake."

"Well," he explained, "I knew that we hadn't finished plumbing this bathroom and that it had to be finished before tomorrow. We have a team of volunteers arriving in just a few hours, and I didn't want them to have nothing to do. So I figured I'd sneak down and finish up before the team arrived."

What a picture of servanthood! Here was a man who was once the most powerful person in the world plumbing a bathroom in the middle of the night. Nobody was supposed to find out. There was no photo op here, no occasion for the world to admire the servanthood of a former president.

This late-night plumber was not seeking to augment his glory, but simply to serve others as a follower of the Son of Man.

How ready are you to imitate the example of President Carter, not to mention the example of Jesus? Opportunities for service abound. You can help build houses for the poor. You can teach Sunday school or become a junior high youth group leader. You can volunteer in your child's classroom at school or help immigrants learn to read English. You can feed the hungry or help them receive vocational training. You can serve your spouse by fixing the screen on the front door or by taking over household duties so she can enjoy precious hours of rest. You can serve your children by reminding them less often of the myriad ways you serve them already.

What motivates our servanthood? Surely not the desire for glory, or even for gratitude from those we serve. We are motivated, on the one hand, by the desire to follow the example of Jesus, the Son of Man who chose the path of the Servant of God. On the other hand, we are prompted to serve as we continue to receive the grace of God, that same grace shown most clearly in the sacrificial love of Jesus. We are to "serve one another" as "good stewards of the manifold grace of God" (1 Peter 4:10, NRSV). This grace, revealed through Jesus and showered upon us through the Spirit, transforms us to give up ourselves in grateful imitation of the serving, suffering Son of Man.

CHAPTER 7

GOD'S ANOINTED ONE

Jesus the Messiah

As the presidential election of 1972 drew to a close, Senator George McGovern was straining for every last vote. Though polls showed him trailing President Richard Nixon by a substantial margin, McGovern didn't let up.

His campaign took him to a church in New York City, where the senator addressed a congregation full of supporters. Opening the Bible to Isaiah 61, he read:

> The Spirit of the Sovereign LORD is on me,
>> because the LORD has anointed me
>> to preach good news to the poor.
> He has sent me to bind up the brokenhearted,
>> to proclaim freedom for the captives
>> and release from darkness for the prisoners,
> to proclaim the year of the LORD's favor. (verses 1-2, NIV)

Then, amazingly, McGovern peered over his Bible and related this prophecy to his own political cause, almost implying that a major Old Testament prophet was endorsing his election as president.

For several reasons the candidate's use of this quotation was ill-advised. He may have forgotten what once happened to Jesus when he read the same passage of Scripture to a religious gathering and then applied it to himself. It wasn't a pretty sight. At least the New York congregation didn't try to throw George McGovern off a cliff, as did those who heard Jesus apply Isaiah's prophecy to himself.[1]

Yet, even implying the support of an Old Testament prophet, McGovern wasn't able to capture the highest office in the nation. He lost to Richard Nixon in a landslide, garnering only 38 percent of the popular vote. It was back to South Dakota and the United States Senate for George McGovern.

But suppose for a moment that in the weeks following the election, supporters of Senator McGovern began regarding him as the true president of the United States. Imagine that they began to address him as "President McGovern," in spite of the fact that he had lost the election, that he had not been inaugurated, and that he seemed uncomfortable with being called "President." Suppose, further, that this title became so closely associated with McGovern that, two decades after his death, the title "President" began to function as his name. Years later, historians would face a bedeviling puzzle: Why did one who failed abysmally in attempting to become president end up being identified in the popular mind as "President McGovern"? And why did this identification become so common that people nearly forgot his given name, George, thinking of him instead as, simply, "President"?

Of course this scenario will never confound future historians, since it didn't happen. But something similar did happen with Jesus, leaving a perplexing enigma for those of us who seek to understand him. How did the man from the lowly village of Nazareth, who by any popular accounting failed to fulfill nearly all of the first-century Jewish expectations for the Messiah, end up being revered as the Messiah? Why did thousands of Jews decide to join with the first believers in Jesus and acclaim him as the promised Messiah? And why did his identification as Messiah become so fixed in the public mind that within two decades of his execution, Jesus would be called Messiah Jesus or, simply, Messiah?

To make matters even more confusing, why did this happen, in light of Jesus' own reluctance to accept this title? If you examine the record, you will find that not once did Jesus use the title "Messiah" in reference to himself, at least prior to his resurrection.

These questions are not intended for mere intellectual amusement. They force us to stop and reconsider what we actually believe about the ministry and identity of this man. They lead us to a deeper understanding of his messianic mission and therefore to a deeper relationship with him. But before we consider how we might relate personally to Jesus as the promised Jewish Messiah, we must first wrestle with his messianic status in light of his Jewish background.

Messiah in the Old Testament

The word *messiah* is a transliteration of the Hebrew term *mashiach*. It means "anointed one," referring to someone who had oil poured on his or her head for a special purpose. The Greek translation of *mashiach* is *christos,* which also means "anointed one." From this Greek term we get the English word *Christ*. When we refer to Jesus as "the Christ," therefore, we are saying that he is the Messiah, the one who was anointed for a special purpose.

In Old Testament times a person was anointed when set apart by people—or by God—for some special task. Kings were anointed as a sign of their authority to rule the nation.[2] Prophets and priests were anointed to symbolize their election by God for service.[3] Thus, when Jews spoke of someone as a "messiah," they indicated that this person had been authorized for leadership. Today, our "anointed ones" are, in a sense, "appointed ones," those who have been publicly recognized as leaders through inauguration, ordination, coronation, or appointment to office.

The Messiah and the Kingdom

Among the Jewish people, the king of Israel was specially recognized as "the LORD's anointed" (1 Samuel 26:16), that is, one installed by God to rule the nation. If the king served the Lord faithfully, then his reign would be blessed, with global sovereignty the ultimate reward for his royal house.[4] The actual kings of Israel, however, generally failed to fulfill God's vision for his anointed one. Though King David had a heart for God, this heart was not inherited by his descendants. Not only did his royal heirs split the nation into two rival kingdoms, but also they led God's people into pagan idolatry. Their regal crimes precipitated the devastation of Israel as foreign empires came to dominate the Promised Land and drag the Israelites into exile.

Yet God had not abandoned his people. Through the prophets, he promised that in time he would forgive Israel's sin, gather her exiled people, and restore the kingdom.[5] In several prophetic passages, God's redemption is characterized as coming through the agency of a special human figure. This "Prince of Peace" will "rule forever with fairness and justice from the throne of his ancestor David" (Isaiah 9:6-7). He appears as a shepherd or even as King David himself, under whose rule the kingdom of Israel will flourish once again.[6]

Although prophetic passages use images that are closely associated with David—the king used as the archetype of the Lord's anointed—most don't actually use the term "messiah." This text from Isaiah, however, envisions the future redeemer as one who will be anointed by God:

> The Spirit of the Sovereign LORD is on me,
> because *the LORD has anointed me*
> to preach good news to the poor.
> He has sent me to bind up the brokenhearted,
> to proclaim freedom for the captives
> and release from darkness for the prisoners,
> to proclaim the year of the LORD's favor. (61:1-2, NIV,
> emphasis added)

As this passage continues, the Lord's anointed restores the kingdom of Israel, empowering the Jews to rebuild their ruined cities and to enjoy the benefits of global rule.[7] Yet the mission of the anointed one mentioned in Isaiah 61 is not pictured in political terms alone. It also touches the depths of the human soul, binding up the brokenhearted and freeing captives, both literally and spiritually.

MESSIANIC EXPECTATIONS

As we saw in chapter 4, Jews in the time of Jesus ached for the coming of God's kingdom. In weekly synagogue gatherings, they prayed that God might initiate his kingdom in their lifetime. Though unified in their longing for God's kingdom, first-century Jews pictured its coming in diverse ways. Some envisioned God's activity occurring through the agency of a human figure, one who could be called "Son of Man," or "Son of David," or "Messiah." Others hoped for direct divine intervention without a human intermediary. Still others expected the coming of more than one messianic figure. The Jewish community at Qumran, whose beliefs are recorded in the Dead Sea Scrolls, looked forward to the advent of two messiahs, a political one and a priestly one.[8]

The common idea that all Jews in the time of Jesus expected the coming of a political redeemer called "the Messiah" oversimplifies a complex historical picture. Kingdom hopes came in a variety of packages. Nevertheless, many Jews in the first century did associate the coming of the kingdom of God with one known as "the Messiah." For example, in a collection of Jewish psalms written in the years before Jesus was born, we find the following:

> See, Lord, and raise up for them their king,
> > the son of David, to rule over your servant Israel
> > in the time known to you, O God.
> Undergird him with the strength to destroy the unrighteous
> > rulers,

to purge Jerusalem from gentiles....
He will gather a holy people
  whom he will lead in righteousness....
And he will be a righteous king over them, taught by God.
There will be no unrighteousness among them in his days,
  for all shall be holy,
  and their king shall be the Lord Messiah.[9]

In this psalm the Messiah fulfills Old Testament hopes for God's kingdom, running the Gentiles out of Jerusalem and reigning over God's holy people.

During the years of Roman domination of Judea, many aspiring "messiahs" attempted to fulfill hopes like these by leading rebellions against Rome and its local minions. At the death of Herod in 4 B.C., for example, anti-Roman revolts erupted throughout the nation, with leaders promoting themselves as God's anointed leaders. In the town of Sepphoris in Galilee, only a few miles from Jesus' hometown of Nazareth, a man named Judas led a makeshift militia in a successful assault against the royal palace. Of course Rome didn't wink at Judas and his gang. Ultimately the Roman army recaptured Sepphoris, taking all of its residents as slaves and burning the city to the ground.[10] At about the same time, another Roman battalion sought out others who had rebelled against the Empire and crucified two thousand rebels.[11]

Consider how these events must have shaped Jewish expectations in the time of Jesus. On the one hand, the people must have yearned even more eagerly for God's true Messiah after the pretenders to the throne had been decimated. On the other hand, the Jewish people would have been more careful in the future, even skeptical of anyone who claimed to be anointed by God to redeem Israel.

All of this talk of Jewish messianic hopes sometimes feels merely academic, altogether distant from our experience as a politically free people in the twenty-first century. The destruction of the World Trade Center on

September 11, 2001, however, helps us climb a bit more fully into the skin of the Jewish people during the time of Jesus. We have felt the sadness and anger that come when an enemy kills thousands of our citizens. We have felt the sting of helplessness and a longing for revenge. We have wept along with people whose loved ones have perished. But if you really want to empathize with Jewish messianic yearnings, take all of those feelings and multiply them a hundredfold. How do you think the residents of Nazareth felt when they journeyed to see the total devastation of Sepphoris and realized that the Romans could just as easily burn their little village to the ground? How would you feel if the terrorists who destroyed the World Trade Center were, in fact, the rulers of our nation? Our feelings of helplessness and fear would be overwhelming. How much we would ache for God's help! We wouldn't cry out for divine deliverance in a few specially organized prayer meetings, but every day, just like first-century Jews, and every week, just like those who gathered in the synagogue. The hope for the Messiah would never be far from our lips or our hearts.

JESUS' HOMETOWN DEBUT

In the midst of an oppressed, fearful, and yet hopeful people who longed for God's kingdom, Jesus appeared, announcing, "At last the time has come!... The Kingdom of God is near!" (Mark 1:15). He backed up this announcement with stunning deeds of power, healing the sick and casting out demons. Soon the crowds were asking, "Could he be the Messiah?"

One Sabbath day, Jesus attended the synagogue in Nazareth. When it was his turn to read, he unrolled the scroll to a hope-filled passage from the prophecy of Isaiah:

> The Spirit of the Sovereign LORD is on me,
> because the LORD has anointed me
> to preach good news to the poor.

He has sent me to bind up the brokenhearted,
  to proclaim freedom for the captives
  and release from darkness for the prisoners,
to proclaim the year of the LORD's favor. (61:1-2, NIV)

As Jesus finished reading, he rolled up the scroll and announced: "This Scripture has come true today before your very eyes!" (Luke 4:21).

Even the overly ambitious George McGovern didn't have the audacity to make this stunning and unambiguous claim. If, as Jesus said, this portion of Scripture had come true before the eyes of those in the Nazarean synagogue, then Jesus was claiming to be anointed by God to usher in the kingdom. Without literally saying, "I am the Messiah," Jesus' intention was unmistakable.

At first, those gathered in the synagogue marveled at what Jesus had said. But when he went on to suggest that his ministry would not flourish among them and that he would be like the Old Testament prophets who ministered even to Gentiles, the tenor of his audience's response changed dramatically. The congregants grabbed Jesus and attempted to hurl him over the edge of a cliff, but somehow he managed to escape.[12]

It might seem to us that Jesus' neighbors overreacted in the extreme. What Jesus said about his ministry bypassing Nazareth and being extended to the Gentiles was discouraging, perhaps even insulting, but hardly cause for a lynching. Yet, when we consider the historical setting, we can understand why the locals tried to rid themselves of Jesus. His claim to be the one to fulfill Isaiah's messianic prophecy might have sounded like good news at first. But then the people remembered how many others had made that same claim. From their perspective, nothing in Jesus' résumé suggested that he could succeed where many others had already failed. The memory of the failed uprising only four miles away at Sepphoris was all too vivid in their minds. The last time a local boy acted on his belief that he was the Lord's anointed, he led a whole town to destruction. Better to throw Jesus off a cliff than to risk allowing him to bring the ire of Rome upon helpless Nazareth.

JESUS' MESSIANIC MISSION

The chilly reception Jesus received helps explain his reticence about identifying himself as the Messiah. Jesus never called himself "Messiah," and when others made this identification in his presence, he immediately switched the title from "Messiah" to "Son of Man."[13] Moreover, he specifically told his more discerning followers not to tell others that he was the Messiah.[14] Only after his death and resurrection did Jesus speak of himself more openly as the Messiah.[15]

As Jesus' experience in Nazareth so dramatically illustrated, speaking of oneself in messianic terms was risky business. But Jesus' unwillingness to identify himself publicly as the Messiah was motivated by more than concern for his personal safety. He wanted to avoid the inevitable misunderstanding that would result from a messianic identification. If he had said, "I am the Messiah," then his Jewish contemporaries would have expected him to expel the Romans from Jerusalem and to begin his political reign. But Jesus, though he was the one through whom God was ushering in his kingdom, did not embrace the militaristic and nationalistic agendas of his peers.

Unlike the Jews who hoped for armed rebellion, Jesus renounced the way of violence. His call to turn the other cheek was not merely sound advice for personal relationships but a summons to Israel in its relationship with Rome.[16] Moreover, Jesus never embraced Jewish nationalism. In word and deed he pronounced judgment upon the temple, which more than anything else symbolized the divine election of the Jewish nation.[17] And though Jesus usually limited his pre-Resurrection ministry to Jews, he foresaw a time when the good news of the kingdom would be received by Gentiles.[18] So even though Jesus saw himself as the Lord's Messiah, he never defined that role in terms of rebel general or national king. Thus he shied away from the title "Messiah" prior to his resurrection because use of this title would have obscured, rather than clarified, his true messianic mission.

A Political Messiah?

It is common for Christians to say that while the Jews expected a political messiah, Jesus was a spiritual messiah, not a political one. But this distinction between the political and the spiritual, so foreign to the biblical worldview, misconstrues Jesus' own intent. To be sure, his mission was spiritual in that it impacted the human spirit and was empowered by the Holy Spirit.[19] Yet Jesus, like the Old Testament prophets before him, believed that spiritual reality permeates the rest of life, including social relationships and political structures. By calling people to turn the other cheek, for example, Jesus was making far more than merely a spiritual statement. His fellow Jews who hoped for a military victory over Rome grasped well the political implications of Jesus' teaching and, therefore, viewed him as a political opponent. Moreover, by proclaiming that God alone was king, Jesus directly undermined the ideological foundation of the Roman Empire, with its confession of the ultimate authority and even deity of Caesar.[20] Therefore the messiahship of Jesus had clear political implications, implications that put him at odds with both Jewish nationalists and Roman imperialists. This helps explain why both sides, so often in conflict, would ultimately conspire to put Jesus to death.

As Messiah, Jesus proclaimed and ushered in the kingdom of God. Consistent with Jewish hopes, this kingdom is not limited to spiritual benefits. Indeed, it confers abundant earthly blessings, including good news for the poor, release for the captives, and freedom for the oppressed. It leads to a complete transformation, not only of individual human spirits but also of human social and political structures. When the day comes that the messianic work of Jesus is finally complete, it shall be proclaimed: "The kingdom of this world is become the kingdom of our Lord and of his Christ, and he shall reign forever and ever."[21]

The Scandal of the Cross

Jesus' messianic calling led him not to military victory over Rome, but to death at the hands of the Romans. This was an unwelcome and virtually incomprehensible vision in the eyes of Jesus' contemporaries, including his closest followers. Remember the scene in Mark 8, when Jesus asked his disciples who they thought he was. Peter boldly proclaimed, "You are the Messiah" (verse 29). Then Jesus interpreted his messiahship by speaking of himself as the Son of Man who would suffer and die. Peter, who appeared to have figured out Jesus' identity, rebuked him for speaking nonsense. Jesus retorted by accusing Peter of seeing with human, not divine, eyes.

As far as we know, Jesus was the first person in history to believe that God's Messiah must suffer and die. His pre-Resurrection attempts to persuade his own followers of this necessity appear to have been unsuccessful. In Luke 24, for example, two of his disciples were walking sadly from Jerusalem to their hometown of Emmaus. They were mourning his death but unaware of his recent resurrection. Suddenly, the risen Jesus joined them in their journey, though they did not recognize him. When Jesus inquired about their obvious sadness, they explained what had happened to their fallen leader:

> He was a prophet who did wonderful miracles. He was a
> mighty teacher, highly regarded by both God and all the
> people. But our leading priests and other religious leaders
> arrested him and handed him over to be condemned to death,
> and they crucified him. We had thought he was the Messiah
> who had come to rescue Israel. (verses 19-21)

They had thought Jesus was the Messiah before his crucifixion, but they abandoned this belief when Jesus died. Despite the fact that Jesus himself had predicted the necessity of his death, his own followers clung to their simple conviction that the Messiah would not die as an essential part of his mission. Death on a Roman cross was beyond comprehension.

It's easy for Christians to miss the scandal of the Cross, that which the apostle Paul calls "a stumbling block to Jews" (1 Corinthians 1:23, NIV). We have become so accustomed to the idea of Christ's death that we struggle to grasp what seems to us like the dimwittedness of Jesus' followers. Yet for most Jews in the first century, and in all centuries for that matter, messiahship and death appear to be utterly incompatible. In fact, we saw the same conviction expressed late in the twentieth century.

On June 12, 1994, thousands of faithful Jews mourned the death of one they had hoped might be the Messiah. Rabbi Menachem Schneerson, known as "the Rebbe" among his followers, was the leader of the Lubavitch Hasidim sect of Judaism. Many believed that he was the long-awaited Messiah, or *Moshiach* in their Yiddish dialect. They had raised billboards in New York City that proclaimed, "Moshiach—Be a Part of It!" The refrain of their favorite hymn cried, "We want Moshiach now! We don't want to wait."[22] But then the unthinkable happened. The ninety-two-year-old Rebbe died of natural causes. As Lubavitchers around the world mourned, a scant few believed that their Rebbe would rise from the dead and complete his messianic work. Most of the faithful, however, accepted his death as proof that Schneerson was not the promised Messiah. For the majority of Jews, both past and present, death and the Messiah simply do not mix.

That's why the two disciples on the road to Emmaus who had once thought Jesus was the Messiah abandoned this hope. Jesus responded to them with obvious exasperation:

> You are such foolish people! You find it so hard to believe all
> that the prophets wrote in the Scriptures. Wasn't it clearly pre-
> dicted by the prophets that the Messiah would have to suffer all
> these things before entering his time of glory? (Luke 24:25-26)

Then, beginning with Genesis and continuing through the whole Bible, Jesus explained the necessity of his suffering and death.

Death and True Messiahship

Don't you wish you could have eavesdropped on that conversation? Biblical scholars throughout the ages have wondered which passages Jesus cited to explain why he, as Messiah, had to die. Surely the prophecies of Isaiah took central place in Jesus' Bible study, especially chapters 52 and 53. There, the good news of God's coming kingdom is inseparably linked to the suffering Servant of God who gives his life as an offering for sin.[23] Drawing from these chapters and many others, Jesus explained that he had inaugurated the kingdom of God, not only through preaching and works of power but also by taking upon himself the sin of Israel so that Israel might be restored in its relationship with God, the true king. Jesus might even have shown how the impact of his death was broader still, opening the way for all people—without regard to national origin—to be reconciled to God and to live under God's reign.[24] Through his death, Jesus unlocked the doors of God's kingdom for all, for Jew and Greek, for slave and free, for male and female.[25]

Though Jesus' understanding of his death boggled the minds of his Jewish contemporaries, he knew that death was a necessary element of his messianic calling. Without dying on the cross, Jesus would not have inaugurated the kingdom of God.

Of course, Jesus' take on messianic sacrifice is all well and good—if it's true. But why would any Jews in the first century have exchanged a heartfelt hope for messianic victory with an unprecedented notion of messianic suffering? For that matter, why should we?

Everything turns upon the axis of the Resurrection. If the crucifixion of Jesus had been the end of his story, that would have been the end of his significance. His followers, like the disillusioned pedestrians on the Emmaus road, would have returned to their homes greatly discouraged, convinced that Jesus was not what they had hoped him to be. They wouldn't have bothered to tell anyone about him, not to mention going throughout the known world to proclaim him as the Messiah. If Jesus had not been raised from the dead, we never would have heard his name, just as we don't know the names of the thousands of Jewish rebels who were crucified at the hands of Rome. Jesus would have become one more anonymous casualty of Roman imperialism.

But Jesus' messianic story does not end with a cross, but with an empty tomb, a tomb that was both an ending and a new beginning. After his resurrection, Jesus appeared to his followers on several occasions, even revealing himself to five hundred of them at a single time.[26] When they saw him, they were convinced, not that Jesus had somehow managed to remain alive through his torturous crucifixion, but that Jesus, who had truly died, was now raised to life by the power of God.

In the next chapter we'll consider the broader implications of Jesus' resurrection. For now, however, we must understand that it confirmed that Jesus was the Messiah, and it provided God's seal of approval on his vision of sacrificial messiahship. Shortly after his encounter with the disciples on the road to Emmaus, Jesus appeared to the rest of his inner circle and explained the necessity of his death and resurrection.[27] Just as the Suffering Servant from Isaiah 53 would be honored by God because of his sacrifice for others,[28] so Jesus was exonerated and glorified through his death and resurrection. Just as God promised to resurrect Israel and restore the nation under the rule of David in Ezekiel 37, so God raised Jesus and showed him to be the true Son of David, the Messiah who ushered in the kingdom of God. The resurrection of Jesus was also a sign of things to come. He was the first fruits of a great harvest, the harvest of all who would accept Jesus as Messiah.[29] Thus, the Resurrection proved that the coming of God's kingdom, which had begun in the life, death, and resurrection of Jesus, would one day be complete.[30]

The Early Claim to Jesus as Messiah

Given the crucial significance of Jesus' resurrection, we should not be surprised that the first Christian sermon focused on this very event as a confirmation of Jesus' messianic status.[31] The response to this sermon may startle us a bit, however. More than three thousand Jews who heard this sermon accepted the astounding truth that Jesus was, indeed, God's Messiah. What began that Pentecost snowballed in the months that followed. Thousands more Jews came to accept Jesus as Messiah, even though it forced them to reconfigure their messianic expectations in a radical way. They recognized that the kingdom of God had begun to make its presence known, but in a way they had never before anticipated.

Moreover, the early believers in Jesus, who still considered themselves to be Jews, understood that the kingdom of God was not just for themselves, but for Gentiles as well. As the risen Jesus had instructed them, the first disciples became the first evangelists, going throughout the known world with the good news that Jesus was the Messiah who had given his life for others and who had been raised by God. Within only twenty years, Jesus was commonly called "Jesus the Messiah," or, in its Greek form, *Iesous Cristos,* "Jesus the Christ" or "Jesus Christ." In time Jesus would simply be called "Christ." Jesus had indeed been anointed by God to preach good news to the poor, to proclaim freedom for the captives, to set the prisoners free, and to usher in the year—indeed, the age—of the Lord's favor.

RECONFIGURING OUR EXPECTATIONS FOR GOD'S WORK TODAY

We should not wonder why it was difficult for Jews to accept Jesus as the Messiah, even after his resurrection. Jesus simply did not do what the Anointed One was expected to do. In fact, he actually seemed to go out of his way to do what the Anointed One was *not* supposed to do, namely, die at the hands of the enemy. Thus, for Jews to acknowledge Jesus as Messiah, they had to completely reconfigure many of their fundamental expectations of God and his work. This process is excruciatingly difficult.

Most of us who confess Jesus to be the Christ also go through seasons of painful reconfiguration. We discover that things we have believed about Jesus need to be pruned away so that truer branches can sprout.

When I began pastoral ministry, I had just emerged from several years of intense graduate study of the New Testament. My faith was strong and my beliefs about Jesus fairly orthodox. But my Jesus was a distant Lord and Savior. For the most part, I thought of him as sitting patiently up in heaven until it was time for his return. Though I believed that Jesus could, in principle, do the same works through the Spirit today that he did during his earthly ministry, I had very low expectations for him to actually do these things.

As a member of the pastoral staff of Hollywood Presbyterian Church, I had colleagues whose Jesus was much more active than mine. My boss and mentor, Dr. Lloyd Ogilvie, actually preached Jesus' promise that the one who believes in him will do both the "same works" of Jesus and even "greater works" (John 14:12). The works of the kingdom were for today. One of my colleagues, Scott Erdman, regularly prayed for the sick and expected Jesus to heal both bodies and souls. Though I was initially wary of Scott's enthusiasm, I couldn't very well discount as naive his convictions about healing, since he had personally experienced divine healing from life-threatening cancer. Soon I found myself joining Scott as he prayed for the sick. Sometimes we saw the Lord heal bodies in ways that reminded me of Jesus' own ministry. In order to make sense of these expectation-rattling experiences, I started studying the Gospels with new eyes, discovering that the kingdom of God was a present reality.

My expectations were being scrambled through my encounter with Jesus as he was revealed in Scripture. Though I found it hard to give up the safe Jesus of my academic past, I was being drawn to a new understanding by the living Jesus. I came to know him as Messiah in a fresh way, realizing that Jesus could still do what he once promised—binding up the broken-hearted, giving sight to the blind, and setting prisoners free. Knowing Jesus in this way injected vigor into my ministry and my personal faith.

Meanwhile, my father was struggling with liver cancer. Yet he, my family, our friends, and I had newfound confidence in Jesus' healing power. I felt sure that the same Healer who had responded so graciously to my prayers for others would surely hear my heartfelt pleas for my own dad. Many godly people from our church were certain that the Lord would heal him. We could almost taste the joy that would accompany this healing. Our expectations of Jesus were built upon Scripture, nourished in prayer, and completely logical.

They were also wrong. Though making his presence known in count-less ways throughout my dad's illness, Jesus did not heal him. He did not fulfill my expectations, nor did he answer my prayers affirmatively. As I grieved over my father's suffering and then his death, I must confess that I felt jerked around by the Lord. If I had only maintained my earlier image of Jesus, the safe, distant, benign, and relatively inactive one, my dad's death would have left my expectations intact. But it seemed that Jesus him-self had completely altered my hopes for him, only to leave me utterly dis-appointed. I was tempted to abandon my new beliefs about the presence of God's kingdom, but I couldn't deny what I had learned from Scripture and had seen with my own eyes. Yet, how could I expect Jesus to be a gracious Healer and at the same time make sense of his failure to heal my father?

If you've been a Christian for several years, you've probably had your expectations of Jesus confounded. Perhaps you're in the midst of such a cri-sis right now. You wonder, as I have wondered, if your confidence in Jesus will ever be restored, if you'll ever be able to frame your expectations of Jesus in light of who he really is.

THE MESSIAH WHO MAKES HIMSELF KNOWN TODAY

Relating to Jesus isn't a one-way street, but a thoroughfare of travel in both directions. The Jesus we seek to know also seeks us and helps us to know him. The encounter on the road to Emmaus illustrates this gracious truth. At times we find ourselves like the two journeying disciples, disheartened because Jesus has failed to meet our expectations. But then Jesus unex-pectedly joins us on the road. In our journey of faith, he makes himself known. Of course, he rarely reveals himself in a visible form. But Jesus nev-ertheless draws near in our distress and helps us know him more truly and more intimately.

Sometimes this happens when we are alone, when the Spirit of Christ speaks to our hearts. During the last months of my father's life, I used to hike in the hills above my parents' home, praying to a God who often seemed hopelessly distant. Yet, on one occasion as I was interceding for my father, I felt the calming presence of the Spirit. Even as I received the inexplicable peace that Jesus promised,[32] I sensed that my father would not be healed of cancer. And even though I struggle now to find words to express it, I also knew deep within my soul that God was with my dad, my family, and me. Divine love flooded my heart. Although I did not see the risen Christ with my eyes, his presence was unmistakable.

Jesus regularly makes himself known through Scripture. As he did with the disciples on the way to Emmaus, so he does with us through the written Word. The Bible, both Old and New Testaments, reveals Jesus to us and opens our hearts to him. As we read the gospel accounts, as we dig into the Old Testament Prophets, as we meditate on the very psalms that Jesus prayed, we experience his messianic work. Our blind eyes are opened; our captive hearts are liberated.

Sometimes Jesus makes himself known to us through the activity of his body, the church. Brothers and sisters in Christ take the place of the physical presence of Jesus. My family and I experienced this dimension of Jesus' presence often during the final months of my father's illness. Close friends and people we didn't even know told us that they were praying for us. As my dad came closer to dying, church members offered to bring dinners for as long as they were needed. For three straight months, church members would appear around five o'clock in the evening with hot meals, some elaborately prepared and others picked up on a hurried commute home. During these bleak days, Jesus appeared to us in the form of his people. Some months after my father had died, my sister admitted that it was only the tangible care of the folks at church that sustained her faith.

Jesus also opens our eyes to see him in the context of worship. In the Emmaus story, Jesus accompanied the two disciples to their home. When they all sat down for supper, Jesus himself assumed the role of host, taking the bread, blessing and breaking it. At that moment the disciples knew who he was. Although it would go beyond the text to say that they celebrated Communion, the wording is purposefully suggestive. Luke wants us to understand that we see Jesus afresh in the breaking of the bread, which we experience in the Lord's Supper. As we remember the death of Jesus, that crucial center of his messianic mission, we draw near to him and he draws near to us through his Spirit.

Moreover, corporate worship enables us to see Jesus in ways both old and new as we sing songs of praise, hear the good news preached, and offer ourselves humbly to the Lord. When we sing, "Crown Him with many crowns, the Lamb upon His throne,"[33] our hearts are lifted with a vision of Jesus' greatness as the Messiah who has given his life for us as the Lamb of God. Or when we sing, "What a Friend we have in Jesus, all our sins and griefs to bear,"[34] we gratefully draw near to him in spite of our sin and shame.

Throughout my years as a pastor, I have known many people who have encountered Jesus in worship, even in times of doubt and discouragement. Gina, a woman who had been attending my church for several weeks, was one of those people. When I first met Gina, she was in the midst of a spiritual crisis that had erupted during a time of great personal loss, the pain of which was intensified by God's apparent unwillingness to answer her prayers. She came to church in the midst of her crisis but continued to find her hopes in God dashed. Her experiences in worship were anything but encouraging.

"From the moment I walk in," she told me, "I start crying. I see all the people around me who seem so full of faith. But whatever faith I once had has disappeared. Throughout the service I weep with sadness over how much I want to know God and how far away he seems. I'm thinking that I should stop coming because it just isn't helping. What do you think?"

"I don't know why God isn't making himself more obvious to you," I responded. "I can imagine how hard this must be. I have known something like this in my own spiritual journey. Many Christians have walked down a path like yours."

Then I told Gina something that might have seemed uncaring. "I believe that your ache for God is actually a sign of his presence with you, however painful it must be. God is allowing you to feel your great need for him. If you stop coming to church, you'll be cutting yourself off from one way God is making himself known. I fear that you will feel less pain, but increasingly drift away from God. So keep on coming to worship. If you need to cry, then cry. If you need to leave early, then leave early. But if you keep on making yourself available to the Lord, I know he will reveal himself to you."

In the months that followed, Gina did remain faithful in worship. There were no dramatic Emmaus road experiences for her. But over time she began to sense God's presence. Like the two disciples on the road, she found herself in a growing relationship with a Jesus who walked with her on her journey. In this process, many of Gina's immature conceptions of Jesus were pruned away so that a more mature faith might blossom. She came to deeper knowledge of and relationship with the Anointed One who binds up the brokenhearted.

JOINING JESUS IN HIS MESSIANIC MINISTRY

Jesus reveals himself not only so that we might know him intimately but also so that we might join him in the work of God's kingdom. As disciples, we are his apprentices who are learning to share in his messianic ministry. We take seriously his promise that "anyone who believes in me will do the same works I have done, and even greater works" (John 14:12). Our works are greater, not in degree, but in number. Millions of believers in Jesus empowered by his Spirit will do far more than he was able to accomplish in his solitary life.

When we confess Jesus as the Messiah, we recognize that he inaugurated the kingdom of God, a kingdom "already, but not yet" present with us. It is already present through the power of the Spirit and in the ministry of the church. Yet it has not fully come. As we wait for Jesus' return as conquering Messiah, we don't sit idly by with nothing to do. Rather, we accept the thrilling challenge of engaging in kingdom work. With Jesus as our model and his Spirit as our inspiration, we preach the good news, pray for the sick to be healed, and seek liberation for the captives.

We who honor Jesus as the Christ are to live as Christians, as "Christ-people" who imitate his messianic work. As we do, we will share many of the joys and sorrows that Jesus himself experienced. There will be times when we pray for the sick and rejoice over their supernatural healing. There will also be times when our prayers appear to fail and when we wrestle with discouragement and doubt. The ministry of the kingdom can be messy. But we continue on, not because the royal road is easy, but because we have been called to follow Jesus, who gave up his life as the Messiah. In offering our lives for the sake of the kingdom, we will gain life in a whole new dimension—the life of the kingdom, the life of Jesus the Messiah.

CHAPTER 8

THE DYING DELIVERER

Jesus the Savior

If ever someone needed a savior, that person was Dr. Beck Weathers. In the spring of 1996, Weathers joined a mountaineering team attempting an ascent of Mount Everest, the world's tallest mountain at 29,023 feet. Through an extraordinary effort, Weathers and his team made it past Base Camp at 17,000 feet, up the treacherous Khumbu Icefall, past Camps 1 and 2, up the deadly Lohtse Face, and past Camp 3. Finally they arrived at Camp 4, 26,000 feet above sea level. From there they would attempt to scale the final 3,000 feet to the highest point on earth. At Camp 4, Weathers and his party had already entered The Death Zone, where, owing to the extreme atmospheric conditions, humans can survive only for a very short time—if they are lucky.

Weathers and his team weren't lucky. Early in the morning of May 10, they began their assault on the summit. The weather was unusually calm at first, a fact that encouraged the climbers. But soon things became more complicated. There were so many teams attempting to summit Everest that day that progress up the mountain was dangerously slow. Then, at 27,500 feet, Beck encountered an unforeseen snag. His eyesight, which had been improved through radial keratotomy surgery, failed all of a sudden. The high altitude changed the shape of Beck's restructured eyes, rendering him almost completely blind. As a result, the team decided that Beck should wait at his current location until team leader Rob Hall returned on his descent, many hours later. Neither man had any reason to believe that Hall would never show up.

As Beck waited on his icy perch, the hours slowly passed. The persistent cold began to weaken his already exhausted body. Several climbers on their way down the mountain offered to help Beck descend, but he declined, choosing to honor his agreement with Hall. As day turned to night, however, this decision proved to be tragically wrong, since Hall did not return and the weather on the mountain quickly turned deadly. A fierce blizzard attacked the summit with blistering winds, blinding snow, and lethal cold. Though Beck had finally joined a small party on their way down to camp, soon he and his comrades were lost and rapidly freezing to death. There Beck remained throughout the night, without any protection other than the bodies of those who huddled with him. Before long, frostbite had claimed his arms and face. His body temperature dropped to a point where death was imminent.

When a rescue party found Beck the next morning, he was lying under a pile of icy snow, deep in a coma, and only minutes from death. Knowing there was no hope for his survival, the rescuers left him in order to search for others. When they returned to Camp 4, they radioed headquarters, which then called Beck's wife, Peach, to inform her of his death. Everest had claimed another victim.

Hours later, Beck miraculously awoke from his coma, blind, without the use of his frozen arms, and completely disoriented. Nevertheless, he managed to begin walking in a direction that he believed led to Camp 4. Falling dozens of times, Beck kept tottering on without knowing exactly where he was going. Astoundingly, he finally stumbled into camp.

Beck's situation was hardly hopeful at this point. As he lay virtually comatose in a tent, he heard the other climbers referring to him as "the dead guy." Their description made perfect sense considering almost nobody in Beck's condition ever survives for long, and there was no way to get him down the mountain for emergency medical assistance.[1] If ever anybody needed a savior, it was Beck Weathers…and you…and me.

Although most of us will never find ourselves in a predicament as obviously terminal as that of Beck Weathers, we are, in fact, rather like him. Every living person is terminal. And the Bible reveals that, apart from Christ, we are dead in our sins and completely without hope.[2] We need a Savior, or else we will perish eternally.

The good news of Scripture is that we do indeed have a Savior, one who cares deeply about our dire condition and who has come to deliver us. In the words of John's first letter in the New Testament, "the Father sent his Son to be the Savior of the world" (1 John 4:14). Jesus of Nazareth is our Savior.

SALVATION IN THE OLD TESTAMENT

If we are to understand what it means for Jesus to be the Savior, we must first examine the Old Testament notion of salvation. The verb "to save" in Hebrew basically means "to rescue" or "to deliver." Most commonly, salvation is associated with deliverance from enemies.[3] In some biblical texts, however, salvation takes on a broader significance. It includes not only deliverance from difficulty but also a state of well-being that pervades one's experience. God's salvation includes the peace that accompanies his kingdom.[4] It can be equated with physical healing or with long life.[5] Yet, contrary to our Christian tendency to think of salvation as life after death, the Old Testament associates this concept almost entirely with experience in this earthly life. When the psalmist cries out to God to be saved when his life is at risk, he thinks in terms of physical rescue, not life after death.[6] When the prophets promise salvation, it is not something up in heaven, but something in the future of this world, something Israel will experience when God brings about their deliverance and blessing.[7]

God the Savior

Rarely does the Old Testament refer to human beings as agents of divine salvation.[8] In the vast majority of texts, God alone is the true Savior. Through Isaiah the Lord says,

> When you go through deep waters and great trouble, I will be
> with you. When you go through rivers of difficulty, you will
> not drown! When you walk through the fire of oppression, you
> will not be burned up; the flames will not consume you. For I
> am the LORD, your God, the Holy One of Israel, your Savior....
> I am the LORD, and there is no other Savior. (Isaiah 43:2-3,11)

Because of God's unique status as Savior, the psalmist confesses:

> I wait quietly before God,
>   for my salvation comes from him.
> He alone is my rock and my salvation,
>   my fortress where I will never be shaken. (Psalm 62:1-2)

Even though the Lord can use human beings such as judges or kings to implement his saving plans, he alone is the Savior, the ultimate source of all salvation.

Salvation in the Future

The Old Testament prophets often use the language of salvation to refer to God's future deliverance of Israel and restoration of his kingdom. Through Ezekiel, for example, the Lord promises:

> I will save my flock, and they will no longer be plundered. I will
> judge between one sheep and another. I will place over them
> one shepherd, my servant David, and he will tend them; he will
> tend them and be their shepherd. (Ezekiel 34:22-23, NIV)

Isaiah proclaims:

> How beautiful on the mountains are the feet of those who
> bring good news of peace and salvation, the news that the God
> of Israel reigns! The watchmen shout and sing with joy, for
> before their very eyes they see the LORD bringing his people
> home to Jerusalem. Let the ruins of Jerusalem break into joyful
> song, for the LORD has comforted his people. He has redeemed
> Jerusalem. The LORD will demonstrate his holy power before
> the eyes of all the nations. The ends of the earth will see the
> salvation of our God. (Isaiah 52:7-10)

Notice that this vision touches not only the Jewish people, but all nations. Though the Hebrew prophets focused primarily on God's saving of Israel, every now and then they glimpsed a broader vision in which all the world would experience divine salvation.[9]

Salvation and Sin

The world's need for a Savior is revealed throughout the Bible, beginning in the very first chapters of Genesis. There, God created all things good. The whole creation was "excellent in every way" (Genesis 1:31). But among the creatures were two that had the choice to maintain this excellence—or not. If the first humans continued to live in right relationship with the sovereign God, then all would be well. If they chose to break this relationship, then they would damage not only their own lives, but the whole creation. Sadly, the man and the woman did indeed elect to disobey their Creator. Preferring to be their own boss, they did what God had forbidden. They rejected God's kingdom in favor of their own self-rule. In the blunt language of classic theology, they sinned.

Human sin marred the excellence of God's perfect creation without completely destroying it.[10] Basic relationships, once so delightfully harmonious, were now marked by painful dissonance. People could no longer live in peace with each other or with God. Even nature became twisted because of human sin. Human beings, designed for immortality, would now experience both physical and spiritual death. There was nothing they could do to mend that which they had shattered. They needed a Savior.

And so do we. The story of the first humans grips our hearts because it is our personal tragedy as well. Like the first people, we have rebelled against God, preferring our own kingdom to that of God. Therefore, we experience brokenness in all of life, including our key relationships with others, with our world, and, most painfully, with God himself.

As a pastor I regularly meet with people whose lives have been blown apart by their sin. Materialism breeds workaholism that ruins personal and familial health. Seemingly harmless flirtation leads to an adulterous affair that devastates a family. Overly harsh or overly permissive parenting bears the sour fruit of adolescent rebellion. And so it goes. Sin pollutes every soul, every relationship, every community, every church, every nation.

The more we try to solve the problem of sin by ourselves, the more we realize how hopeless it is. Like Beck Weathers, we just can't save ourselves. We need someone who can deliver us, not only from certain death, but from sin itself. We need a Savior who can restore our relationship with God as our solitary Sovereign so that we might live life as it was meant to be within his kingdom, both in this world and in the next. We all share the same need. In a nutshell, we need Jesus the Savior.

JESUS THE SAVIOR

In chapter 2 we examined the angel's instruction to Joseph concerning the pregnancy of his fiancée, Mary: "[Y]ou are to name him Jesus, for he will save his people from their sins" (Matthew 1:21). We discovered that Jesus' name embodies his mission, since it means "Yahweh saves." Through Jesus, the God who once made a covenant with Israel will save his people, forgiving their sins, gathering them from their exile, and restoring his kingdom.

God intended the salvation that was coming through Jesus to impact the nation of Israel, fulfilling the heartfelt prayers of the Jewish people for God's kingdom. But he sent Jesus to be not only the Savior of Israel but also "the Savior of the world" (1 John 4:14). Jesus came to deal with the deepest human problem that infects both Jew and Gentile: the problem of sin. As the apostle Paul writes to Timothy, "Christ Jesus came into the world to save sinners" (1 Timothy 1:15).

For Jesus the Savior, the way of salvation was the way of the cross. His mission was not only to proclaim the kingdom of God and to demonstrate the presence of that kingdom, but especially to erase that which kept the Jews, and indeed all people, from living under God's reign. He did this in a most paradoxical manner, taking upon himself the ultimate penalty for sin, about which God had warned the first humans.[11] Since human sin led to death, Jesus chose to die in place of humanity. "God was in Christ," Paul tells us, "reconciling the world to himself, no longer counting people's sins against them" (2 Corinthians 5:19). And what exactly did God do in Christ? "God made him who had no sin to be sin for us, so that in him we might become the righteousness of God" (2 Corinthians 5:21, NIV). Though Jesus was himself sinless, God regarded him as if he were sin itself. God rejected him, nailing to the cross everything that kept us from true fellowship with God.[12] As a result, we can experience right relationship with God, the kind of relationship Jesus alone had with his heavenly Father. We can have peace with God through the blood of Jesus, "shed on the cross" (Colossians 1:20, NIV).

You might wonder why the death of Jesus counts for us. Indeed, this is one of the most profound questions one can ask. I can't even begin to provide a satisfactory answer here, other than to note a couple of crucial points. First, because Jesus was fully human, he was able to bear the penalty for sin that had been levied upon humanity. Although sinless himself, Jesus nevertheless shared in our humanness and could therefore stand in our place. Second, even as a lamb could be sacrificed to signify God's forgiveness in the Old Testament era, so Jesus was "the Lamb of God who takes away the sin of the world" (John 1:29). As Savior, he took the place not only of the sacrifice but also of the high priest who offered it, and even of the temple, the place of the sacrifice.[13]

Ultimately, answers to the question of why the death of Jesus counts for us fail to capture the intricacy of God's design. Logic and analogy take us only so far. In the end we are left with the revealed truth that God was in Christ, reconciling the world to himself through the death of Jesus. His death counts for us because God determined that it would.

DID JESUS' PLAN WORK?

Salvation from sin and its results through the death of Jesus on the cross sounds wonderful. But is it true?

Some years ago the Indian spiritual guru Bhagwan Shree Rajneesh accused Jesus of being a "crackpot" because he was trying to save the world but couldn't even save himself.[14] The Bhagwan's denigration echoed that of Jewish leaders during Jesus' crucifixion: "He saved others; he cannot save himself. Let the Messiah, the King of Israel, come down from the cross now, so that we may see and believe" (Mark 15:31-32, NRSV). As Christians we naturally resent such insults. But if we step back from what now seems so obvious, we must admit that Jesus' critics have a point. It's not immediately evident that a person's death brings salvation to anyone, let alone to the whole world. Before we acknowledge Jesus as Savior, we ought to know why he deserves this title. That's especially true given the fact that we need Jesus to save us from a terminal illness called sin. We need a plan of salvation that actually works, not simply wishful thinking, no matter how pious or poetic it might be.

As Beck Weathers lay dying on Mount Everest at 26,000 feet, his wife, Peach, received a second call from headquarters. Beck was still alive, she was told, but his condition was so serious that he would surely die soon. Inexplicably, Peach Weathers felt hopeful. She formulated a plan for her husband's salvation. She would get somebody to fly a helicopter up near the summit of Everest to save Beck and to rush him to a hospital. That was a fine plan, except for its fatal flaws. Peach had no access to a helicopter. She did not know an American pilot, not to mention a Nepalese one, not to mention a Nepalese one who would be willing to risk his life to save a complete stranger. It's probably fortunate that Peach didn't know a pilot because, if she did, she would have learned that no helicopter had ever flown above 20,000 feet. Beck was stuck at 26,000 feet without the ability to descend to an altitude where a helicopter could rescue him. Peach's plan to save Beck was well and good, except for one problem: It would never work.[15]

Why do Christians believe that Jesus' plan of salvation worked? Why should one believe that the death of Jesus is the source of eternal life? Why should we trust in a Savior who seemed to be unable to save himself? Whatever would lead us to accept something so paradoxical as this? Only one thing: the Resurrection.

Had Jesus simply died on the cross, nobody would have considered him to be any kind of savior, let alone the Savior of the world. His disciples, discouraged and disillusioned, would have dropped the matter of Jesus like a hot potato that had scorched their hands. Once burned by their failed Messiah, they would not have picked him up again. Surely they wouldn't have invented some bizarre theory about his death being the source of salvation for the world.

But a few days after he died, Jesus showed up again. He appeared to his disciples, not as one who had somehow managed to survive the deathly ordeal of crucifixion, but as one who had defeated death itself. The life of God was surging in his veins and was available to all who would put their trust in him. So convinced were Jesus' followers of his resurrection and its implications for salvation that they devoted themselves, often at great personal cost, to telling others how they, too, might be saved. When the Jewish leaders commanded the disciples to cease preaching about him, Peter replied:

> We must obey God rather than human authority. The God of
> our ancestors raised Jesus from the dead.... Then God put him

in the place of honor at his right hand as Prince and Savior.
(Acts 5:29-31)

Because God raised Jesus from the dead, we can have confidence that
Jesus is, indeed, the Savior. He did not choose to avoid the Cross, since his
death was essential to his saving effort. The paradoxical plan of salvation, in
which Jesus took our sin and gave us his righteousness in exchange, suc-
ceeded. The plan actually worked.[16]

Looking back on Peach Weathers's naive plan to save her husband,
nobody today would believe that it worked, except for one simple fact:
Beck showed up again. He lives today with his wife whose efforts led to his
deliverance. Though Peach faced impossible odds, somehow her plan suc-
ceeded. Calling every national leader she could think of, eventually she per-
suaded a couple of them to get the U.S. State Department to appeal to the
government of Nepal. Yet, even when Nepalese officials offered their help,
no helicopter pilot would agree to fly high enough to save Beck. They knew
all too well that it was a suicide mission because the air above 20,000 feet
was simply too thin to support helicopter flight. Finally the Nepalese em-
bassy found one man, Madan Khateri Chhetri, who sensed a moral duty
to try to rescue Beck, even though the attempt would put his own life in
mortal danger.

Meanwhile, with help from other climbers, Beck somehow made it
down to Camp 3, at 21,300 feet. This was still far above the limit of previ-
ous helicopter flight, but it put him close enough for Madan to make an
attempt. Contrary to all reasonable expectations, this brave Nepalese pilot
somehow managed to fly up high enough to rescue Beck. Narrowly miss-
ing certain death, Madan whisked his passenger away to a hospital in
Katmandu, the capital of Nepal. Although Beck's physical condition was
extremely critical, he managed to survive. His wife's crazy plan worked, and
Beck is living proof.[17]

Jesus is living proof that the plan of salvation through his death worked.
Jesus was not a crackpot. He didn't save himself from wrongful execution

because that would have scuttled his plan for world salvation. He chose freely to die so that he might become, indeed, the Savior of the world.

THE SAVIOR IN A MULTICULTURAL WORLD

It's not politically correct to proclaim Jesus as the Savior of the world these days. Postmoderns might allow us to claim Jesus as our own personal Savior, but to confess him as Savior of the world fails to render homage to the multicultural and relativistic gods of our contemporary world.

Many Christians struggle to proclaim Jesus as the Savior in a world that is filled with so many other potential saviors. I know how awkward it can be to tell a Muslim or a Jew or a secularist what I truly believe about Jesus. It can feel insensitive to say, "Yes, I actually think Jesus intends to be *your* Savior too, even though you don't agree with me."

Sometimes Christians talk about the challenge of multiculturalism as if it were something new, a result of modern technology or twenty-first-century globalism. To be sure, the technology-driven shrinking of the earth has contributed to our gaining a greater appreciation for the variety of religions in the world. But, in fact, the awkwardness of proclaiming Jesus as the Savior in a multicultural world is nothing new. If anything, it's much easier for us to profess Jesus as the Savior than it was for Christians in the first century.

The earliest Christians were Jews who lived within an environment that had no interest in human, crucified pseudo-saviors. Moreover, those who first heard the preposterous claim that Jesus was the Savior would have winced at the application of a title for God to a human being. We'll explore this point in the following section.

As hard as it was to proclaim Jesus as Savior in the Jewish context, early Christians found equally difficult challenges as they reached out to Gentiles in the Roman Empire. The Mediterranean world of the first century was filled with saviors. Gods from every nation were exalted as personal and national saviors. One of Jesus' chief competitors, for example, was the

Greek god of healing, Asclepius, whose reputed miraculous cures earned him the title of "savior" and led to the establishment of hundreds of temples in his honor. If Christians had simply offered Jesus as one more savior among the pantheon of saviors, their good news would have been inoffensive. But their claim that Jesus was *the* Savior of the world was quite another thing altogether. It insulted the deeply held convictions of worshipers of Asclepius, Isis, Zeus, Mithras, and dozens of other so-called saviors.

Offending religious people wasn't the only problem the early Christians faced. Proclaiming Jesus as the Savior was also a potentially treasonous offense, since the Roman emperors were often identified as saviors. Julius Caesar was called "savior of the whole world." Nero, who was infamous for his persecution of Christians, was known as "the savior and benefactor of the whole world."[18] Thus, those who announced Jesus as the Savior risked not only social ostracism but also persecution and even martyrdom. The daring boldness of the first Christians should encourage us to speak plainly of Jesus as Savior, even if we risk offending people. The pressures of our multicultural world are nothing new.

THE SAVIOR AND HIS DIVINITY

None of the titles we have examined so far suggest that Jesus was anything more than a man, a special man, to be sure, but a human being nevertheless. One can claim Jesus as Rabbi, Prophet, Holy One, Son of Man, and Messiah without the slightest thought that he may be divine. All of these titles, however honorific, refer to human beings.[19]

Using the title of Savior, however, we tread upon new turf. In the Roman world, human beings could be called saviors, as we have noted, but this title for the emperors was often enmeshed with their deification. In the Jewish world, however, "Savior" was a title reserved for God alone. Earlier in this chapter we saw that people who implemented divine salvation could be referred to as "saviors," but this usage was rare. Moreover, a faithful Jew would never say of a human being what the angel said of Jesus, that "he will save his people from their sins" (Matthew 1:21). This sort of salvation belonged to God alone.

But wait a minute! *Jesus* means "Yahweh is salvation." Yet Matthew 1:21 indicates that Jesus is the one who will bring salvation. A paraphrase of this verse can help us hear its irony more clearly: "You are to name him 'Yeshua'—'Yahweh is salvation'—because he, Yeshua, will offer salvation from sins to his people, the salvation which Yahweh alone supplies." The human being named "Yahweh saves" will save. What does this say about the relationship between this human being and Yahweh himself? Moreover, when we remember God's claim through Isaiah, "I am the LORD, and there is no other Savior" (Isaiah 43:11), what does this suggest about Jesus, who will save God's people?

The earliest Christians answered this question by regarding Jesus as more than a mere man. In a way words could only begin to express, Jesus the Savior was divine. We would be wrong, however, to envision the earliest Christians as somehow thinking in the complex terms of later theology. They did not talk of God as Trinity or refer to Jesus as fully God and fully human. Nevertheless, by proclaiming Jesus as Savior—and not only as Savior but as Savior from sin and as the Savior of the whole world—the early believers expressed their belief that Jesus was far more than a human being. If he accomplished that which God alone could do, then the implications were clear: He is the Savior just as God is the Savior. Who else could claim this title, other than a man who was, somehow, God?[20]

TRUSTING JESUS AS SAVIOR

How should we respond to Jesus the Savior? The essence of our response is embodied within the title itself. We respond to the Savior by allowing him to save us. This almost sounds silly, of course. Who, needing to be saved, would reject a potential savior? When Madan Khateri Chhetri set down his helicopter upon the Everest glacier, Beck Weathers almost flung himself into the vehicle. His action made perfect sense because Beck knew his desperate need for a savior.

Before we fling ourselves into the arms of Jesus as Savior, we first need to recognize that we need his help. Unlike Beck Weathers, however, sometimes we are reticent about our need to be saved. Some of us are like Dave, a man who made an appointment to see me.

When Dave came to talk with me, he was not a Christian, but he was searching for meaning in his life. As we talked, I laid out the good news of Jesus in simple terms. But Dave was not happy with the gospel.

"I find all of this rather insulting," he said. "You say that Jesus died for my sins, that he wants to be my Savior, but I don't think I'm that bad. Sure, I've made some mistakes in my life, but nothing all that terrible. I'm a pretty good person. I try hard. I think God accepts me already. I don't need a Savior. I just need some guidance, some help to live better."

No matter what I said, no matter what Scripture passages I cited, Dave would not be convinced of his need to be saved from anything. He considered himself good enough without Jesus' help and didn't need Jesus or anyone else to be his Savior.

Although I have met a few people like Dave, most people I know are only too aware of their need to be saved. Perhaps in the idyllic days of young adulthood they maintained delusions of personal grandeur. But life, not to mention the Holy Spirit, has a way of putting these delusions to rest. They tried self-help and found it to be lacking. They made a bunch of money, but it didn't satisfy. They got some therapy, but they still felt a deep ache inside. In time, most of us come to the point where we acknowledge our need for a Savior.

So how do we receive the salvation of Jesus? Simply by trusting him, by putting our faith in his saving work. As Paul explains in Ephesians 2, "by grace you have been saved through faith, and this is not your own doing; it is the gift of God" (verse 8, NRSV). We receive God's grace—poured out in the sacrificial death of Jesus—"through faith." Biblical faith is not merely believing the facts about Jesus, though we do believe them. Rather, biblical faith is acting upon what we affirm by putting our full trust in Jesus to save us. As we acknowledge our helplessness, our need for Jesus to be our Savior, we place our souls in his gracious hands. He alone saves us apart from anything we have done other than receive his gift of salvation through faith. Since I have written this book primarily for Christian readers, I expect that you know from personal experience what it means to be saved by grace through faith.

LIVING WITH JESUS AS OUR SAVIOR

The crucial question for those of us who have accepted Jesus as our Savior is: Do I live each day trusting him as my Savior? Remember that the biblical notion of salvation is broader than simply life after death. It touches every part of earthly life, every relationship, every need, every problem. I know many Christians who, after trusting Jesus for salvation, return to the familiar mode of self-reliance. As they struggle with sin, they look to self-improvement strategies, not to Jesus. If their marriages are hurting, they try everything they can think of to make things right, other than relying upon the healing Jesus offers. Please understand that I am not criticizing the use of counselors, doctors, pastors, small groups, and other avenues that lead toward wholeness. Jesus can and does use these means, and so many others, as channels of his saving power. But the decisive question for us has to do with *primary* trust. When I struggle, in whom do I put my fundamental trust? In myself? In my family? In some professional? Or in Jesus?

I must confess that I am preaching to myself right now. When I face some thorny challenge in my ministry, for example, my first inclination is to solve the problem myself. I analyze it, formulate strategies, worry about it, and lose sleep. I try to be my own savior.

How I wish my first instinct were to take my challenge to Jesus in prayer, to offer it to him. I'm learning to do this, however slowly. When it comes to the matter of my eternal soul, I have no problem trusting Jesus completely. I have long since given up any silly notion that I can save myself in the eternal sense. But something in my psyche still resists allowing Jesus to be Savior in every aspect of life. I pray that I will come to trust Jesus to be my Savior each moment of each day, knowing that "I can do everything with the help of Christ who gives me the strength I need," but that I can do "nothing" when I live apart from reliance upon him (Philippians 4:13; John 15:5).

I pray the same for you. If this chapter helps you to trust Jesus more completely as your Savior, then my effort in writing will have been richly rewarded.

PERVASIVE GRATITUDE

Throughout this chapter I have used the story of Beck Weathers as an illustration of salvation. My source for his amazing experience was, primarily, his own autobiographical account, *Left for Dead*. The last section of Weathers's book is a statement of acknowledgments, similar to what one usually finds in a preface. But Weathers gives this section the place of honor. It's the conclusion of his story.[21]

What is most striking about this section, in addition to its placement, is its length. Weathers goes on and on thanking those who had something to do with his miraculous rescue and his journey from death's door back to life. Never in all of my life have I found such a long statement of thanksgiving in a book. That Weathers should finish his story by saying "thank you" comes as no surprise, really. When one has been saved from the brink of death, and when that salvation required extraordinary efforts from many people, gratitude flows freely and generously.

I've seen this same kind of gratitude in people who have experienced the salvation of Jesus. Consider the case of Grant, for example. Before I knew him well, I was impressed by his zeal for evangelism. More than almost any other Christian I had known, Grant sought to tell people about Jesus and his salvation. His zeal, however, was couched in gentleness and humility. I never had the sense that Grant wanted to preach down at people, but rather that he wanted to share with them what meant more to him than anything else in life.

One day I sat down with Grant to hear his story. He began nervously, explaining that he wanted to be completely honest with me. Then he unfolded a tale that could have made tabloid headlines. To put it bluntly, for years Grant's life had been devoted to his quest for sex and money. And he managed to get a lot of both. Though he was married, Grant regularly cheated on his wife. He was rarely home, spending all his time with his financial pursuits—when he wasn't pursuing some young woman, that is. As Grant shared his story with me, his eyes reflected his shame. When he described his unfaithfulness to his wife, he cried over how he had dishonored her.

But after many years of self-centered living, Grant was getting bored. Moreover, he began to suffer the consequences of his poor choices. His business was failing, as were most of his primary relationships. When a Christian friend shared the gospel with Grant, he knew that he needed God more than anything else, but he was convinced that he would never be worthy of God. Of course, in a sense, Grant was correct. There was nothing he could do to make himself worthy of God. But he was wrong to conclude that, therefore, God would never have anything to do with him.

As the years passed, Grant continued to yearn for God, but he was too overwhelmed by his shame to believe that God would ever save him. Finally the truth of the gospel broke through. Grant realized that he did not have to make himself good enough for God. He understood that Jesus had died on the cross for him and that through Jesus he could be saved completely from his sin. Like Beck Weathers who desperately looked for a human "savior" high upon Everest, Grant flung himself into the strong arms of his Savior.

As Grant got to this point in his story, he was weeping steadily. His tears were no longer from shame, however, but from gratitude. He knew what it was to be lost, and he knew the joy of being found. His experience of Jesus the Savior transformed his life. From the moment he first put his trust in Jesus, Grant committed his life to telling others what he had learned. Yet he did this not out of some sense of obligation or in an effort to repay Jesus for grace. Rather, in the centuries-old words of the Heidelberg Catechism, Grant determined to present himself as "a living sacrifice of thankfulness" to Jesus.[22]

When we know Jesus as our Savior, gratitude will pervade our lives. It will fill our hearts. It will motivate our actions. It will flow from our lips. It will resound in our worship with words sung throughout the ages:

> *O sacred Head, now wounded,*
> *With grief and shame weighed down,*
> *Now scornfully surrounded*
> *With thorns, Thy only crown.*
>
> *O sacred Head, what glory,*
> *What bliss till now was thine!*
> *Yet, though despised and gory,*
> *I joy to call Thee mine.*
>
> *What Thou, my Lord, hast suffered*
> *Was all for sinners' gain;*
> *Mine, mine was the transgression,*
> *But Thine the deadly pain.*
>
> *Lo, here I fall, my Savior!*
> *'Tis I deserve Thy place;*
> *Look on me with Thy favor,*
> *Vouch-safe to me Thy grace.*
>
> *What language shall I borrow*
> *To thank Thee, dearest friend,*

For this Thy dying sorrow,
Thy pity without end?

O make me Thine forever;
And should I fainting be,
Lord, let me never, never
Out-live my love for Thee.[23]

CHAPTER 9

THE RULER OVER ALL

Jesus the Lord

Several years ago I served as the Protestant representative on an ecumenical panel commissioned with the task of comparing our various religious traditions. In front of an audience of a hundred people, a Catholic priest, a Greek Orthodox priest, and I tried to sort out the similarities and differences between our theological traditions.

After a while we came to the contentious issue of faith and works. As I laid out the Protestant perspective, I leaned heavily upon Paul's teaching in Ephesians that we have been saved by grace through faith.[1] Salvation, I explained, is not something we earn, but something we receive as a gift from God. "Yet," I was just about to say, "the Bible calls us to express our salvation in good works."

I never had the chance to finish my thought, however. Before I could say anything positive about good works, a Catholic man in the crowd interrupted me.

"How can you say that we're saved by grace alone?" he shouted. "How can you ignore good works? You Protestants always divide what God keeps together!"

When I had the chance to speak again, I explained that Paul goes on in Ephesians 2 to join salvation by grace with good works. We are saved by grace through faith, he states, in order that we might live as "God's masterpiece...created...anew in Christ Jesus, so that we can do the good things he planned for us long ago" (verse 10). Works do not precede salvation as a prerequisite, but they follow from it as a necessary result of being saved by grace.

Protestants too often separate salvation from works, rightly stressing that we are saved by grace alone, but wrongly ignoring the truth that we are saved in order to do good works. To put it another way, we tend to proclaim Jesus as our Savior from sin and its consequences but ignore Jesus as Lord of our lives on earth.

LORDSHIP IN THE FINE PRINT

The danger of separating Jesus as Savior from Jesus as Lord was driven home for me many years ago when I was a camp counselor for high-school students. The leaders of the weeklong conference placed a high priority on helping those teenagers who were not Christians to put their faith in Jesus. Wednesday night was crucial. Everything up to that point was designed to help students understand their need to be saved. At the Wednesday night meeting, the speaker would lay out the gospel and invite students to become Christians.

The big night arrived. As he presented this invitation, he articulated the benefits of salvation: forgiveness for sins, the assurance of eternal life, intimacy with God, purpose for living, and so forth. Then, asking everyone except the counselors to put their heads down, the speaker urged those who wanted to accept Jesus as their Savior to raise their hands. Dozens of hands shot into the air.

At the subsequent counselors' meeting, we rejoiced over what had happened. Many of the students for whom we had been praying had put their faith in Christ. Almost all of the people who didn't raise their hands were already believers. We were excited to realize that almost all the campers were now Christians.

One counselor in the meeting was somewhat less enthusiastic, however. "We've encouraged people to accept Jesus as Savior," he said, "but what about Jesus as Lord? We seem to have buried that in the fine print at the bottom of the contract. We haven't called students to commit their lives to Christ."

"Don't worry," he was reassured by the speaker. "We'll do that tomorrow night. I'll be preaching about Jesus as Lord of our lives. I'll be sure to give the kids a chance to commit their lives to him."

Indeed, the following night the speaker delivered a compelling message about what it means to acknowledge Jesus as Lord. Then he asked the campers to bow their heads and to raise their hands if they were willing to live under the lordship of Christ. The other leaders and I expected to see virtually every student raise his or her hand, but that didn't happen. Among the two hundred campers, only about twenty put a hand into the air. Of those who claimed Jesus as their Savior, only about one-tenth would acknowledge him as Lord of their lives.

This was a most distressing situation. By offering salvation through Jesus on Wednesday night and calling for commitment to his lordship on Thursday night, we had allowed students to believe that they could accept Jesus as Savior while at the same time reject him as Lord. We had separated what God had joined together. How could our high schoolers "grow in the grace and knowledge of our Lord *and* Savior Jesus Christ" if they accepted his salvation but not his lordship?[2]

The earliest Christians identified Jesus as Savior, to be sure, but not apart from acknowledging him as Lord. In fact, the confession of Jesus as Lord is perhaps the oldest, most basic statement of Christian faith. As we delight in our salvation through Jesus, we must never neglect his lordship. Jesus the Savior…Jesus the Lord…the two go hand in hand, inseparably joined by God himself.

But this raises an obvious question: What does it mean for Jesus to be Lord? And how are we to live in light of this reality?

If we're to understand what it means for Jesus to be Lord, we must investigate the meaning of the word *lord* in its biblical context. This is particularly important in our time of history because the English word *lord* has fallen into disuse and even disfavor. Most of us don't use the term outside of religious contexts, or, if we do, it usually has a negative connotation.

Consider popular culture, for example. I can't think of any positive hero who bears the title "lord." But there are several negative ones. George Lucas added that title to the archvillain in the Star Wars saga, Darth Vader, or as he is often called, "Lord Vader." J. K. Rowling reinforced the negative sense of the title *lord* in her Harry Potter stories. The wizard who is so evil that most people refuse even to speak his name is called "Lord Voldemort." Then there's Lord Sauron in Tolkien's fantastic trilogy, the wicked ruler who calls himself the "Lord of the Rings."

Negativity about lordship in popular culture reflects an abiding suspicion in our society at large. As democratic people we are wary of lords, and we carry forward the historic opposition to the feudal rule of monarch and nobility. The very concept of lordship—the idea that one person holds ultimate authority over another—is anathema to us. So when we hear the title "lord," we tend to get rather squeamish, if not critical.

But such was not the case for people living in the first century. Those who said *mar* in Aramaic or *kyrios* in Greek, both of which mean "lord," could simply have been showing respect to an elder or to some other highly regarded person. Their situation was similar to that of modern Spanish speakers who can use the word *señor* to mean "sir" or "mister" as well as "lord" or even "Lord," when referring to God. When the Samaritan woman at the well referred to Jesus as "lord" in Aramaic, she was speaking to him with simple human respect: "Please, *sir,*…give me some of that water!" (John 4:15, emphasis added). She certainly was not imagining him to be the Lord God in the flesh.

Throughout the Gospels, Jesus is called "Lord."[3] We should not read more into this than was originally intended. People were not deifying Jesus but simply honoring him. The disciples of Jesus may well have called him

"Lord" to indicate his authority over them as their teacher.[4] When Jesus referred to himself as "Lord," he no doubt meant it in this sense.[5]

In the Gospels, Jesus was called "Lord" because he was a person worthy of respect. His disciples called him "Lord" because he was their master teacher. There was nothing particularly novel or controversial in these uses of the title. But what began so innocuously during the earthly ministry of Jesus morphed into something far more intriguing—and problematic—after his crucifixion and resurrection.

LORD WITH A CAPITAL *L*

As we look for the earliest post-Easter uses of "Lord" as a title for Jesus, we stumble upon a curious prayer in Paul's first letter to the Corinthians: "Our Lord, come!" (1 Corinthians 16:22). What appears at first glance to be Paul's own composition turns out to be something that Paul borrowed from the earliest Christian communities. How do we know this? First, Paul's letter to the Corinthians is one of the earliest of all New Testament writings, having been penned within twenty years of Jesus' death and resurrection. Anything in this letter counts as early Christian belief. Second, the phrase "Our Lord, come!" stands out starkly in 1 Corinthians because it is not written in Greek like the rest of the letter, but in Aramaic. The Greek letters of 1 Corinthians 16:22 spell out two Aramaic words, *marana tha* (from which we get the English word *maranatha*). Since Paul would not have composed a prayer in Aramaic for the Greek-speaking Corinthians, he must have been quoting something that came from the Aramaic-speaking churches in the eastern Mediterranean, those who were among the very earliest believers in Jesus. He expected the Corinthians to understand the meaning of *marana tha,* presumably because he had passed along this prayer as a part of his earlier instruction of the Corinthian church. *Marana tha* was such a common prayer that those who did not speak Aramaic could, nevertheless, use it, much as we pray the Hebrew phrase *halelu-yah* without confusion.

This linguistic analysis confirms that the very earliest Aramaic-speaking Jewish Christians referred to Jesus as *marana,* "our Lord." But after Jesus' death and resurrection, they were not using "Lord" merely as a title of respect. They were actually praying to Jesus as Lord, asking him to come again. This is astounding, especially if you consider that those who prayed in this manner were, for the most part, Jews. For all of their lives they had prayed to God, and to God alone. Now they were praying to one they knew had been human. Moreover, "Lord" was a title for God, indeed, the representation of God's own special name, Yahweh.[6] Never in Jewish history, before or since, did people pray to a dead rabbi or address him with the name reserved for God alone. Yet this is exactly what we find among the earliest believers in Jesus. The acclamation of Jesus as Lord had moved far beyond the polite human address used in the Gospels.[7] Jesus was no longer simply one lord among many, but someone who could be addressed as *the* Lord, with a capital *L.*

Refuting a Popular Theory

It's important to realize the early origin of the prayer to Jesus as Lord because it refutes a popular but erroneous theory about the development of early Christian Christology. If you were to wander into your local secular bookstore and randomly pick up a book about Jesus, you would likely read something like the following: "The real Jesus was just a man, a wandering teacher who never considered himself to be divine. His earliest followers thought of Jesus as completely human and nothing more. But as Christianity began to move beyond the Jewish realm into the pagan world of the Roman Empire, a change occurred. Under the influence of Hellenistic religions, which often envisioned people as a mix of humanity and divinity, Jesus began to be thought of as a god, and then even equated to the Lord of Judaism. But the deification of Jesus was a late, secondary addition to genuine Christianity and therefore can be dismissed as untrue." If not expressed in those exact words, the message would be very nearly identical to this one.

Variations of this theory appear in so many books that the theory is assumed to rest on the solid ground of academic scholarship. In fact, however, this theory has been built upon the quicksand of scholarly prejudice. Many who write books on Jesus begin their investigation with a basic assumption: Jesus was not and could not have been God. As they sift through the biblical evidence, they emphasize anything that highlights the humanity of Jesus while ignoring or discounting anything that suggests his deity. The theory that Jesus was deified under the influence of Roman paganism, and that this happened long after his death, plays perfectly into the bias of many writers. It gives them a Jesus they can conform to their own preconceptions. They adopt the theory of his late deification and proclaim it confidently—in spite of convincing evidence to the contrary.

The simple prayer in 1 Corinthians 16:22 shows that at least some of the earliest Christians considered Jesus to be a Lord to whom one ought to pray. Clearly they believed him to be far more than merely a human being. Of course these earliest Christians could have been wrong in this belief. They might have considered to be divine one who was, in fact, merely a human being. But the idea that Jesus' deity is somehow an appendix to genuine early Christianity must be rejected as wishful thinking on the part of those who can't stomach the Jesus who is clearly portrayed in the New Testament.

Early Belief in Jesus as Lord

We can say with confidence that the confession of Jesus as Lord with a capital *L* goes back to the earliest strata of Christian belief. Another passage from one of Paul's letters both confirms this conclusion and helps explain how the first believers came to such an astounding appraisal of Jesus' divine identity. In his letter to the Philippians, Paul wrote:

> Let the same mind be in you that was in Christ Jesus,
> who, though he was in the form of God,
>   did not regard equality with God
>   as something to be exploited,

but emptied himself,

   taking the form of a slave,

   being born in human likeness.

And being found in human form,

   he humbled himself

   and became obedient to the point of death—

   even death on a cross.

Therefore God also highly exalted him

   and gave him the name

   that is above every name,

so that at the name of Jesus

   every knee should bend,

   in heaven and on earth and under the earth,

and every tongue should confess

   that Jesus Christ is Lord,

   to the glory of God the Father. (2:5-11, NRSV)

Notice that the translators of this passage format it as poetry. Indeed, the Greek version of this text suggests that it was an early Christian song of worship. Moreover, the differences between the language of this passage and Paul's writing elsewhere indicate that Paul did not actually compose this song but instead borrowed it from earlier worship traditions, much as a Christian preacher today might incorporate lyrics from a familiar hymn into a sermon.

The ancient hymn quoted in Philippians 2:5-11 gives us access to some of the earliest Christian beliefs about Jesus. Even if Paul had composed this song himself, his composition came within about two decades of Jesus' resurrection and should be counted among the earliest Christian beliefs. But we have in this text another case where Christians before Paul apparently proclaimed Jesus as Lord with a capital *L*. There's no question here about their intention. God himself has given Jesus "the name that is above every name" so that every person in all creation should bow before Jesus in worship, the very worship that is reserved for God alone (verses 9-10, NRSV). The name above all names is Jesus, the name that means "Yahweh is salvation," the name of the one who is also called Lord, the very name of God himself. Without question, this passage from Philippians proclaims Jesus as the Lord, the one who has the most exalted name and who is worthy of universal worship. Who else could Jesus be than a man who is somehow also God himself?

The first stanza of this passage suggests that Jesus was divine even prior to his becoming human. Before the Incarnation he was "in the form of God" and had "equality with God" (verse 6, NRSV). Space does not allow me to explore in detail the meaning of these phrases other than to point out the obvious: Jesus' deity was something he possessed prior to his birth. Yet he "emptied himself" and "humbled himself" both in becoming human and especially in dying on a cross (verses 7-8, NRSV). He did not allow his deity to insulate him from the humiliation that was necessary to bring about human salvation.

According to Philippians 2, because Jesus humbled himself even to the point of death, "[t]herefore God also highly exalted him and gave him the name that is above every name" (verse 9, NRSV). This passage envisions the resurrection of Jesus as more than simply his return to life on earth. It is his exaltation, his victory, the beginning of his triumphant reign as Lord of lords.

Why did the earliest Christians come to call Jesus "Lord" with a capital *L*? Once again we find ourselves in an Easter parade, in the celebration of Jesus' resurrection from the dead. When God raised Jesus, not only did he prove the efficacy of salvation through the cross, but he also exalted Jesus as the Messiah, the Savior, and even the Lord who was worthy of worship. In light of the Resurrection, the first Christians came to recognize the Lordship of Jesus. Apart from the Resurrection, they would never have imagined something so fantastic and, in a way, so contrary to their Jewish monotheistic intuitions.

But, I should add, the earliest believers in Jesus didn't postulate his lordship merely because he rose from the dead. Rather, in light of the Resurrection, they began to see clearly what Jesus had already communicated. We have no record that Jesus ever said anything quite as blunt as "I am the Lord God." Yet the "I am" statements in the gospel of John—"I am the good shepherd" (John 10:11) or "[B]efore Abraham was, I am" (John 8:58, NRSV)—suggest the identification of Jesus with Yahweh, whose name means "I Am" (Exodus 3:14).

The same could be said of Jesus' statement that "The Father and I are one" (John 10:30). Furthermore, by healing the sick and forgiving sinners without depending on the mediation of a priest or the temple, Jesus acted in a role that Scripture reserves for God alone.[8] Throughout his ministry, Jesus implied that the long-awaited return of Yahweh to Zion was happening in and through him.[9] Without saying "I am Yahweh," Jesus spoke and acted in a way that suggested no other conclusion, but still it's clear that his first followers didn't grasp this point until after his resurrection.

From the text of the New Testament we discover that, shortly after the resurrection of Jesus, those who previously had referred to him respectfully as "lord" ("sir") during his earthly life now began to call him "Lord" in a sense they had previously reserved exclusively for God. They prayed to him as they prayed to God alone. They worshiped him as they worshiped God alone. Without denying his genuine humanity, the earliest Christians spoke of and related to the resurrected Jesus as if he were not just a special human being, but, somehow, the Lord himself, the God of Israel.

JESUS IN A FOREIGN CULTURE

As the first-century Christians began to preach the good news of Jesus to Gentiles in the Roman world, they faced a number of tricky challenges. As we have seen, Jesus came to Israel to announce, to enact, and to inaugurate the kingdom of God. The concept of the kingdom of God was deeply rooted in Jewish soil, especially in the language and hopes of the Hebrew prophets. Yet, after his resurrection, Jesus instructed his disciples to spread the good news throughout the world. This presented early Christian evangelists with a pesky challenge. How could they pass on Jesus' good news about the kingdom of God, a concept that was completely alien to the ears of non-Jews? How could the gospel of Jesus, which more easily made sense to Jews steeped in their own religious traditions, be transplanted from its Jewish pot into the vast, pagan garden of the Greco-Roman world?

Translating words and concepts from one language to another is always a tricky business, as any world traveler can tell you. Consider these valiant attempts to translate foreign phrases into something that English-speaking tourists can understand:

> Elevator notice in Bucharest, Romania: "The lift is being fixed for the next day. During that time we regret that you will be unbearable."

> Menu at a Polish hotel: "Salad a firm's own make; limpid red beet with cheesy dumplings in the form of a finger; roasted duck let loose; beef rashers beaten up in the country people's fashion."

> Advertisement by a Hong Kong dentist: "Teeth extracted by the latest Methodists."

> Sign in a Copenhagen airline ticket office: "We take your bags and send them in all directions."[10]

If it's tricky to translate such relatively simple ideas as these from one language to another, imagine the challenge faced by the early Christians.

First-century preachers discovered that the message of the kingdom of God could be translated quite nicely into good news about Jesus as Lord. The Jewish notion of living under God's reign was repackaged as a call to accept the rule of Jesus. Greco-Roman people knew what lordship was all about, from their social relationships, their religious practices, and even their governmental propaganda. For example, when a Roman soldier named Apion wrote home to his father, he addressed him as "father and lord." He then reported that "I give thanks to the Lord Serapis because, when I was endangered at sea, he rescued me immediately."[11] Serapis was a Hellenistic version of the Egyptian god Apis. When early Christians invited people to acknowledge Jesus as not just one lord among many, but *the* Lord above all lords, they were calling them to submit to Jesus as a son submitted to his father or as a servant obeyed his master. Moreover, they were claiming that Jesus was the one true Lord. Acknowledging the Lord Jesus necessarily involved rejecting other so-called lords, including Serapis, Isis, Zeus, and the others who filled the Greco-Roman pantheon.

Of course, as is always the case in cross-cultural communication, the translation from the kingdom of God to the lordship of Jesus left something behind. Jesus as Lord represented the sovereignty of God, more or less, but did not convey the full good news of his kingdom, including such essential components as healing, forgiveness, and reconciliation with God. Therefore the proclamation of Jesus as Lord was complemented with the good news of Jesus as Savior and Redeemer.

THE *REAL* LORD—JESUS OR CAESAR?

Translating the kingdom of God into the good news of Jesus as Lord may have been an effective evangelistic strategy, but it was also a risky one. If early Christian evangelists had simply announced Jesus as one lord among many, they would have faced little opposition. But they insisted that Jesus was *the* Lord, the one and only Sovereign over all creation. This was not only politically incorrect in the eyes of Roman multiculturists, but treason in the eyes of Roman imperialists.

Beginning with Julius Caesar, Roman emperors became the object of worship after their death, if not during their lifetime. Caligula, who reigned when Christianity was in its infancy, was perhaps the first emperor to be convinced of his own deity and to encourage worship of himself during his lifetime. His successor, Claudius, was called "Lord" and "Savior of the World." The next emperor, Nero, had his predecessor deified and allowed himself to be identified as "Lord of the whole world." By the end of the first century, Emperor Domitian demanded to be addressed as "our Lord and God," and he punished all who refused to give him such honors.[12]

Lest we think that the Roman emperors would have been happy to share the title "Lord" with Jesus, we need to consider the case of Polycarp, a Christian who lived from the late first century into the middle of the second. A leader of stature, he ultimately drew the ire of Roman officials for his Christian faith. The proconsul where he lived sought out Polycarp in order to have him executed. As he confronted the prospect of being burned alive, however, Polycarp had the chance to escape martyrdom. All he needed to do was to say that Caesar was Lord and to offer incense in Caesar's honor.[13] But Polycarp remained faithful to Jesus, devoting himself even in death to his one and only Lord.

Thus we see how problematic and even life threatening it was for early Christians to confess Jesus as the Lord. Among Jews this confession was seen as a blasphemous confusion of a human being with the one true God. Among Romans it came to be regarded as a treasonous offense against the emperor. There can be little doubt, therefore, that when the early Christians professed Jesus as the Lord, they meant it with all of their hearts and intended to live completely under his gracious lordship.

THE LORDSHIP OF JESUS TODAY

Growing up in a well-known Southern California church, I became involved in one of the first "contemporary" worship services around, the sort of service that is now found in churches across the country. Guitars and simple praise songs took the place of the majestic organ and classic hymns that guided the traditional services. The contemporary service even met at an untraditional time, 8:19 each Sunday morning, and was called, simply, "The 8:19 Service."

I remember vividly the excitement of the first 8:19 service. I sat in the front row with my family, enjoying music with a beat and a service led with a more informal style. The pastor who preached that morning didn't hold forth from the pulpit. Rather, Dr. Darrell Guder spoke from a spot on the floor just a few feet in front of where I was sitting. And he didn't just preach. He encouraged dialogue—a radical concept for church in 1970.

Dr. Guder began his sermon with a question: "What does the Lord and his lordship mean to you?" He waited, but nobody spoke. We weren't accustomed to actually answering questions in church. Looking around, Dr. Guder rested his eyes upon me. "Mark," he said probingly, "what does this phrase mean to you: 'The Lord and his lordship'?" Then he stuck a microphone in my face.

I don't think I had ever been so shocked in church. A jumble of thoughts filled my terrified mind. Finally I choked out an answer, "The Lord and his lordship means that Jesus is the Lord, and we're his servants, and he's the one we're supposed to serve." Relieved, I let out a deep sigh and waited for Dr. Guder's response. To my great delight, he liked what I said.

In retrospect, I like it too. If Jesus is Lord, then we are his servants. This would be true even if Jesus were lord merely in the sense of being our master. But since he is also Lord with a capital *L,* we owe him unhesitating dedication and uncompromising obedience.

Truly responding to Jesus as Lord involves far more than merely saying the words, "Jesus is Lord." As he himself said,

> Not all people who sound religious are really godly. They may refer to me as "Lord," but they still won't enter the Kingdom of Heaven. The decisive issue is whether they obey my Father in heaven. (Matthew 7:21)

This remains the "decisive issue" for those of us who claim Jesus as Lord today. Will we flesh out this claim in tangible works of obedience? Will we serve Jesus not simply as one lord among many, but as the Lord of all and as our solitary Master?

Our culture discourages us from accepting the lordship of anything, other than our own autonomy, of course. But, although we pretend to control our own lives, in truth we all serve one or more "lords" outside of ourselves. People in the suburb where I live seem to be running their own lives as they work eighty-hour weeks to support their affluent lifestyles. But often, even when they realize how miserable they are and how much they'd like to change their schedules, they can't get off the treadmill they have made for themselves. They have given their lives to the "lords" of workaholism and materialism. Even their leisure time, what little of it remains, is ruled by the lords of the cell phone and the pager.

Most Christians who confess Jesus as Lord do indeed try to serve him, but we also try to sneak in at least one other lord. Our other lord might be career achievement or financial security, family or friends, social status or even success in ministry. But in the end, we discover that Jesus had it right all along: "No one can serve two masters. For you will hate one and love the other, or be devoted to one and despise the other" (Matthew 6:24). Jesus wants to be Lord of our lives, and he isn't willing to share this position with anyone or anything else.

Devotion to Jesus as Lord has never been without cost. In the first few Christian centuries, it cost many believers their lives. In many countries today, confessing the lordship of Christ still leads to persecution or even martyrdom. Those of us who live in the Western world very rarely face such risks, at least not today. But even for us, solitary allegiance to the lordship of Jesus can be costly. You may recall the bitter public debate over the nomination of John Ashcroft as attorney general of the United States. Senator Ashcroft, a man of unquestionable skill and integrity, had been forthright about his Christian faith throughout his career. He claimed that his commitment to God helped him to be a better citizen and political leader.

But speaking at a Christian college a year before his nomination, Ashcroft had praised the Americans who revolted against British tyranny under the slogan "We have no king but Jesus." Ashcroft's public commitment to Jesus as King drew the wrath of politicians, media pundits, and even some religious leaders. If John Ashcroft believes such things about Jesus, they argued, that's fine for him. But he should not be the nation's chief law enforcement official. In their view, commitment to Jesus as King—or we might equally say, commitment to Jesus as Lord—eliminated Ashcroft from the list of people qualified to serve as attorney general.

You and I will probably never be threatened with death because we confess Jesus as Lord, nor will our Christian commitment become the target of national criticism. But we will inevitably struggle with people or institutions that want to claim lordship over us. Many families in my church have encountered such a claim in youth sports. "Your child plays on Sunday mornings," they are told, "or she doesn't play." All of a sudden parents and children are forced to consider how to acknowledge Jesus as Lord of the Sabbath in a culture that completely disregards both the Sabbath and its Lord.

Consider another situation, something that Christians in the business world often encounter. A woman in my church had a lucrative position in a growing company. Peg liked her job and her professional prospects. Everything looked promising, until the day when her boss asked her to tell a couple of "insignificant" lies. She didn't have to break any laws; she simply had to misrepresent the truth for the sake of office politics. When Peg refused to lie, her boss turned on her. "The choice is yours," he said. "You can work for this company and do what's best for the company, or you can quit." For Peg's boss, either you revered the company as lord, or you did not work for the company. Stunned and disappointed, Peg knew she had no choice. Since Jesus was her only Lord, she resigned, sadly but with unquestioning conviction.

Whether at work or at home, whether in public or in moments when no one is looking, we who claim Jesus as Lord face the continual challenge of living under his lordship.

A Life of Worship

For most of my life, Americans lived with relatively little awareness of Islam. But the growing population of Muslims in the United States combined with the prominence of Islam in world events has changed all of that. Now scenes of Muslims praying to Allah fill the news. We have all seen the pictures of men, women, and children kneeling on their prayer mats, with their faces lowered to the ground.

This Muslim posture for prayer, something relatively unfamiliar to Western Christians, is a position we will someday assume when we worship Jesus as Lord. Remember Paul's picture of the future described in Philippians 2? Because Jesus humbled himself, becoming human and even submitting to physical death,

> Therefore God also highly exalted him
>   and gave him the name
>   that is above every name,
> so that at the name of Jesus
>   every knee should bend,
>   in heaven and on earth and under the earth,
> and every tongue should confess
>   that Jesus Christ is Lord,
>   to the glory of God the Father. (verses 9-11, NRSV)

The time will come, this passage reveals, when everyone will bow before Jesus the Lord in humble worship. But those of us who recognize his lordship today don't have to wait. Indeed, we shouldn't. If we confess Jesus as Lord, then we will respond by worshiping him today just as we will in the future.

The biblical sense of worship is embodied in the posture of bowing to the ground. The basic words for worship in both the Old and New Testament mean, literally, "to bow down in humble submission before another."

When we worship God, we offer ourselves as if we were in the presence of a human king:

> Come, let us worship and bow down.
> > Let us kneel before the LORD our maker,
> > for he is our God.
> We are the people he watches over,
> > the sheep under his care. (Psalm 95:6-7)

Throughout the Old Testament, worship of this kind belongs to the Lord alone.[14] To worship anything or anyone else is idolatry. But because the New Testament reveals that Jesus is the Lord with a capital *L*, he, too, receives worship. The book of Revelation paints a stirring picture of heavenly worship:

> And then I heard every creature in heaven and on earth and
> under the earth and in the sea. They also sang:
>
> > "Blessing and honor and glory and power
> > > belong to the one sitting on the throne
> > > and to the Lamb forever and ever."
>
> And the four living beings said, "Amen!" And the twenty-
> four elders fell down and worshiped God and the Lamb.
> (5:13-14)

Jesus, the Lamb of God who has been exalted as Lord, deserves praise, thanks, adoration, and the humble offering of our very lives.

In biblical worship, though we bow in utter humility, we don't focus upon our unworthiness before God. It is true, of course, that apart from God's gracious action of making us worthy, we are not worthy to be in God's holy presence.[15] But Jesus has opened up the way for us so that we might worship God with freedom and boldness.[16] As recipients of his grace, we are made worthy to enter the direct presence of God without fear or hesitation.

Moreover, the focus of our worship should never be on ourselves, but on God. The English verb "to worship" comes from an old English word that means "to offer worth to" or "to recognize the worth of" someone or something. When we worship, we celebrate the supreme worth of the Lord:

> You are worthy, O Lord our God,
> > to receive glory and honor and power.
> For you created everything,
> > and it is for your pleasure that they exist and were created.
> > > (Revelation 4:11)

> The Lamb is worthy—the Lamb who was killed.
> > He is worthy to receive power and riches
> > and wisdom and strength
> > and honor and glory and blessing. (Revelation 5:12)

Perhaps one of the greatest impediments to genuine worship in the church today is our focus on seeking a special experience or blessing as we worship. To be sure, when we approach God, we come with a yearning to experience him afresh. Often, in the context of worship, our minds are expanded by God's greatness, and our hearts are inspired by his goodness. The experiences and feelings associated with worship can be marvelous indeed. But they are not the goal. We don't worship the Lord primarily to get filled up spiritually, to get blessed, to get healed, or to *get* anything at all. Rather, we worship to give honor, glory, and blessing to God and to the Lamb. When we worship truly, we focus all that we are upon God. We invest our whole selves in fulfilling the greatest commandment of all, to "love the Lord your God with all your heart, all your soul, all your mind, and all your strength" (Mark 12:30).

All of us, at times, find this to be a tremendous struggle. Our hearts can be weighed down with worry. Our souls are sometimes tainted with unconfessed sin. Our minds are distracted with the busyness of life. We can begin to wonder why we don't feel anything when we worship. What happened to the joy of the Lord that used to flood our hearts? At this point we face a watershed decision. If we continue to be preoccupied with ourselves, then we will drift even further from genuine worship. We might try to conjure up joyful feelings, but even if we're successful, they quickly dissipate. We might begin to blame our worship leaders and start looking for another church to inspire us with a novel worship style. But the novelty soon wears off once again, and we're back in our emotional slump.

If you are struggling to worship God, don't focus on yourself, your lack of feelings, your failures. Worship is not a place to criticize yourself or those who seek to lead you before God's throne of grace. Worship is, fundamentally, not about us at all. It's all about God, a God who took on mortal flesh so that we might live eternally. It's about a God who has exalted Jesus, giving him the name above all names and inviting all creation to bow before him as Lord.

No matter how unworthy we are apart from Christ, no matter how unworthy we might feel at any given moment, Jesus has made us worthy to worship him, to ascribe worth to him as Lord, to offer our lives to him as a living sacrifice.[17] Ultimately, our response to Jesus as Lord is a divinely inspired duet in which obedient service and humble worship unite their voices to exalt Jesus as Lord of all.

CHAPTER 10

AN INVITATION TO THE
FATHER'S HEART

Jesus the Son of God

As I stood before my congregation on May 9, 1993, everything felt so familiar, yet so new. With my wife standing next to me and my infant son in my arms, I was not so much the pastor of the church as a father offering his child for baptism. Involvement in this sacrament was nothing new for me, since I had baptized dozens of people before that spring morning. But I had always been on the giving, not the receiving, end. As I stood there with Nathan in my arms, I felt unexpectedly nervous and excited.

My associate pastor, Larry, asked Linda and me to reaffirm our faith in Jesus Christ and our commitment to raise our son to know and serve the Lord. Then Larry baptized Nathan and prayed for him that he might someday confess Jesus as his Lord and Savior and that he might live as a disciple all his life.

Though I had always desired to raise Nathan to be a Christian, his baptism was a defining moment for me. It riveted my mind and quickened my heart. More clearly than ever before, I understood that God had entrusted my son to Linda and me so that we might raise him to know and to love Jesus.

During the first six months of Nathan's life, we had been preoccupied with other duties, the basic responsibilities that overwhelm new parents, things like feeding, diapering, and trying to get some sleep. All of that was necessary, of course. But at the moment of Nathan's baptism, I saw my parental obligations in a bright new light. Yes, Linda and I were to make sure that our son's basic needs were taken care of. In time we'd help him learn to speak and to read, to play soccer and to clean his room, to be a good citizen and a diligent student. Yet all of these matters would take second place to the most important responsibility: to raise him in the love of Christ so that one day he might put his faith in Jesus and live as a faithful disciple. The events of May 9, 1993, defined who I was and what I was to do as a father. That defining moment continues to shape my priorities and practices as Nathan's dad.

The defining moment of Jesus' earthly life also came in the context of baptism. For about thirty years he had lived a relatively normal and obscure life. But as he waded into the Jordan River to be baptized by John, everything was about to change forever. When Jesus came up from the water, the heavens opened and the Holy Spirit descended on him in the visible form of a dove. Then Jesus heard a voice, the very voice of God, speaking to him. "You are my beloved Son," it said, "and I am fully pleased with you" (Mark 1:11).

From that moment on, Jesus left behind his ordinary life as a Galilean craftsman. Following the guidance of the Spirit, he went out alone into the wilderness where he was tempted by Satan. Then he returned to Galilee with a startling message. "'At last the time has come!' he announced. 'The Kingdom of God is near! Turn from your sins and believe this Good News!'" (Mark 1:15).

What happened to Jesus in his baptism defined who he was and what he was to do. It changed the course of his life and, in time, human history. It was the defining moment of all defining moments.

JESUS AS GOD'S BELOVED SON

What exactly did Jesus hear when God said, "You are my beloved Son, and I am fully pleased with you" (Mark 1:11)? I'm not asking about Jesus' auditory experience. Presumably he heard an actual voice speaking in Aramaic. I'm asking instead about what Jesus *understood* when he heard that he was God's Son. If the heavenly voice defined him and his ministry, what definition did Jesus adopt?

Those of us who are Christians might find this question to be so obvious that it's almost silly. Jesus heard that he was the Son of God, of course. He learned that he was divine, if he didn't know it already. He understood that he was, in the language of later theology, God the Son, the second person of the Trinity, fully God and fully human.[1]

I believe all of these things to be true of Jesus. But I don't think any of these truths occurred to him when he heard God proclaim him publicly as his Son. Nor would those who were standing around, who also likely heard the voice from heaven, have thought that Jesus was somehow divine because he was the Son of God. Jews in the first century had a clear idea of what it meant for someone to be a son of God, and this had nothing to do with deity. It had everything to do with the coming kingdom of God, however. We can see this clearly in Jesus' own response to his defining moment. After his sojourn in the wilderness, what did he do? Did he set up a throne and expect to be worshiped as God? Did he go around telling everyone who would listen that he was divine? No, instead he began to preach the good news of the kingdom of God. That was his job description as Son of God: to declare and to inaugurate the kingdom.

THE SON OF GOD IN JUDAISM

If we are to understand the connection between Jesus' identity as Son of God and his ministry of the kingdom, we must, once again, set all of this in its Jewish context. The Old Testament uses the phrase "son of God" in various ways. Israel can be identified as God's son, as in the case of God's statement through the prophet Hosea: "When Israel was a child, I loved him as a son, and I called my son out of Egypt" (Hosea 11:1). The Lord also refers to the children of Israel as his sons and daughters.[2]

In extrabiblical Jewish writings, God's children are not just Israelites in general. They are specifically those who are righteous. According to an apocryphal book known as the Wisdom of Solomon, the righteous person "calls himself a child of the Lord" and "boasts that God is his father."[3] The ungodly seek to test this bold claim by hurting and even killing the righteous person:

> Let us see if his words are true,
>> and let us test what will happen at the end of his life;
> for if the righteous man is God's child [literally "son"],
>> he will help him,
> and will deliver him from the hand of his adversaries.[4]

This sounds strikingly similar to what the Jewish leaders said of Jesus as he was dying on the cross: "He trusted God—let God show his approval by delivering him! For he said, 'I am the Son of God' " (Matthew 27:43).

By far the most significant use of the title "Son of God" both before and during the time of Jesus was as a title for the human king of Israel, beginning with David. When the Lord established David and his progeny upon the throne, he said of David's son, "I will be his father, and he will be my son.... [M]y unfailing love will not be taken from him" (2 Samuel 7:14-15). Moreover, in Psalm 89 God speaks fondly of David, promising to extend his kingdom rule:

> And he will say to me, "You are my Father,
>> my God, and the Rock of my salvation."
> I will make him my firstborn son,
>> the mightiest king on earth.
> I will love him and be kind to him forever. (verses 26-28)

Jews who read this psalm did not attribute divinity to David or his royal heirs. They understood "son of God" in the sense intended, as a title for the king who was close to God's heart and who reigned with God-given authority.

So, if a Jew in the time of Jesus heard that Jesus was the Son of God, the natural inference would be that he was the rightful Davidic king of Israel, not that he was divine. We see this clearly in the beginning of the gospel of John, where one of Jesus' disciples says, "Teacher, you are the Son of God—the King of Israel!" (John 1:49). Nathanael isn't saying two different things about Jesus. In his mind, "Son of God" means the same thing as "King of Israel."

Jews in the time of Jesus tended not to express their messianic hopes with the title "Son of God." They preferred "Messiah" or "Son of David" instead. But since they believed that the Messiah would be the king of Israel and that he would be a descendant of David, the title "Son of God" would have had strong messianic overtones whenever it was used. When Nathanael announced that Jesus was "the Son of God, the King of Israel," he knew quite well that Jesus had absolutely no actual authority as king. Herod remained the nominal ruler under Roman imperial authority, but Jesus was the true King, the Son of God who had been anointed by God to inaugurate the kingdom.

The Messianic Son of God

It should not surprise us to discover that the titles "Messiah" and "Son of God" are closely related. The gospel of Mark starts with the straightforward statement: "Here begins the Good News about Jesus the Messiah, the Son of God" (Mark 1:1). When Peter confesses his belief that Jesus is the Messiah, he says, "You are the Messiah, the Son of the living God" (Matthew 16:16). Similarly, though with different intent, the high priest supervising Jesus' trial says, "I demand in the name of the living God that you tell us whether you are the Messiah, the Son of God" (Matthew 26:63). Of course, Jesus' answer would not have satisfied the high priest, who certainly didn't embrace Jesus' sense of messiahship. But the terms were clear to all parties involved. The Messiah was the Son of God and vice versa.

We have noted that, at his baptism, it was made clear that Jesus was God's Son. However, we know so little about the life of Jesus prior to his baptism that we ought to avoid speculation about his messianic consciousness during his first thirty years. From the moment of his baptism onward, however, Jesus saw himself as the one anointed by God to usher in the kingdom. What happened as he came out of the Jordan River clarified for Jesus his calling as Messiah and Son of God.

The descent of the Spirit upon Jesus after he was baptized fulfilled the messianic visions of Isaiah, who proclaimed many centuries earlier:

> Out of the stump of David's family will grow a shoot—yes,
> a new Branch bearing fruit from the old root. And the Spirit
> of the LORD will rest on him—the Spirit of wisdom and
> understanding, the Spirit of counsel and might, the Spirit
> of knowledge and the fear of the LORD. (Isaiah 11:1-2)[5]

In another passage, the Lord says,

> Look at my servant, whom I strengthen. He is my chosen one,
> and I am pleased with him. I have put my Spirit upon him.
> He will reveal justice to the nations. (Isaiah 42:1)

Here, God not only gives the Spirit to his chosen servant, but he is also "pleased with him." It is no coincidence that Jesus heard the divine voice say, "I am fully pleased with you" (Mark 1:11). These words did more than merely communicate divine delight in Jesus. They also identified him as the chosen Servant of Isaiah, the one who will bring God's salvation and who will suffer vicariously for others.[6]

The divine message given at Jesus' baptism also echoed Psalm 2. In this psalm, the focus is upon the Lord and "his anointed one" or Messiah (see verse 2). At first God speaks: "I have placed my chosen king on the throne in Jerusalem, my holy city" (verse 6). In response, the anointed king proclaims,

> The LORD said to me, "You are my son.
> Today I have become your Father.
> Only ask, and I will give you the nations as your inheritance,
> the ends of the earth as your possession." (verses 7-8)

God identifies the king as his son, not to suggest that the human ruler is divine, but rather to mark him as God's chosen representative, the one who is crowned with divine authority. The baptism of Jesus served rather like the coronation of the Jewish king. It was the sign that his messianic work had received the divine seal of approval.

Notice, however, that God did not echo Psalm 2 completely when speaking to Jesus at his baptism.[7] After saying "You are my son," he omits the line, "Today I have become your Father" (Psalm 2:7). The implication of this omission is clear. Jesus was not adopted as God's Son on the day of his baptism as the king was adopted, so to speak, on the day of his coronation. No, Jesus had been God's Son prior to his baptism. The voice from heaven simply stated what had been true for all time.

INTIMACY BETWEEN SON AND FATHER

Without question, Jesus understood the events of his baptism as pointing toward a messianic mission. This explains why he promptly set out to preach the good news of the kingdom and to enact this good news in works of healing and deliverance. But even though Jesus recognized the messianic dimension of his divine sonship, he understood himself as the Son of God in a more thorough and shocking sense. He assumed an intimacy with God that no Jewish person had ever considered.

We see this most vividly when Jesus called God "my Father." He addressed God with the Aramaic word *abba,* meaning "father" or "my father," something no Jew had done before. God was the Father of Israel in a general sense, but never "*my* Father" in a most personal and intimate way. More than thirty years ago biblical scholars believed that "abba" was a child-like name for a father, something akin to "Daddy." But further research has shown that "abba" was employed by both toddlers and fully grown children. Thus it was a term both of intimacy and respect.

Nevertheless, Jesus' reference to God as "my Father" astounded his Jewish contemporaries, no doubt intriguing his followers while dismaying his opponents. How could a human being speak of God, whose name could not even be mentioned out loud, in such an intimate and personal way? How could any human, even the Messiah himself, say something like Jesus once said about himself?

> My Father has given me authority over everything. No one
> really knows the Son except the Father, and no one really knows
> the Father except the Son and those to whom the Son chooses
> to reveal him. (Matthew 11:27)

Jesus as "the Son"

This passage illustrates another striking feature of Jesus' sense of divine sonship. Here, and in many other gospel passages, Jesus referred to himself as "the Son" in an absolute sense. This peculiar turn of phrase suggests that Jesus considered himself as something more than the Son of Man, the Son of David, or even the Son of God in an ordinary messianic sense. He was *the* Son, the one who had a unique relationship with God, his Father.

The heavenly announcement at Jesus' baptism suggested this. You may recall that Jesus was not just the Son in whom God was pleased, but the "beloved Son" (Mark 1:11). There is one place in the Old Testament where a son is identified specifically as "beloved." This occurs in one of the most poignant stories of the Bible, when God tested Abraham by calling him to sacrifice his son Isaac. In his instruction to Abraham, God says, "Take your son, your only son—yes, Isaac, whom you love so much—and go to the land of Moriah. Sacrifice him there as a burnt offering on one of the mountains, which I will point out to you" (Genesis 22:2). The word translated as "whom you love so much" actually denotes Isaac's uniqueness as well as his father's love for him. When the Hebrew Scripture spoke of someone as a "beloved son," this meant both "greatly loved son" and "only son." When God called Jesus his "beloved" Son at his baptism, this word conveyed both God's profound love for Jesus and Jesus' unique status as the only Son of God.

Jesus' manner of speaking about God indicated that his relationship with God—"my Father"—was unique. He claimed divine intimacy unknown to others. As John puts it in his gospel, "No one has ever seen God. But his only Son, who is himself God, is near to the Father's heart; he has told us about him" (John 1:18).

An Invitation to Sonship

No Jew before Jesus had ever had the audacity to speak of God as "my Father." Jesus' bold familiarity with the Almighty reflected his sense of being the unique Son of God, the one who is close to the Father's heart. But Jesus didn't guard his close relationship with God as something for himself alone. In fact, he did just the opposite. He invited others to join him in calling God "Abba."

This point is marvelously illustrated in the passage of the Sermon on the Mount that includes what we call "The Lord's Prayer":

> But when you pray, go away by yourself, shut the door behind you, and pray to your Father secretly. Then your Father, who knows all secrets, will reward you.... Pray like this:
>
> Our Father in heaven,
>   may your name be honored....
>
> If you forgive those who sin against you, your heavenly Father will forgive you. (Matthew 6:6,9,14)

The unprecedented intimacy that Jesus shared with his heavenly Father was something into which he invited his followers. They, too, could have a personal relationship with God as their Father, One with whom they could share all of their secrets. They, too, could refer to God as "Abba," just as Jesus had done.[8]

What a shocking invitation! It's one thing to recognize that Jesus, as the unique Son of God, had a uniquely intimate relationship with his heavenly Father. It's another thing altogether to consider that mere human beings, people like the disciples, or like you and me, could pray to God as "Abba." Yet this is exactly how Jesus taught his disciples to pray. So striking was this instruction that even Greek-speaking Christians knew and used the Aramaic word *abba* in prayer even decades after Jesus' death and resurrection.[9]

A Shocking Rejection

As we marvel over the intimacy that Jesus shared with his Father and the fact that he invites us to know God as our Abba, too, we stumble across something even more shocking. The beloved Son of God, the one who is near to the Father's heart, was forsaken by his heavenly Father. In his hour of deepest despair, the Son of God was rejected by the Father who loved him.

This part of the story begins with Jesus praying in the Garden of Gethsemane: "'Abba, Father,' he said, 'everything is possible for you. Please take this cup of suffering away from me. Yet I want your will, not mine'" (Mark 14:36). In the hours before his crucifixion, Jesus was crying out to his heavenly Father, asking for the "cup of suffering" to be removed. But the Father's answer was negative. Jesus would suffer not only the physical torment of crucifixion but also the emotional and spiritual anguish of being forsaken by God, his own, loving Abba.

Hours later, after Jesus had been tried, tormented, and tortured, he hung upon a Roman cross. There he cried out once again to his Father, "*Eloi, Eloi, lema sabachthani?*' which means, 'My God, my God, why have you forsaken me?'" (Mark 15:34). Jesus heard no answer, no reassuring voice from heaven as he had heard when he was baptized. The response to his sorrowful prayer was only silence, the silence of divine rejection. The Father had forsaken his only Son.

Our limited minds can only begin to imagine what the Son and the Father experienced in this moment. I remember an occasion in my youth when my dad punished me harshly for something I wasn't guilty of. I felt far worse than I did at other times when he disciplined me for actually breaking the rules. Or I think of how, as a father, I have ached when disciplining my own children.

When my son Nathan was two years old, he had a dangerous habit of wandering away from Linda and me when we were in public places. Once he took off at a park when Linda had turned her back. He was lost for several scary minutes—scary to Linda, that is. Nathan seemed to enjoy his brief flirtation with freedom. Our attempts to teach Nathan to stay near us just weren't working.

One day when Nathan and I were alone in a large, secluded park, he took off on his own. It occurred to me that if he could experience the natural consequences of his actions—the horrible feeling of being lost—that experience might cure him of his wandering. So I followed him but kept out of sight. For several minutes Nathan was happy as could be, enjoying his unfettered exploration. But, all of a sudden, it dawned on him that he was alone. I was not there beside him. He looked around, uncertain at first, then worried, then fearful. Soon he started rushing about randomly, trying desperately to find me. From my hiding place nearby, I felt all of Nathan's pain. I wanted to jump out and run to his rescue, but I knew that if I did so too soon, he'd never learn his lesson. If anything, I'd reinforce his bad habit of wandering off. The seconds I spent in hiding were excruciating. My son was crying for me, and I was able to come to him, but I didn't. Finally, when it seemed that Nathan had really learned his lesson and when, frankly, I could take it no longer, I jumped out from behind my tree. I called out to Nathan and ran to him. We both shared a giant hug and a big cry.

I'm glad to report that this experience cured Nathan's risky wanderings, and I don't think it left any permanent scars on his psyche. But hiding behind that tree was one of the hardest things I ever had to do. To allow my son to feel that I was not there for him when he needed me, even for a couple of minutes, just about broke my heart.

Then I think of God the Father, who loved his Son with a love infinitely greater than mine. I try to imagine what it cost the Father and the Son to experience the dissolution of their intimacy while Jesus hung on the cross. My mind cannot comprehend it, nor my heart encompass it. These things are both too horrible and too wonderful for me.

Why did the Father reject his Son? Unlike the situation with my son Nathan, Jesus had done nothing to merit divine rejection. He lived as a human being, yet without sin to the very end.[10] The punishment he received on the cross was not his own, but ours. As Paul explains, "God made him who had no sin to be sin for us, so that in him we might become the righteousness of God" (2 Corinthians 5:21, NIV). God treated Jesus, the sinless One, as if he were sin itself, rejecting and forsaking him. Jesus experienced what we deserve as sinners. Why? So that "we might become the righteousness of God," or, to paraphrase, so that we might experience the kind of parent-child intimacy with God that Jesus alone had known.

Earlier in this book we saw that Jesus' sense of mission as the Son of Man and as the Messiah was shaped to a considerable extent by Isaiah's prophecy of the Suffering Servant of God.[11] The heavenly voice at Jesus' baptism, we noted in this chapter, intentionally echoed a line from Isaiah that spoke of the Servant as filled with the Spirit and pleasing to God.[12] From the very beginning of his messianic mission as Son of God, Jesus was on his way to fulfilling the unique calling of the Suffering Servant. Remember what Isaiah had predicted concerning this Servant:

> Yet it was our weaknesses he carried; it was our sorrows that
> weighed him down. And we thought his troubles were a pun-
> ishment from God for his own sins! But he was wounded and

crushed for our sins. He was beaten that we might have peace.
He was whipped, and we were healed! All of us have strayed
away like sheep. We have left God's paths to follow our own.
Yet the LORD laid on him the guilt and sins of us all.
(Isaiah 53:4-6)

This describes exactly what Jesus experienced on the cross. He experienced
the ultimate penalty for sin—separation from God—for our sake.

Why did the Father forsake the Son? Because that was necessary for
Jesus to complete his mission as the messianic Son of God. Through being
rejected by the Father, Jesus took upon himself the penalty for our sin, and,
in the process, he exploded that which keeps us from intimate fellowship
with God. Without his sacrifice, Jesus could still teach us to pray to God as
Abba, but we would never know the fullness of the Father's love for us. Sin
would always impede our relationship with God. Yet the paradoxical suffering of the Son of God not only showed us the Father's love, but it also
showered that love upon us. Here is how Paul explained it:

> For we know how dearly God loves us, because he has given us
> the Holy Spirit to fill our hearts with his love.
>
> When we were utterly helpless, Christ came at just the right
> time and died for us sinners.... God showed his great love for
> us by sending Christ to die for us while we were still sinners....
> So now we can rejoice in our wonderful new relationship with
> God—all because of what our Lord Jesus Christ has done for us
> in making us friends of God. (Romans 5:5-6,8,11)

The shocking good news is that we are not only God's friends, but we are
also his beloved children through the saving work of Jesus. To all who
received Jesus, Scripture says, "he gave the right to become children of
God" (John 1:12). As children, we can call God Abba, just as Jesus did. As
children, we can know the love of God that will never let us go.

Living as Children of God

Each of us has a keen yearning for intimacy with God the Father. You and I are just like a four-year-old boy I saw one day in my favorite bagel store. This boy had come for breakfast with his dad. I could tell from their interaction that it was a special "daddy and me" occasion, and the boy was beside himself with glee.

The dad told his son to go and find a table for them while he stood in line waiting to place their order. The boy searched for a minute before he found just the right table, a small table for two with chairs placed on opposite sides. Then the boy did a most curious thing. He grabbed one of the chairs, which was almost bigger than he was, and slowly dragged it around to the other side of the table. He labored for a couple of minutes until both chairs were on the same side, without a hairbreadth between them. This boy didn't just want to share bagels with his father. He wanted as much closeness with his dad as was physically possible.

Can you relate to this boy? I can, in many ways. When I was a young child, my father and I had an exceptionally close relationship. I felt closer to him than most of my friends did with their fathers. But, as I entered adolescence, I began the natural process of withdrawing from my father, and he wasn't able to bridge the gap. We still got along well, but there just wasn't much closeness between us. For several years we shared almost no physical affection, other than an occasional handshake or a very stiff hug.

One day my dad was driving a bunch of my teenage friends and me to an early-morning Bible study. Our Rambler American was particularly full that morning, so I ended up sitting in the middle of the front seat, a bench seat that could barely contain three people. Both my father and the person sitting on my right were relatively large, so I was wedged in between them. As we drove I began to be aware of the feeling of my dad's warm body next to mine. It felt so inviting and reassuring. My dad seemed so strong, so available, so present to me. I could have sat there for hours.

I yearn for that kind of closeness with God. Sometimes I long to be wedged in next to my heavenly Father, to feel his presence as I once felt that of my earthly father. Yet, because my own dad was reticent in sharing himself and his love for me, I hesitate to approach God. If I seek closeness with my heavenly Father, will he be there for me? Or will he remain exalted in heaven, loving me in principle, but rarely loving me in a way that truly touches my heart? Fortunately for me and others who have a similar question, Jesus provides the answer we all long for.

As we already noted, Jesus teaches us to pray to God as our Abba. He encourages us to approach God intimately and share our deepest secrets with our heavenly Father. And to help us have confidence in God's love, he paints a poignant picture of a father who loves his children with reckless abandon.[13]

A father has two sons, the classic "good boy" and his younger brother, the infamous "bad boy." The younger son, overcome by self-interest, asks his father for his share of the inheritance, even while the father is alive. It's as if he says, "Let's pretend that you're dead, Dad, so I can get my share of the money right now." Astoundingly, the father goes along with this insulting plan. As soon as he gets the money, the younger son gets as far away from home as possible. In a distant land, he wastes all his money on frivolous debauchery. For good reason, we know him as the "prodigal" son, the extravagantly wasteful son.

Just about when he runs out of money, famine hits the land where he is living. The only job the unwise young man can find is the worst possible one for a Jewish boy: feeding pigs. He's so hungry that he considers eating the pig slop. Then it dawns on him that his father's servants have a higher standard of living than this. He decides to return home, to confess his unworthiness, and to throw himself upon his father's mercy. Maybe, if he is lucky, he can become one of the hired servants. With this plan in mind, he heads for home.

When his boyhood home is visible but still far in the distance, the son sees some curious commotion. A man is running in his direction. To his horror, he sees that this man is his father, who has been waiting for his return. Surely the son is about to receive the lecture of his life. Maybe the father won't even let him come near his home. Why else must he meet his son so far from the house? As the son nervously practices his confession, all of a sudden his dad reaches him and throws his arms around him. The father is so filled with love and compassion that he can't stop kissing his son. The perplexed young man isn't even able to proceed with his confession speech because his dad interrupts him, showering him with signs that he is completely welcomed back into the family. A festive party lets everyone know that the son has returned into his father's good graces. Though we tend to label the son as prodigal, the father is the truly prodigal one, the one who loves extravagantly. This father loves not just the lovely people who deserve it, but those who are least worthy of being loved.[14]

And that's how our heavenly Father loves us, Jesus says. No matter what you've done, no matter how you've rejected God's love, he seeks intimacy with you just as much as you seek intimacy with him, and even more. Because the Son of God took upon himself the due penalty for your sin, you can approach the Father with freedom and confidence. As the New Testament book of Hebrews urges, "So let us come boldly to the throne of our gracious God. There we will receive his mercy, and we will find grace to help us when we need it" (Hebrews 4:16).

The parable of the extravagant father touches deeply those of us who have intentionally wandered away from God. But it also speaks to those of us who relate, not to the younger son, but to the older "good boy." Jesus doesn't forget about this son, the one who would never have insulted his father by demanding his inheritance and who would never waste money on loose living. When the older son learns that his younger brother has returned and that the prodigal is the guest of honor at a sumptuous feast, he feels both angry and jealous. He refuses to join the celebration.

Once again, the father goes out to meet his son. He pleads with the "good" son to come into the party. But the older boy objects that he has never been the recipient of such extravagance, even though he has always been faithful and responsible. To this the father responds, "Look, dear son, you and I are very close, and everything I have is yours" (Luke 15:31). Fatherly grace is available, not only for the younger son, but for the elder brother as well.

So it makes no difference whether your sin has been extravagant or miserly, egregious or subtle, infamous or secret. Whoever you are and whatever you have done, the love of God is available to you, and not just available, but freely and generously given. God invites all of us into the grand party of his love.

I have always appreciated the story of this prodigal family. When I have taken God's blessing and squandered it, this parable has given me the courage to return to God. Yet I have struggled to take this story into my heart, to know in my soul that God loves me like the father in the parable. To this day I can still doubt God's love at times. But an experience several years ago brought me closer than ever to knowing his love—a love that exceeds all human knowing.

When my wife and I finally completed our seemingly endless years of education and professional training, we were past prime childbearing years. It wasn't a total shock, therefore, when Linda had a hard time getting pregnant. Yet we yearned for a child. After a couple of years of frustration we sought medical assistance. Of course we also brought our hearts' desire before God, praying often for the blessing of a child. Months of medical help and hundreds of prayers produced nothing but disappointment, until a magical moment in April 1992. Linda was finally pregnant!

The following months were like a blur as we got ready to add a baby to our lives. We prepared a room, filling it with everything a newborn could need. We took classes on giving birth and caring for a newborn. Finally, between worship services on the Sunday before Christmas, Linda found me and whispered, "My water broke this morning."

With unmatched excitement, we set off for Hoag Hospital where our baby was to be born. Linda's labor progressed slowly during the evening, and she wasn't ready to deliver until the sun was coming up the next morning. After a physical effort that was truly mind-boggling, Linda gave birth to our son, Nathan.

Like many new parents, I was completely unprepared for what I felt at that moment. I had always been fond of other people's children, even babies. I expected to love my own similarly, perhaps a little more passionately. But when I first held Nathan, my heart exploded volcanically. I felt a fierceness of love that I had never known before. I knew in that moment that I would do anything for my son. No sacrifice would be too great. If someone had offered me literally everything in the world in exchange for that little boy I had held for only a few seconds, I would have rejected the offer without hesitation.

After Linda and Nathan were finally settled in, I drove home for a shower and change of clothes. As I drove, I began to thank God for all of his blessings, for a healthy delivery, for a great doctor, for a fine hospital, and mostly for answering our prayers by giving us a baby. I thanked the Lord for the love I felt for Nathan, for the new joy of loving so completely. Then I heard the Lord speak to me, not audibly, but almost so: "The way you love your son, that's how I love you." I gasped in astonishment. Something I had known in principle suddenly flooded my heart as the Spirit inundated me with the Father's love.

I am aware that my love for Nathan, no matter how powerful it feels, barely begins to approximate the all-surpassing love of our heavenly Father. God's love for me—and for you—excels all human loves. God loves you more ferociously and tenderly than you love anyone or anything. Jesus, the Son of God, lived and died to reveal that love and to invite you into the Father's heart.

Will you accept this invitation? Will you live today—and for the rest of your life—in a loving relationship with the God of the universe, the one Jesus teaches you to call Abba? Your Father is waiting with open arms for your response.

CHAPTER 11

GOD'S PERFECT CAMPSITE

Jesus the Word of God

I'm on a quest for the perfect campsite. I haven't found it yet, but I've come close. When my family and I go camping each summer, I keep my eyes open, always hoping to discover the ultimate place to camp. I'll know it immediately as soon as I see it.

This campsite will occupy an exquisitely beautiful setting near a lake or a stream. It will be secluded and quiet, except for the sounds of nature. Perhaps most important, it will be completely free of mosquitoes. Buzzing is one sound that the perfect campsite will not have.

Several years ago when my wife and I were backpacking in the Sierra Nevada mountains of California, we thought we had finally found it. The campsite was situated in remote Hutchinson Meadow, a lovely alpine garden close to a stream filled with golden trout. Through a lush canopy of pine branches we could see the lofty peaks of the Sierras piercing an azure sky. Yes, this could have been the perfect site, except for one minor drawback—mosquitoes, millions of them, ravenous for blood, *our* blood.

After battling these buzzing vampires for two nights, Linda and I cut short our stay and headed for safer ground. There was no perfect campsite at Hutchinson Meadow, in spite of its exceptional beauty.

But we didn't give up on our quest. Some time later we discovered what I consider to be our best campsite so far. Once again in the High Sierra, we left the marked trail and hiked cross-country to Bottleneck Lake. Finding a suitable campsite near the lake, we feasted our eyes on a vast panorama of soaring, snow-covered mountains. There were no mosquitoes, or any other pests, for that matter. And for the duration of our stay, we didn't see another human being. I suppose the only drawback to this glorious spot is that it requires a grueling, eight-mile hike to get there. But, I must say, it comes pretty close to the ultimate campsite.

My wife and I are not the only ones who are drawn by the idea of finding just the right spot to pitch a tent. According to the gospel of John, even God's Son, the Word of God in the flesh, was seeking a perfect campsite. And he found it here on earth. If we translate John 1:14 very literally, it reads, "And the Word became flesh and pitched a tent among us." This peculiar reference to a tent is not accidental, but an intentional echo of Jewish speculation about the nature of God. If we're to understand who Jesus is as the Word of God and what his camping out among us is all about, then we must first examine Jewish traditions about both God's Word and God's wisdom.

THE WORD AND WISDOM OF GOD

From the very beginning of the Bible, the Word of God is active. In Genesis 1, God speaks all things into existence, testifying to the creative power of his Word. Psalm 33 calls us to praise God in relation to his Word's power and trustworthiness:

> For the word of the LORD holds true,
> > and everything he does is worthy of our trust....
> The LORD merely spoke,
> > and the heavens were created.
> He breathed the word,
> > and all the stars were born. (verses 4,6)

Moreover, the Word of God reveals divine truth. More than one hundred times the Hebrew text of the Old Testament says that "the word of the LORD came" to someone in order to reveal God's purposes to or through that person.[1]

Although the biblical writers sometimes spoke as if God's Word were a thing in itself, almost separate from God, they were simply utilizing a creative turn of phrase. The Word of God is none other than God's own expression, God's power and thought focused in speech.

The Old Testament contains similar language about the wisdom of God. Jewish sages, who speculated upon divine wisdom and its activity on earth, sometimes pictured wisdom as a female figure alongside the Lord. In Proverbs, for example, wisdom speaks in her own voice:

> The LORD formed me from the beginning, before he created
> anything else. I was appointed in ages past, at the very first,
> before the earth began.... And when he marked off the earth's
> foundations, I was the architect at his side. I was his constant
> delight, rejoicing always in his presence.... Happy are those
> who listen to me, watching for me daily at my gates, waiting
> for me outside my home! For whoever finds me finds life and
> wins approval from the LORD. (8:22-23,29-30,34-35)

Once again, though this text uses language in a creative way, we mustn't think of God's wisdom as distinct from the Lord himself. Wisdom, pictured as a heavenly woman, is an aspect or expression of God. This is reflected in Jewish thought about divine wisdom that developed after the completion of the Old Testament. As one writer professed,

> For wisdom is more mobile than any motion; because of her
> pureness she pervades and penetrates all things. For she is a
> breath of the power of God, a pure emanation of the glory of
> the Almighty; therefore nothing defiled gains entrance into her.

> For she is a reflection of eternal light, a spotless mirror of the
> working of God, and an image of his goodness.[2]

Given the Jewish belief that God created all things through his Word, combined with this picture of wisdom as the divine partner in creation, it was natural for the notions of word and wisdom to be closely associated or even combined in the Jewish mind. We see such an association in the prophet Jeremiah, for example:

> But God made the earth by his power,
>   and he preserves it by his wisdom.
> He has stretched out the heavens
>   by his understanding.
> When he speaks, there is thunder in the heavens. (10:12-13)

Because divine wisdom finds expression in divine speech, a Jewish writer in the second century B.C. addresses the Lord,

> O God of my ancestors and Lord of mercy,
> who have made all things by your word,
> and by your wisdom have formed humankind....[3]

Word and wisdom become two sides of the same coin, the coin of the Jewish wisdom tradition with its theological investigations.

WISDOM'S CAMPSITES

According to the wisdom tradition in the centuries prior to the birth of Jesus, God was thought to be once again looking for a perfect campsite, a place where his wisdom might dwell on earth. A Jewish sage named Jesus Ben Sirach composed a treatise in honor of wisdom. In this document, written about two hundred years before Jesus of Nazareth was born, wisdom herself speaks:

> Over waves of the sea, over all the earth,
>> and over every people and nation I have held sway.
> Among all these I sought a resting place;
>> in whose territory should I abide?
> Then the Creator of all things gave me a command,
>> and my Creator chose the place for my tent.[4]

Wisdom's tent, as it turns out, was the "holy tent,"[5] what we often call the tabernacle. This unique tent was designed by God to be the place of Israel's sacrifices, and that design was revealed to Moses as part of the Law.[6]

Another Jewish sage envisioned a related but different campsite for God's wisdom. In the vision of Baruch, wisdom exists in heaven, far away from human comprehension. But the one who created all things makes wisdom readily available to his chosen people:

> This is our God;
>> no other can be compared to him.
> He found the whole way to knowledge,
>> and gave her to his servant Jacob
>> and to Israel, whom he loved.
> Afterward she appeared on earth
>> and lived with humankind.[7]

In what form does wisdom appear this time? Baruch explains,

> She is the book of the commandments of God,
>> the law that endures forever.
> All who hold her fast will live,

and those who forsake her will die.

Turn, O Jacob, and take her;

walk toward the shining of her light.[8]

Divine wisdom takes the form of the Law revealed by God to Moses upon Mount Sinai, in which the instructions for the tabernacle play a central role. Yet, according to Baruch, wisdom is to be identified with the Law, not with the sacred tent. Her perfect campsite, one might say, is the Law itself, the source of both life and light.

THE WORD IN JOHN'S PROLOGUE

Now that we've examined Jewish speculation about God's wisdom and Word, let's read the first few verses of the gospel of John:

> In the beginning the Word already existed. He was with God,
> and he was God. He was in the beginning with God. He
> created everything there is. Nothing exists that he didn't
> make. Life itself was in him, and this life gives light to
> everyone. (1:1-4)

This passage resounds with the language of the Jewish wisdom tradition. Virtually everything John says about the Word Incarnate was attributed to wisdom by the Jewish sages. Like John's description of the Word, wisdom was also said to exist in the beginning, to be present at creation, and to be active as an "architect" at God's side.[9] Even as John envisioned the Word to be the source of life and light, the same was said of wisdom.[10] And, as the sages often spoke of wisdom's visit to earth, so John described the coming of the Word into the world.[11]

But John does not accept the sages' picture of the perfect campsite for wisdom. Though specifically mentioning in his prologue that "the law was given through Moses," John does not view either the Law or the tabernacle as the definitive location for wisdom on earth. God's Word and his wisdom came in an altogether different mode, in the human being known as Jesus of Nazareth.

John 1:14 begins, "So the Word became human and lived here on earth among us." I mentioned earlier that we could translate this sentence literally, "And the Word became flesh and pitched a tent among us." Why would John use such a peculiar verb? Why does the Word Incarnate "pitch a tent"? I suggest that John was consciously echoing and revising Jewish speculation about wisdom. Remember what Jesus Ben Sirach had written about wisdom's camping trip on earth:

> Then the Creator of all things gave me a command,
>> and my Creator chose the place for my tent.
> He said, "Make your dwelling in Jacob…"
>
> In the holy tent I ministered before him,
>> and so I was established in Zion.[12]

John, on the contrary, sees God's Word, so closely associated with wisdom, as pitching a tent among us in a flesh-and-blood human being, in Jesus himself.

This is an astounding assertion, something unprecedented in Jewish reflections about the spoken Word or the wisdom of God. Surely theologians had considered God's Word to be active in human lives, especially among the prophets. And those who sought wisdom could be filled with her, even becoming her children. But no Jew would have gone so far as to say that the divine Word actually became a human being or that wisdom herself took on human flesh.

John makes this very claim, adding, "We have seen his glory, the glory of the One and Only, who came from the Father, full of grace and truth"

(John 1:14, NIV). Jesus, as the Word Incarnate, shines with the very glory of God. He is full of that which God alone can fully contain, namely grace and truth. Yet Jesus, a genuine human being made of flesh and blood, is the embodiment of God's Word and wisdom. He is wisdom's perfect campsite.

A NEW VIEW OF GOD'S WORD

The picture of God's Word and wisdom taking on human form was a new sprout from Jewish theological soil. Though John was the only New Testament writer to use the particular language we find in John 1:14—"the Word became flesh and pitched a tent among us"—the identification of Jesus as God's wisdom occurs elsewhere in the New Testament. Paul writes that "Christ is the mighty power of God and the wonderful wisdom of God" (1 Corinthians 1:24). Moreover, his description of Christ in Colossians echoes Jewish wisdom speculation in a way very similar to John's prologue:

> Christ is the visible image of the invisible God. He existed
> before God made anything at all and is supreme over all cre-
> ation. Christ is the one through whom God created everything
> in heaven and earth.... He existed before everything else began,
> and he holds all creation together.... For God in all his fullness
> was pleased to live in Christ. (1:15-17,19)[13]

Where, we might wonder, did the early Christians get the mind-blowing idea that Jesus was the Word and wisdom of God in human flesh? The answer "by divine revelation" is correct, I believe, as far as it goes. But how, I wonder, did God reveal the true nature of Jesus as the Word made flesh?

I would suggest that Jesus himself sowed the seeds that later sprouted into his identification with divine wisdom.[14] In many of his sayings, Jesus spoke as if he were not just a wise man, but wisdom herself. When defending some of his actions against criticism, he said, "[W]isdom is proved right by her actions" (Matthew 11:19, NIV). Consider also Jesus' stirring invitation,

> Come to me, all of you who are weary and carry heavy burdens, and I will give you rest. Take my yoke upon you. Let me teach you, because I am humble and gentle, and you will find rest for your souls. For my yoke fits perfectly, and the burden I give you is light. (Matthew 11:28-30)

Now compare this with what we find in the writings of the Jewish sage Jesus Ben Sirach:

> My child, from your youth choose discipline,
>> and when you have gray hair you will still find wisdom.
> Come to her like one who plows and sows,
>> and wait for her good harvest....
> Put your feet into her fetters,
>> and your neck into her collar.
> Bend your shoulders and carry her,
>> and do not fret under her bonds.
> Come to her with all your soul,
>> and keep her ways with all your might....
> For at last you will find the rest she gives,
>> and she will be changed into joy for you....
> Her yoke is a golden ornament,
>> and her bonds a purple cord.[15]

Later in this same writing, wisdom herself is quoted:

> Come to me, you who desire me,
>> and eat your fill of my fruits.

> For the memory of me is sweeter than honey,
> and the possession of me sweeter than the honeycomb.[16]

Can there be any doubt that Jesus intentionally echoed the call of wisdom, offering an invitation as the literal incarnation of the wisdom of God?

It's unlikely that Jesus' followers equated Jesus with the divine Word or wisdom prior to his resurrection. But, in the bright light of this event, the seeds Jesus had sown took root, sprouted, and flourished. Guided by the Spirit, the early Christians saw that Jesus was not merely a man possessed of divine wisdom, but the embodiment of wisdom herself. Jesus was not merely one who spoke the Word of the Lord, but he was that Word in the flesh.

RESPONDING TO JESUS THE WORD

If Jesus was indeed the Word of God in human form, then he was also the ultimate revelation of God. That's exactly what John celebrates in the prologue to his gospel. In Jesus, we can see "the glory of the One and Only," the unique glory of God (John 1:14, NIV). Furthermore, though "no one has ever seen God," the Word Incarnate has unique, privileged access to the Almighty. As the "only Son, who is himself God," Jesus "has told us about him" (John 1:18). He is the unique revealer of God's nature through his words, his works, and his very being as the Word Incarnate. Therefore we can know God and know about God with confidence, even though the fullness of God's nature eludes our comprehension. But God has condescended to our weakness, revealing himself in human form so that we might know him.

The notion of Jesus as the Word Incarnate fits poorly within our postmodern world. Our culture, and perhaps even our own culturally conditioned intuition, would resist many implications that follow from Jesus' identity as the Word of God. I would suggest, however, that it is precisely these implications that we need to embrace, allowing them to shape both our relationship with Jesus and our life as his disciples. Let me briefly highlight two countercultural implications of the incarnational theology presented in the first chapter of John.

Becoming People of the Logos

First, if Jesus is the Word Incarnate, then we must use our minds to think carefully and energetically. The Greek term translated in John 1 as "word" is *logos*. It has a broad range of meanings, including "spoken word," "speech," "reason," or "rationality." A form of *logos* shows up as the latter half of many familiar English words, like *sociology* and *theology*. Indeed, theology involves thinking rationally about God and expressing those thoughts in words (though not in words alone, of course). If Jesus is the *Logos,* then we ought to exercise our God-given intellect to think theologically about God, about Jesus, and about every important facet of life.

This commitment to being people of the *Logos* runs counter to our culture's obsession with feelings. Our world has enthroned emotion as the measure of all things. Postmodernism has replaced the Cartesian formula "I think, therefore I am" with a new credo: "I feel, therefore I am, maybe. At any rate, I feel, and that's all that really matters." This emotional and skeptical orientation to life has infected the Western world, including Christianity. I know Christians who relish their emotional relationship with Jesus, but invest very little mental effort in trying to understand him. For them, Christianity is primarily, if not exclusively, a matter of feelings.

If Jesus is the Word of God, then we must reject the view that equates genuine Christian faith with our feelings. We do well to hold suspect anything that sacrifices truth for the sake of fleeting emotions. Jesus does indeed promise that wonderful feelings will be given to those who believe in him, feelings like overflowing joy and supernatural peace.[17] But these are the by-products—not the core—of a genuine, truth-filled relationship with Jesus the Word.

Since you've read to this point in this book, you probably don't need me to tell you to think about your faith. So to you I offer a word not of admonition, but of encouragement. Keep on thinking about Jesus. Read theology that challenges your mind. Engage in serious conversation with others about matters of faith. And above all, study the Scriptures, the written Word of God that reveals the incarnate Word of God to us.

Becoming People of Revelation

Here is a second crucial point about Jesus: The Word of God became flesh in order to reveal God to us.[18] Jesus offers a unique and uniquely truthful picture of God because he is the divine Word made flesh. We can know God in light of his self-revelation through the incarnate Word, as well as the entire written Word of God.

Christian faith is based on God's revelation in history. Though God often whispers in our hearts when we are quiet enough to listen, our faith does not rest on our subjective experience. It stands upon the rock of God's self-revelation throughout the ages. We see this in every part of the Bible. In the Old Testament, for example, Abraham and Sarah didn't conjure up a god to meet their needs; their culture supplied plenty of household gods already. Rather, the sovereign Lord freely disclosed himself to them, changing their lives forever.[19] The same could be said for Moses, whose sojourn in the wilderness was interrupted by God's self-revelation at the burning bush.[20] Through the Law and the Prophets, through exceptional miracles and daily blessings, God revealed himself to his people. The New Testament continues the story of God's self-revelation, with attention focused on Jesus as the unique, ultimate Revealer.

Divine revelation lags in popularity these days. In our postmodern world, we are encouraged to invent our own gods, not to be told by anyone else—God included—what God is like. We claim the right to piece together a religion that meets our personal needs and conforms to our preferred values. Take a little of Christian grace, a bit of Eastern meditation, a bunch of generic love, and—voilà!—you have your own tailor-made religion. The whole idea of revelation seems foreign, even offensive, because it assumes that we receive truth from an outside authority, one who is superior to ourselves and who, therefore, has the right to tell us what our religious beliefs ought to be.

I can't tell you how many times, when talking with folks about some perplexing aspect of God's revealed character, I have heard them say, "Well, I'm just not comfortable with a God like that. *My* God isn't that way." They simply assume the right and the ability to determine what God is and isn't like. Wow! If there really is a God who lives outside of our imaginations, then it's rather audacious of us to define God's nature on the basis of what we're comfortable with.

Furthermore, if God has actually bothered to reveal himself through something other than our personal inclinations, it's rather foolish to try to invent God from scratch. Wouldn't it be better to pay attention to God's self-revelation in history, in Scripture, and, most of all, in Jesus? In the final analysis, I wouldn't want to trust my life to the pint-sized God of my own creation. Though the idea of revelation might insult my self-centeredness, it actually relieves me of an impossibly heavy burden—the need to invent God and get it right.

Let me hasten to add, however, that a commitment to revelation does not imply our own infallibility in interpreting that revelation. God has revealed himself definitively in Jesus, but that does not mean that I have understood this revelation fully or even correctly in many details. I'm quite sure that, as hard as I've tried to avoid it, this book you're now reading has a few mistakes in it. They don't reflect a lack of effort on my part. But in spite of my best intentions, I am still a limited, fallible, finite human being.

It's important to make this sort of confession, I believe, because Christians are often accused of arrogance. And rightly so at times. We often confuse the fact of revelation with the false fact of our own ability to grasp this revelation perfectly. We ought to avoid this confusion at all costs. So although we seek to understand what God has revealed and to communicate our findings to others, we must do all of this with genuine humility. If anything, the revelation of God in Christ should set us free from presumption, helping us realize that every truth we grasp is a gift from God. Jesus, who humbled himself in his incarnation, calls us to imitate his humility.

When I think of a humble yet confident witness to Jesus as the Word Incarnate, I remember my friend Krister Sairsingh. I first got to know Krister when we were students at Harvard. He was a Christian with a most amazing story.

Krister, whose given name was actually Krishna—in honor of the Hindu god—was raised in a respected Hindu family. He took his religion seriously, a situation that led him to a crisis in his teenage years. Although he had put his faith in the Hindu gods, they didn't satisfy Krister's thinking or the longing of his soul. After a friend told him about Jesus, he was haunted by the teachings and personality of the man from Nazareth. During a season of deep intellectual and personal struggle, Krister would often cry out to God for help. He wanted to know the truth.

Finally Krister realized that the good news about Jesus was true, that Jesus was indeed the only Lord and Savior. Krister put his faith in Jesus, even though it dishonored his family and forced him into passionate debates with them. How could he give up his own faith and take on something so foreign? And how could he claim that Jesus is not just *one* way but *the* way to God?

When I first got to know Krister, he was trying to finish his doctoral work in religion at Harvard. Though he was a brilliant scholar, his confident faith in Jesus was a stumbling block for many faculty members, especially since his decision to abandon Hinduism dishonored the idol of multicultural relativism. It took years for Krister to convince the religion faculty at Harvard that he was worthy of a Ph.D. degree, even though his academic work was exemplary.

Remarkably, through all of his trials, in countless presentations, panels, and personal interactions, Krister's confidence in Christ never spilled over into pride. When he spoke of Jesus, he did so with genuine humility. One never had the sense around Krister that he was some brilliant know-it-all, even though his intellect was dazzling. I'd be amazed if Krister ever offended anyone by talking about Jesus, though he shared his faith freely and frequently.

Krister's story convinces me that we can be solidly committed to God's revelation through the Word Incarnate and still speak with true humility. This will be especially true if we realize that, in the end, everything we are depends on God's grace offered to us in Christ. Let us now turn to this point.

EVERY DAY IS CHRISTMAS

As John reflects on the impact of the Word made flesh, he writes, "We have all benefited from the rich blessings he brought to us—one gracious blessing after another" (John 1:16). This translation rightly renders the sense of the Greek, which literally reads, "From his fullness we have all received, grace upon grace." On the one hand, we respond to the incarnation of the Word by receiving him as the unique revelation of God. On the other hand, we respond by receiving the grace he offers: grace upon grace, one gracious blessing after another.

Grace is something undeserved and unmerited. By definition, it can't be earned. This is what Jesus gives us as the Word Incarnate. He gives us true knowledge of God, even though we deserve to remain lost in our ignorance. He gives us eternal life, even though we have earned the death penalty for our sin. He gives us joy, peace, and a life full of blessing, not because we deserve it, but because of his grace.

Several years ago on Christmas Eve, I was preaching on the prologue of John's gospel. This text was most appropriate, of course, since at Christmas we celebrate the coming of the Word of God in human flesh. The first installment of this sermon would be preached at our 4 P.M. service, a service for young children and their families. My tradition had always been to preach on the same topic during all three Christmas Eve services but to direct the first sermon to children. Usually I found some child-friendly illustration that fit the main point of the sermon.

As I wrestled with how to illustrate the concept of "grace upon grace," I stumbled upon a happy plan. When it was time for my sermon, I walked to the center of the stage, which was covered with brightly wrapped Christmas presents. Each present, I told the congregation, represents some gift of God, some specific instance of what we call "grace." I asked the children if they could think of some wonderful gift God has given us. Immediately a hand shot into the air. "My mom and dad," said the child. I took one of the presents, called it "Mom and Dad," and put it on the floor in front of me. "My dog," said another child. I took a present, called it "our pets," and put it on top of the first present. Whenever a child mentioned a gift from God, another present would go on the pile. Before too long I had a stack of presents so tall that I couldn't reach the top. There we had it, gifts stacked upon gifts, grace upon grace.

The gifts of Jesus don't come just one day a year. He gives grace upon grace each day. Every day is Christmas, so to speak, because we continually receive gifts of divine grace. Moreover, every day is Christmas because we live constantly in light of the Incarnation, which we celebrate at Christmastime.

If we live in light of the Incarnation, we will stop trying to earn God's favor. By definition, grace can only be freely given, not earned. As recipients of divine grace, we will live in freedom, not fear. We will offer our lives to God, not because we have to, but because we want to, because that's what our gratitude produces.

So let me urge you to delight in the blessings that the Word Incarnate has showered upon you. Take time to remember his manifold gifts, his "grace upon grace" in your life. Let this day be like Christmas, a day to celebrate the incarnation of the Word of God, the one who embodies the very wisdom of God. Jesus reveals the Father's glory and pours out the Father's grace.[21]

Allow your heart to worship Jesus with the words of the beloved carol:

Yea, Lord, we greet Thee,
Born this happy morning,
O Jesus, to Thee be all glory given;
Word of the Father,
Now in flesh appearing!

O come, let us adore Him,
O come, let us adore Him,
O come, let us adore Him,
Christ, the Lord![22]

CHAPTER 12

THE BRILLIANCE OF GOD

Jesus the Light of the World

Simeon was a godly man, both in heart and in action. Throughout his long life he had loved nothing more than to worship in God's house. Like other faithful Jews in the first century A.D., Simeon longed for the coming of the Messiah. But unlike his contemporaries, he had ample reason to believe that his longing would be fulfilled. None other than the Spirit of God had told Simeon that he would not die before he had seen God's Anointed One.[1]

It's not hard to imagine what this aging man might have envisioned when he reflected on this promise: the triumphant entry of a victorious general into Jerusalem, the cleansing of the city of all vestiges of Roman rule, the crowning of the Messiah who would sit on the throne of David. How Simeon's heart must have burned within him as he waited for the Savior to come!

Then it happened. Just as the Spirit had once spoken when promising that Simeon would see the Messiah, so the Spirit spoke again. Unmistakably, Simeon heard the voice of God in his heart, telling him to go quickly to the temple. In spite of his old age, Simeon sprinted to his destination.

Upon arriving he scanned the crowds for evidence of the Messiah, but he saw nothing unusual, only the teeming masses that generally filled the temple courts. He noticed a young couple who had brought their baby to be presented to the Lord, as was required in the Law. Immediately, Simeon heard the inner voice of God once again: "He's the one. This is the one you've been waiting for."

It's easy to picture Simeon's surprise. At first taken aback, the old man quickly recovered his bearings. God was showing him the promised Messiah, not in his regal glory, but in his infancy. Approaching the young couple, Simeon introduced himself and asked if he might hold their child. They agreed, sensing they could trust him.

When Simeon took their child, it wasn't like anything they had ever seen before. He seemed to be transfixed as he gazed at the face of their little boy. Finally Simeon lifted his eyes to heaven and prayed:

> Lord, now I can die in peace!
>> As you promised me,
> I have seen the Savior
>> you have given to all people.
> He is a light to reveal God to the nations,
>> and he is the glory of your people Israel! (Luke 2:29-32)

We can only imagine how Simeon's heart was moved in this moment. Feelings of awe, wonder, and gratitude must have saturated his soul. Likewise for the parents of the baby. In spite of all the wonders they had recently experienced, they must also have been amazed by Simeon's words. How had he known that Jesus was so special? And what did he mean by calling him "a light to reveal God to the nations"?

Some thirty years later, the baby once held by Simeon had grown up. He returned to the temple, where he amazed the crowds with his teaching. All of a sudden he raised his voice and said something strangely similar to what Simeon had once declared about him: "I am the light of the world," he stated. "If you follow me, you won't be stumbling through the darkness, because you will have the light that leads to life" (John 8:12).

What an audacious claim! It's one thing to be called the light of the world by somebody else. It's another thing altogether to refer to oneself as the Light of the World, and to do so in public, especially in the temple! After all, in Jewish tradition, Jerusalem was to be a light for the nations, with her illumination emanating from the temple, the place where God's own glory shines.[2] For Jesus to proclaim that he was the true Light that would open the spiritual eyes of the Gentiles was virtual blasphemy.

What did Jesus mean by referring to himself as "the Light of the World"? What did Simeon picture when he called Jesus "a light to reveal God to the nations"? Once again, we turn to the Old Testament to gain insight into this promised Jewish Messiah.

THE LIGHT OF THE WORLD IN THE OLD TESTAMENT

According to Genesis 1, God made light as the first of his creative activities.[3] He then added the light-giving bodies in the heavens, the source of actual light on earth.[4] When God appeared to his people, he often took the form of light-producing fire.[5] And, though the Israelites never worshiped the sun itself as a god, they could refer to the Lord using the powerful imagery of "a sun and shield" (Psalm 84:11, NIV).

God appeared as the sun to the prophet Habakkuk:

> I see God, the Holy One, moving across the deserts from Edom
> and Mount Paran. His brilliant splendor fills the heavens, and
> the earth is filled with his praise! What a wonderful God he is!
> Rays of brilliant light flash from his hands. (3:3-4)

In Hebrew poetry, God's grace was pictured as the shining of his face.[6] And he was a God who could be called, simply, "light."[7]

But the symbol of light took on special significance in the prophecies of

Isaiah, who associated divine light with the coming of the Messiah and his kingdom:

> The people who walk in darkness will see a great light—a light
> that will shine on all who live in the land where death casts its
> shadow. Israel will again be great, and its people will rejoice as
> people rejoice at harvesttime.… For a child is born to us, a son
> is given to us. And the government will rest on his shoulders.
> These will be his royal titles: Wonderful Counselor, Mighty
> God, Everlasting Father, Prince of Peace. His ever expanding,
> peaceful government will never end. (Isaiah 9:2-3,6-7)

Yet, according to Isaiah's vision, the light of God's kingdom would shine not only upon Israel, but upon the whole world. To his Servant the Lord said, "You will do more than restore the people of Israel to me. I will make you a light to the Gentiles, and you will bring my salvation to the ends of the earth" (Isaiah 49:6). The Servant's task would be shared with Jerusalem as well, according to God's command:

> Arise, Jerusalem! Let your light shine for all the nations to see!
> For the glory of the LORD is shining upon you. Darkness as black
> as night will cover all the nations of the earth, but the glory of
> the LORD will shine over you. All nations will come to your light.
> Mighty kings will come to see your radiance. (Isaiah 60:1-3)

Jerusalem's light would not be self-generated but would be a reflection of the "everlasting light" of God (Isaiah 60:19).

WHO IS THE LIGHT OF THE WORLD?

Simeon's claim that Jesus is "the Savior…given to all people" and "a light to reveal God to the nations" reverberates with the prophecies of Isaiah. The baby Jesus will grow up to fulfill the role of God's Servant, the "light to the Gentiles" who will bring divine "salvation to the ends of the earth" (Isaiah 49:6). Jesus affirms the same reality in different language. As "the light of the world," he offers "the light that leads to life" (John 8:12). This life is not mere physical existence. It is eternal life, abundant life, the life of the kingdom of God.

As the Light of the World, Jesus also reveals God's truth. He shines into the darkness of human ignorance and sin. Although the darkness resists the light of Jesus, it cannot overwhelm that light.[8]

From our vantage point as Christians, we can easily take Jesus' claim to be the Light of the World for granted. After all, if he's Savior, Lord, and Word Incarnate, why not Light of the World as well? Of course, if we were to put ourselves in the place of those Jews who first heard this claim, we might begin to share in their amazement. But Jesus said something else, which, I believe, needs even less cultural translation to shock us. We find this saying in the Sermon on the Mount:

> You are the light of the world—like a city on a mountain,
> glowing in the night for all to see. Don't hide your light under a
> basket! Instead, put it on a stand and let it shine for all. In the
> same way, let your good deeds shine out for all to see, so that
> everyone will praise your heavenly Father. (Matthew 5:14-16)

Did you catch that? Jesus said *you* are the light of the world! In the context of Matthew, Jesus was speaking to his disciples. As his disciples today, we rightly hear this statement as a description of our own identity. *We* are the light of the world. Do you believe it?

Notice that Jesus does not say, "You *should be* the light of the world." He doesn't describe a worthy goal; he describes present reality. From his enlightened perspective, we already *are* the light of the world. The question is not who we ought to be, but whether or not we will live out who we already are. We can try to hide from the world, to cover our light with a basket. But that's rather silly, Jesus notes. Light is meant to be displayed. If we're the light of the world, then we had better shine out brightly.

Jesus adds that, as the light of the world, we are also "like a city on a mountain" (Matthew 5:14). This allusion is not just to any city of high elevation, but quite obviously to Jerusalem, the city perched upon Mount Zion. Remember Isaiah's encouragement, "Arise, Jerusalem! Let your light shine for all the nations to see! For the glory of the LORD is shining upon you" (Isaiah 60:1). Appropriating this imagery, Jesus says that we who follow him are the New Jerusalem, the shining city that illuminates all nations.

Those of us who like tidy ideas might be unsettled by Jesus' creatively untidy use of light imagery. How can we be the light of the world if Jesus is also the Light of the World? This question was answered, I believe, in the verse from Isaiah 60 that I just quoted. Jerusalem was a light for the nations, not because she glowed internally, but because the glory of God was shining upon her. Her light, therefore, was reflected. Similarly, we can be the light of the world when we reflect Jesus, the Light of the World.

Several years ago I made our identity as the light of the world the topic of my Christmas Eve sermon. But how could I explain the twofold sense of the light of the world to a bunch of children who were beside themselves with excitement because it was Christmas Eve? As I thought and prayed, the Holy Spirit gave me a solution. I had to do a little bit of shopping, but once I had the right equipment, my illustration was perfect.

As my sermon began, the lights in the sanctuary were turned off. A large box wrapped as a Christmas present sat on the Communion table. It was illuminated by a spotlight that shone upon it with blinding brilliance. Pointing to the light I explained how Jesus is the Light of the World.

"Like this spotlight," I said, "Jesus shines in the darkness. He helps us see God's wonderful gifts of salvation and eternal life. At Christmas we celebrate the coming of Jesus, the Light of the World.

"But that's not the whole story," I continued while walking over to the brightly wrapped package. "Jesus also said that we are the light of the world. That's right. You and I are the light of the world, just like Jesus.

"I know some of you are wondering how this can be true. 'I'm not much of a spotlight,' you're thinking. 'How can I shine into the world like Jesus does?'

"Well," I continued, "rather than explain how this works, let me show you instead. This is how you and I can be the light of the world, just like Jesus."

Immediately I lifted the large package from the Communion table. It wasn't really a package at all, but a wrapped box without a bottom, a cover hiding my surprise prop. What people saw at first wasn't so much the prop itself, but what it produced. Instantly the whole sanctuary was flooded with beams of brilliant light. Hundreds of glowing quadrilaterals twirled around the room, reflecting off the windows, bouncing playfully on the walls. You've probably figured out by now what I had put on the Communion table. That's right, a disco ball—a spinning, shining monument to a 1970s dance craze.

After my unexpected light show made its impact, I explained to the children what they were seeing.

"I know many of you have never seen anything like this before. You ask your parents on the way home about this thing. I'm sure they've got some stories to tell. That spinning ball is called a disco ball. It's covered with several hundred small squares of glass, and an electric motor makes it spin around. When the spotlight hits the mirrors, light is thrown in all directions, covering every part of the room. It certainly gets your attention, doesn't it?

"You and I are like the mirrors on this ball. We can shine into the world, not because we have light inside of us, but because Jesus shines *on* us. We reflect his light. Our church is just like this disco ball, a collection of Jesus reflectors. Jesus has put us in the world, in our families and our schools, in our neighborhoods and soccer teams, so that we might reflect his light into our world."

If you come from a segment of Christendom that frowns on dancing, you may not appreciate my use of a disco ball. But it's a vivid illustration of the point made by Isaiah about Jerusalem and by Jesus about us. Jesus is the Light of the World in a unique way. But he has chosen to shine his light on us as we reflect his love and grace.

How Do We Shine?

In practical terms how do we shine as the light of the world? How do we angle the mirror of our lives so that people around us might see God's light reflected in us? Jesus answered this question clearly. On the one hand he said, "Don't hide your light under a basket" (Matthew 5:15). Don't live in such a way that your Christian faith is a secret. That's the negative part of the answer. Positively, Jesus stated, "[L]et your good deeds shine out for all to see, so that everyone will praise your heavenly Father" (Matthew 5:16).

We mustn't misinterpret Jesus' point. He is not encouraging us to seek attention for ourselves, to create photo ops to highlight our personal accomplishments as some political candidate might. Not too many verses later in Matthew, Jesus says we should not do our good deeds publicly in order to be seen by others.[9] The crucial issue has to do with our motivation. When we do good deeds, are we seeking our own glory or the glory of God? Are we intending to reflect Jesus or pretending to be incandescent all by ourselves?

I have sometimes heard Christians utilize Jesus' statement to justify their avoidance of talking to others about the Lord. "Jesus tells us to do good deeds," they say, "and that's it. We don't have to say anything but simply do good things. That will give glory to God." But if we do good deeds, yet never give credit to God, how will people know to praise the heavenly Father? If we invest our lives in all sorts of worthy causes, but do so as if by our own inspiration and strength, how will anyone know that God should get the credit? One of the ways we position our mirror to reflect God's light is by using our words to give credit where credit is due. As in the ministry of Jesus himself, our *words* and our *works* combine to bear witness to the kingdom of God.

I can think of dozens of people I know who live with their mirror set at just the right angle to reflect God's light into their part of the world. I think of business executives who operate at work according to biblical standards. I think of government officials who refuse to do what is wrong even when it's politically expedient. I think of teachers in public schools who shine with Christ's love, even though they are legally limited in what they can say to their students.

One of these teachers is a man named Brian. For years he was the music teacher in a tough inner-city school in Orange County, California. A man of ample talent and devotion, Brian could certainly have found a safer, better-equipped, and wealthier school in which to work. He could also have found an easier teaching position, one that didn't require so many extracurricular hours arranging musical scores, laying down taped instrumental tracks, and overseeing choral rehearsals. But Brian did not regard his job as merely a way to make a living. He did what he did first and foremost to reflect the light of Christ into a dark corner of this world. And reflect Christ he did, through his love for his students and his willingness to speak of his faith when asked. Brian did plenty of good works, to be sure, but nobody who knew him could fail to see in his behavior a reflection of the love of God.

Christians have been doing this sort of thing for centuries. Elizabeth Gurney was born into a wealthy British banking family in 1780. She was expected to marry, to bear plenty of children, and to live the proper and sheltered life of British aristocracy. The first two she accomplished rather well, marrying Joseph Fry and raising eleven children. But the third expectation, living a proper and sheltered life, Elizabeth Fry failed most gloriously to fulfill.

When she was eighteen years old, Elizabeth heard the gospel of Jesus Christ and committed her life to him. In time, the Spirit of Christ led her into a most unexpected ministry: prison reform. In the early nineteenth century, English prisons were notorious for their inhumanity. They were teeming with filth, sickness, brutality, and suffering. Women prisoners, often convicted of relatively minor offenses, were jammed into tiny, polluted cells along with murderers and other violent criminals. Children of female inmates were usually housed with their mothers to share their dreadful quarters. All of this seemed an abomination to Elizabeth Fry.

At first she shined the light of Christ into the dark prisons by making daily visits to the prisoners, seeking to care for their physical needs. Realizing that her personal efforts were inadequate, Elizabeth founded the Association for the Improvement of Female Prisoners in 1816. Her stated purpose was

> to provide for the clothing, instruction, and employment of the
> women; to introduce them to a knowledge of the Scriptures;
> and to form in them, as much as possible, these habits of sobri-
> ety, order and industry, which may render them docile and
> peaceable whilst in prison, and respectable when they leave it.[10]

Elizabeth continued to care for inmates in a personal way, often at great risk to her own safety. Through her efforts, a remarkable change was observed in her local prison. Prison officials began to show interest in reform, as did members of the national government. In time, she not only addressed the House of Commons and the queen of England, but she met with many leaders throughout Europe.

In the end, Elizabeth Fry impacted the prison system not only in England, but throughout the European continent as well. Her willingness to shine the light of Christ into the fiercely dark world of English prisons brought justice to many and much honor to Christ.

A PHOSPHORESCENT WITNESS

I have used the image of the disco ball to explain how we can be the light of the world at the same time we acknowledge Jesus as the unique Light of the

World. Elizabeth Fry and my friend Brian are two small mirrors on the giant disco ball of Christian history.

But I'd like to employ another analogy here, one that focuses on a different aspect of our reflective witness. Allow me to suggest that we are like the small phosphorescent cross that was affixed to my bed during my youth.

There was nothing particularly fancy about that cross. It was a simple design made out of plastic. In the daylight it looked white, with a slightly yellow undertone. But when the cross was exposed to light during the day, it would glow at night with an otherworldly greenness. I don't mean to imply that it was scary, however. My cross actually provided me with many nights of peaceful sleep.

Now I have a confession to make. As a young boy, I was terrified of vampires. I'm afraid I took in too many Dracula films during Saturday-afternoon episodes of "Chiller." Though I knew in my head that vampires were not real, my heart and my dreams remained unconvinced. But I also knew that vampires couldn't bear the presence of a Christian cross. So I glued my little plastic cross to my bed, and there it glowed, warding off vampires better than a garlic pizza.

But my cross wouldn't glow adequately unless it had been exposed to ample light during the day. If for some reason my curtains had been drawn when the sun was shining, then a few hours of artificial light in the evening would energize the cross for just a brief, diffuse glow at bedtime. If I happened to awake in the middle of the night, haunted by a vampire dream, my cross would be of little use to me, having long since lost its luminescence.

I hope you don't mind being compared to a plastic, phosphorescent cross. But it helps make an important point about our calling. You and I will only be able to reflect Christ if we are spending ample time absorbing his light. We are not incandescent, self-generating sources of light. We are phosphorescent, able to glow brightly only if we have spent enough time in the presence of Christ's divine light. If we choose, on the contrary, to live in darkness, even though we are Christians, then we'll be unprepared to shine when our light is needed.

I'll admit that the New Testament doesn't speak directly of vampires and phosphorescent crosses, but a passage from the first letter of John comes pretty close:

> This is the message he has given us to announce to you: God is
> light and there is no darkness in him at all. So we are lying if we
> say we have fellowship with God but go on living in spiritual
> darkness. We are not living in the truth. But if we are living
> in the light of God's presence, just as Christ is, then we have
> fellowship with each other, and the blood of Jesus, his Son,
> cleanses us from every sin. (1:5-7)

According to this text, we who are Christians must choose to live accordingly, by "living in the light of God's presence" and shunning the darkness that used to feel like home. In a similar passage, Paul instructs us to leave behind the darkness in which we once lived and to "[l]ive as children of light" (Ephesians 5:8, NIV). He explains, "Take no part in the worthless deeds of evil and darkness; instead, rebuke and expose them" (Ephesians 5:11).

Guarding Our Eyes

Jesus himself teaches us to avoid darkness by watching carefully what we place in front of our eyes. Notice the connection he makes between being a light in the world and what we see with our eyes:

> No one lights a lamp and then hides it or puts it under a bas-
> ket. Instead, it is put on a lampstand to give light to all who
> enter the room. Your eye is a lamp for your body. A pure eye
> lets sunshine into your soul. But an evil eye shuts out the light

and plunges you into darkness. Make sure that the light you
think you have is not really darkness. If you are filled with light,
with no dark corners, then your whole life will be radiant, as
though a floodlight is shining on you. (Luke 11:33-36)

Jesus' main point is easy to see. That which becomes the focal point of
our vision will soon flood our hearts. To state the matter more broadly,
whatever occupies your consciousness will soon fill your consciousness. So
if you want to be filled with light, then you had better focus on light, not
darkness. If you want to reflect Jesus into a dark world, then you must first
be filled with his light by focusing the eyes of your heart upon him.

Of course our literal eyes can sometimes open our hearts to darkness.
My boyhood fear of vampires was a direct result of having watched too
many Dracula movies. Adulterous desires, if not actions, often result from
eyes that have wallowed in lust. Envy and covetousness follow when we see
something wonderful that belongs to our neighbor and not to us and then
allow our minds to be captivated by what we crave. Without a doubt, we
must govern our gaze if we seek to be filled with the light of Christ.

But the seeing metaphor can easily apply to thinking as well. What
things fill your mind? About what do you daydream in your secret moments? How much time in a given day do you set aside for meditating on
the Word of God? Remember Paul's encouragement to the Philippians:

Fix your thoughts on what is true and honorable and right.
Think about things that are pure and lovely and admirable.
Think about things that are excellent and worthy of praise.
(4:8)

This does not mean, of course, that we should live in denial or keep our
heads buried in the sand of cultural ignorance. Indeed, if we're to shine the
light of Jesus effectively into our world, then we need to know exactly
where the darkness is and how it ought to be exposed. But as we observe

the world around us, we must avoid focusing our hearts on evil in a way that panders to our own desires.

The important point, it seems to me, is that we invest ourselves in relating to Christ. If you'll pardon a switch of metaphors from light to grapevines, Jesus says in John 15 that we will be fruitful in life only if we remain connected to him. "For," he cautions, "apart from me you can do nothing" (John 15:5). When we make our home in him, however, then we are in a position to live fruitful, productive, and joyful lives. Then we are ready to shine with his light into the world around us.

Living in Light of the Future

As Christians we are to live in light of the future. On the one hand, we are to live with the future in mind, with the promise of God's kingdom guiding our present existence. On the other hand, we are to live now in the glow of the future, a future that promises to blaze with divine light.

According to the apostle Paul, we will have endurance for faithful living in this age if we remember that God has "qualified [us] to share in the inheritance of the saints in the kingdom of light" (Colossians 1:12, NIV). God has already "rescued us from the dominion of darkness and brought us into the kingdom of the Son he loves" (Colossians 1:13, NIV). Therefore, we can live now in light of the kingdom of God as it begins to dawn upon the horizon, casting its light into the present.

The biblical picture of the future is replete with divine light. Consider the vision of the new heaven, the new earth, and the New Jerusalem in the Revelation of John:

> No temple could be seen in the city, for the Lord God
> Almighty and the Lamb are its temple. And the city has no
> need of sun or moon, for the glory of God illuminates the city,
> and the Lamb is its light. The nations of the earth will walk in
> its light, and the rulers of the world will come and bring their

glory to it. Its gates never close at the end of day because there is no night....

[T]he throne of God and of the Lamb will be there, and his servants will worship him. And they will see his face, and his name will be written on their foreheads. And there will be no night there—no need for lamps or sun—for the Lord God will shine on them. And they will reign forever and ever. (21:22-25; 22:3-5)

The future prepared for those of us who know Christ is a bright one indeed. When God fully restores and transforms creation, the whole world will be filled with his light. All nations will glorify God, and God's people will reign forever in the radiance of God's own presence.

In that dazzling moment the messianic work of Jesus will be completed. He will sit on the throne of David forever, hailed as the "Wonderful Counselor, Mighty God, Everlasting Father, Prince of Peace" (Isaiah 9:6). In that moment, the Son of Man will finally receive his due. He will be given "authority, honor, and royal power over all the nations of the world, so that people of every race and nation and language would obey him. His rule is eternal—it will never end. His kingdom will never be destroyed" (Daniel 7:14).

In that great moment, "every knee will bow, in heaven and on earth and under the earth, and every tongue will confess that Jesus Christ is Lord, to the glory of God the Father" (Philippians 2:10-11).

And we, Scripture tells us, will "share in the inheritance of the saints in the kingdom of light" (Colossians 1:12, NIV). More than that, we "will shine like the sun in [our] Father's Kingdom" (Matthew 13:43). Even more than that, we will see the glorious Christ and "share in all his glory" (Colossians 3:4).

These promises sound like nothing more than wonderful theological symbolism until their reality captures our hearts. Then the hope of the future can inspire action in the face of opposition, confidence in the midst of strife, joy in the kiln of suffering. This is precisely what happened with my mother-in-law.

When she was first diagnosed with cancer, Marion fought the disease with all available treatments. She was only in her early sixties, with the promise of many wonderful years ahead. But when surgery and chemotherapy had run their course and her cancer had not disappeared, Marion faced a life measured in months rather than years.

As her body was quickly deteriorating, my mother-in-law evinced a powerful faith in Christ. She was hungry for heaven, to live with God in the light of eternity. When doctors offered the possibility of more chemotherapy, a treatment that probably wouldn't have worked and certainly would have destroyed what little quality of life she had left, Marion refused. She wasn't afraid to die. In fact, she seemed at times to relish the thought, not because she had a morose personality, but because she had such confidence in Jesus.

I'll never forget the evening of February 18, 1988. As I entered the room where Marion was resting, I could tell she was having a hard time breathing. What was left of her body, and there wasn't much left by then, struggled to take in the air she needed. As I sat there with her, my wife, Linda, and our family, Marion turned to me, somehow managed a smile, and said, "Hi, Mark." Then she slipped back into a calm sleep. I didn't know those would be her last words.

For Marion, death was a great relief and the beginning of a grand adventure. For Linda and me, and for our family, it was one more excruciating loss. Within the span of eighteen months we had seen liver cancer take the lives of my father and Linda's mother. At times everything seemed almost unbearable.

But during those dark days I began to live more consciously in light of the future. Until I said "good-bye" to my dad and Linda's mom, I really didn't think too much about heaven. I believed in it, theoretically, but it just didn't make much of a difference to me. Death has a way of altering one's perspective, of course, as did Marion's abiding faith in the face of death. Because of her example, I live today with greater confidence in God's future. The hope of heaven gives me the strength to keep going when I'm weak or discouraged. And someday, a day many years away, I hope, it will allow me to look death in the face and say, "O death, where is your victory? O death, where is your sting?" (1 Corinthians 15:55).

On that momentous day two millennia ago, an aged man named Simeon peeked into the future. He saw a little baby who was the Messiah, the "light to reveal God to the nations" (Luke 2:32). Because he had seen Jesus, this aged saint was now ready to die.

Just as Simeon's vision of Jesus prepared him to die, I pray that the manifold vision of Jesus presented in this book has prepared you to live. The life of God's kingdom, the life of the future, is available to us now, though incompletely. Jesus invites us to experience that life, what he calls "life in all its fullness" (John 10:10).

Jesus, who didn't "cling to his rights as God," became human and took our sin upon himself (Philippians 2:6). As Messiah, Son of Man, and Savior, he played the role of the Suffering Servant, giving his life for our sake. Therefore he has been exalted to the highest place. He is King of kings and Lord of lords.

Jesus, the incarnate Word of God, has revealed himself to us through Scripture, the written Word of God. As we study the Bible, we will continue to grow in our relationship with Jesus. We will know him more truly and completely.

But knowledge of Jesus is not the end of the process. We know him more clearly in order to love him more dearly. The more we grasp the astounding fact that the sinless Son of God became sin for us so that we might experience intimate relationship with his heavenly Father, the more we will love Jesus with all that we are.[11]

And this love will draw us to Jesus, so that we might follow him in heart and in action. As disciples of Jesus the Rabbi, we will learn his teachings and imitate his way of life. We will obey his commands and do his works.[12] We will be excited to tell others about our Lord so that they, too, might be transformed through relationship with him.

I hope this book has helped you to see Jesus more clearly as he is revealed in Scripture. I hope it has drawn you into more intimate relationship with your living Lord. But don't let the end of this book be the end of that process. Getting to know Jesus better is a lifelong endeavor.

May you continue to see Jesus more clearly so that you might love him more dearly and follow him more nearly—not just today and not just tomorrow, but day by day, until you see Jesus face to face. Then you will know him completely.[13] What a day that will be!

Questions for Study
and Growth

Responding to the Revealed Jesus

Chapter 1: Jesus Revealed

1. At what times in your life have you felt an especially strong longing to know Jesus better? How were your longings satisfied?
2. Have you ever heard of the Jesus Seminar? How do you feel about efforts to understand Jesus that play fast and loose with Scripture?
3. In your reading of the four Gospels, what aspect of Jesus' identity has stood out most prominently? In what way did that particular aspect touch you personally?
4. In what ways do you find yourself trying to make Jesus conform to your own ideas and expectations?
5. What are the names or titles that people frequently use for you? What do these titles reveal about who you are as a person?
6. Which names and titles for Jesus do you tend to use most frequently? Why? Are there other titles for him that you tend not to use? Why?
7. Have you ever had a transformational encounter with the living Jesus? When? What happened?

8. As you begin reading this book, what expectations or hopes do you have? In what specific ways would you like to grow in your relationship with Jesus?

Chapter 2: The Challenge of Naming

1. Before you read this chapter, what did the name Jesus suggest to you? Did you associate this name with certain experiences, ideas, or feelings? What experiences from your past influenced your understanding of the name Jesus? Are these associations primarily positive or negative? Why?

2. Read the story of Joseph's visit from the angel (Matthew 1:18-25). Try to put yourself in Joseph's position. What would you have felt if you had received this amazing announcement, followed by the angel's specific instructions? What would you have thought?

3. Do you tend to think of Jesus as being Christian or Jewish? What has influenced that perception? In what way(s) is the Jewishness of Jesus important to your faith?

4. Can you envision Jesus as an ordinary man, one who is fully human, even though in the miracle of the Incarnation he is also fully God? In what ways do you think of Jesus as having problems, pains, and real temptations?

5. What difference does the idea that Jesus experienced real suffering, real temptation, real grief, and real joy make for you? How do his experiences as a human help you in your own struggles?

6. What is your response to the notion that the salvation Jesus made possible was not limited to the saving of individual souls after death? Is this a troubling idea to consider, a challenging idea to ponder, or an encouragement to you? Why?

7. When were you most surprised by Jesus? What was the situation, and what led to the surprise?

8. In what way(s) would you like to be surprised by Jesus right now? Are you yearning to know him better in some specific way? If so, write down your thoughts and refer to them in prayer over the next week. Ask yourself: "Am I open to whatever surprise Jesus might want to give me?"

Chapter 3: The Paradigm-Shattering Teacher

1. When you hear the word *rabbi,* what ideas, images, or feelings come to mind? Where do these come from? Personal experience? Movies? Books?
2. In the past, have you ever experienced a paradigm shift in your relationship with Jesus? When did it happen, and what are the details of the "shift" that occurred?
3. Read the first chapter of the gospel of Mark. In what ways was Jesus like the other rabbis of his day? In what ways did Jesus break the rabbinic mold?
4. What is your response to the idea that you belong to Jesus the Rabbi, not primarily because you chose him, but because he first chose you?
5. Do you ever find it hard to let Jesus be the sole authority in your life? What other authorities compete with him for your trust and submission? (Consider career, possessions, status, wealth, relationships, success, personal goals and aspirations, etc.)
6. Have you ever trusted Jesus even in the midst of contradictory advice? When? What helped you to stay true to Jesus as your Rabbi?
7. What is your response to the idea of submitting to Jesus? What is attractive about this idea? What is unattractive or even daunting? What is the primary obstacle that would prevent you from fully submitting to his authority?
8. In what areas of your life, if any, is the authority of Jesus being compromised? Are you choosing to follow others rather than Jesus? Why? What might help you to follow Jesus no matter what?

CHAPTER 4: MESSENGER OF THE KINGDOM OF GOD

1. Jesus' contemporaries thought of him as a prophet. Do you? Why or why not?

2. In the past, how have you understood Jesus' proclamation of the kingdom of God? Is the conception of the kingdom in this chapter new to you? If so, what is new?

3. In the teachings of Jesus, the kingdom of God is "already but not yet." When in your life have you experienced "already but not yetness"?

4. In what ways have you experienced the kingdom of God as a present reality?

5. Have you ever experienced personal repentance like that of Zacchaeus or Chuck Colson? If so, when? What led you to repent? What was the outcome?

6. What are the "kingdoms" in your life that compete with the kingdom of God? What might it mean for you to leave these "kingdoms" behind and follow Jesus?

7. Is Jesus calling you to some specific ministry right now? If so, what is keeping you from saying yes to him? If not, are you open to hearing his call?

CHAPTER 5: HOLINESS INSIDE OUT

1. How would you define holiness? When you think of holiness, what images come to mind?

2. Read the following passages from the Gospels: Matthew 11:18-19; Mark 2:15-17; Luke 7:36-50; 19:1-10. What do you learn from these texts about Jesus and his conception of holiness? What do you learn about the views of holiness that were held by Jesus' contemporaries? How did Jesus explain his scandalous behavior?

3. In the time of Jesus, sharing a meal with someone was a sign of intimate fellowship. What actions in our culture serve this same function?

If we were to imitate the holiness of Jesus, what might we do to reach out to unholy people?

4. Many of us have, at least in part, a Pharisaic bent when it comes to holiness. We can look down upon those whose sins we scorn and avoid fellowship with them. Why is it so easy to fall into this pattern? What might change our hearts and our actions?

5. Have you ever experienced Jesus as "a Friend for sinners"? When? What impact did this have upon your life?

6. In your attempt to imitate the holiness of Jesus, which do you find harder to do: to communicate God's standards for sin or to have fellowship with sinners? Why? What might bring greater balance to your life?

7. Is it really possible "to love the sinner and hate the sin"? What should we do if a person insists that true love means endorsing his or her lifestyle, even if that lifestyle is clearly contrary to Scripture?

CHAPTER 6: ROYAL REGENT AND SUFFERING SERVANT

1. What sense did you have of the title "Son of Man" before you read this chapter? How has this chapter challenged or altered your thinking?

2. Read Daniel 7 completely and carefully. What is the role of the Son of Man? What is the relationship of the Son of Man to the faithful people of God?

3. Carefully read chapters 52 and 53 of Isaiah. What is the role of the Servant of God? How is the work of the Servant connected to the coming of God's kingdom?

4. Read the following gospel passages that use the title "Son of Man": Matthew 8:19-20; 16:13-28; 24:23-31; 25:31-32; Mark 2:1-12; 10:32-45; 14:61-62. What do these passages reveal about Jesus' understanding of his mission as the Son of Man? How are these passages similar to and/or different from the descriptions in Daniel 7 and Isaiah 52–53?

5. What difference should it make in your life to realize that Jesus came as the Son of Man to serve you by giving his life for you?

6. How do you really feel about serving in imitation of Jesus? What draws you to sacrificial service? What repels you?

7. Where might God be calling you to serve today?

CHAPTER 7: GOD'S ANOINTED ONE

1. How would you have defined the word *messiah* before you read this chapter? In what ways has this chapter influenced your understanding of this title?

2. Read Isaiah 61 in the *New International Version*. What does this chapter reveal about the "anointed one" and his mission? What is the relationship between the work of the anointed one and the work of God himself?

3. Read Luke 4:16-30 in the *New International Version*. What does this story reveal about the messianic ministry of Jesus, the anointed one?

4. Read Mark 8:27-38. What does this story reveal about the messianic ministry of Jesus? Why does Jesus shift the focus from his identity as the Messiah to his role as the Son of Man?

5. Were there any political aspects to the ministry of Jesus? If so, what dimension of his ministry was political?

6. In what way(s) might your belief in Jesus as the Messiah impact your own political views and actions today?

7. Read Ezekiel 37. How does this text impact our understanding of Jesus as the Messiah? What light does it shed upon the meaning of his resurrection?

8. In what way(s) has Jesus revealed himself to you? Have you had experiences that are in any way like that of the two disciples on the road to Emmaus (see Luke 24:13-27)? If so, what happened to you?

9. What difference might it make in your life if you took seriously the call to join Jesus in his messianic ministry, the ministry of the kingdom of God?

Chapter 8: The Dying Deliverer

1. Without a doubt the story of Beck Weathers is exceptional in the extreme. But have you ever experienced salvation in some literal sense, apart from being saved by Jesus? If so, what happened? How did you feel before you were saved? How did you feel afterward?
2. Read Isaiah 43 and Ezekiel 37. What sense of salvation emerges from these texts? What does salvation include?
3. What difference does it make in your daily life that Jesus is your Savior?
4. How, practically speaking, can we proclaim Jesus as Savior in a multicultural world without causing unnecessary offense? Of course, some people might be offended by any statement that Jesus is the Savior. But are there ways of telling the truth about Jesus that minimize the offense while maximizing the truth? What are these ways? What should we avoid in our witness to Jesus the Savior?
5. Do you find it easy or hard to trust Jesus as your Savior on a daily basis? Why? What keeps you from trusting him more? Or, conversely, what helps you to trust him more?
6. Have you ever experienced profound gratitude for the salvation you have in Jesus? What happened to motivate this exceptional gratitude?
7. Who in your life needs to hear and to believe the good news about Jesus the Savior? In what ways could you be a deliverer of this news? Take time to pray for those in your life who do not yet know Christ, specifically making yourself available to God as a channel of his grace.

CHAPTER 9: THE RULER OVER ALL

1. In your life, has there been a balance between knowing Jesus as Savior and knowing him as Lord? If not, which has received greater emphasis? Why?

2. Can you think of examples, positive or negative, of how the word *lord* is used today? When we tell people that Jesus is Lord, what might they think or feel?

3. Have you ever heard the idea that the deification of Jesus was a late addition to early Christian belief? How do 1 Corinthians 16:22 and Philippians 2:5-11 help you respond to this mistaken idea?

4. Read Philippians 2:1-11 carefully. According to this text, what difference should the humiliation and exaltation of Jesus make in our lives?

5. Have you ever felt uncomfortable speaking of Jesus as Lord? When? Why?

6. What "lords" compete with Jesus in your life? What might help you to reject these false lords and to be more completely submitted to Jesus as your one true Lord?

7. When you attend a worship service, what do you expect to happen? How does the discussion of worship in this chapter compare with your expectations?

8. What keeps you from focusing on God and God's glorification in worship? What helps you focus on God and not yourself?

CHAPTER 10: AN INVITATION TO THE FATHER'S HEART

1. The baptism of Jesus was a defining moment in his life. What have been some defining moments in your life? What did you take away from these experiences?

2. Study 2 Samuel 7:14-15, Psalm 2, and Psalm 89. What do these passages show us about what Jewish people meant when they considered a human being to be a "son of God"?

3. People respond in different ways to Jesus' invitation to regard God as a Father. For some, it is great news. For others, however, the idea of God as Father is fraught with difficulty. This is especially true for people whose human fathers were not very loving. As you think of God as your heavenly Father, describe your thoughts and feelings.

4. When have you experienced a childlike intimacy with God?

5. What encourages you to long for deeper intimacy with God?

6. In the parable of the prodigal son (and father), to whom do you relate most easily? To the younger son? To the older son? Why? What difference does this make in the way you respond to the divine Father who is portrayed in the parable?

7. When have you felt God's love for you most intensely?

CHAPTER 11: GOD'S PERFECT CAMPSITE

1. Read Proverbs 1:20-33; 3:13-20; 8:34–9:6. Then read John 1:1-18. In what ways is wisdom in Proverbs like the Word in John? What are the differences?

2. To what extent is your faith in Christ a matter of feelings? To what extent is it a matter of thinking? What can believers do to find an appropriate balance between thinking and feeling?

3. How would you respond to people who claim the right to formulate their own religion?

4. How would you respond to Christians who claim the right to disregard the parts of biblical revelation that make them uncomfortable?

5. Which aspects of the Christian faith make you feel uncomfortable? Which do you find the hardest to believe or to practice?

6. How can you share your faith in God with others without coming across as being arrogant?

7. In what way(s) have you received "grace upon grace" in your life?

8. What difference might it make in your life if you lived each day with an awareness of Jesus as the Word of God Incarnate?

CHAPTER 12: THE BRILLIANCE OF GOD

1. Read the story of Simeon in Luke 2:22-35. Put yourself into the shoes of the principal characters. How would you feel, and what would you think if you were Simeon? if you were Mary and Joseph?

2. How would you explain the paradox that Jesus is the Light of the World and that we are also the light of the world? What other analogies, aside from that of a disco ball, can you think of to illustrate this truth?

3. In what part(s) of the world does God want you to reflect his light? In what way(s) are you doing this right now? What more could you do to reflect the light of God more consistently and brightly?

4. As you think about Christians you know, who reflects the light of Christ most brilliantly? In what way(s) do they reflect his light? What accounts for this brilliance?

5. What fills your heart? Are you allowing the light of Jesus to illumine your thoughts, your feelings, and your dreams? Why or why not? What can you do to become even more filled with divine light?

6. Do you spend much time thinking about the life of the future, about heaven? Why or why not? What difference might it make in your life if you lived more intentionally in light of God's glorious future?

7. What in this book has been most striking to you? What has had the greatest impact on your relationship with Jesus?

8. What can you do to continue to grow in your knowledge of and relationship with Jesus?

APPENDIX

Was Jesus Married?

A Close Look at His Relationship with Mary Magdalene

In the wake of the incredible popularity of Dan Brown's best-selling novel *The Da Vinci Code,*[1] people often ask me if Jesus really *was* married. *The Da Vinci Code* advocates the thesis that Jesus married the woman we know as Mary Magdalene, that they had a child together, and that the church covered up this "truth."

Many readers of *The Da Vinci Code* are buzzing about the possibility of Jesus having been married. In a survey conducted by the Beliefnet Web site, nineteen percent of respondents said they believe Mary Magdalene was in fact Jesus' wife.[2]

In a novel as skillfully crafted as Brown's, it's easy to forget that a novel is, by definition, fiction. Great storytelling is just that. But great storytelling also has the power to capture our imagination. So, for the benefit of those who are wondering, let's examine the historical evidence for and against Jesus' purported marriage. Are the assertions made in *The Da Vinci Code* substantiated in the historical record?

Examining the Evidence

Finding the facts about Jesus' marital status isn't easy, since there is little overt historical evidence that addresses this question. The earliest and most reliable records of Jesus' life—the New Testament Gospels—do not tell us explicitly whether Jesus was married. They don't mention his having a wife, nor do they state that he remained single.

The silence of the New Testament Gospels on this question has given rise to a riot of conflicting voices. Some interpret the omission of specific information as a plot to cover up the truth about Jesus and Mary Magdalene. But others see the silence of the gospels as proof that Jesus could *not* have been married. It does seem rather fantastic to imagine that if Jesus had been married to Miriam of Magdala—or to any other woman, for that matter—that this fact would have been overlooked in all of the earliest records of Jesus' life.

There are those who claim that the earliest Christians conspired to hide the fact of Jesus' marriage because to admit that he married would confirm that he was not divine. But this view overlooks the significant fact that a large number of these supposed conspirators gave their lives because they believed Jesus to have been divine. Would they have died for something they knew to be a lie? I rather doubt it.

Nevertheless, the view that the silence of the New Testament Gospels should be taken as strong evidence *for* the marriage of Jesus must not be dismissed. Let's follow this argument to see where it leads.

CLUES FROM THE NEW TESTAMENT

The New Testament contains no explicit answer to the question of Jesus' marital status. It neither mentions his wife, nor that he was unmarried. In fact, whenever the New Testament Gospels refer to Jesus' natural relatives, they speak of his father, mother, and siblings, but never mention a wife.

Although almost all scholars of all religious persuasions take this as strong evidence of Jesus' singleness, a few have proposed that, in fact, Jesus was married. In 1970, for example, William E. Phipps published *Was Jesus Married? The Distortion of Sexuality in the Christian Tradition.*[3] Phipps argued that the silence of the New Testament indicates Jesus was in fact married because virtually every Jewish man in Jesus' day did marry, especially those who were considered rabbis.

A major problem with this argument is that it makes no room for an exception. Jesus was not required by law—either governmental or religious—to marry. And, though he was in many ways a normal Jewish man,[4] in other ways he was utterly unusual. If Jesus and his family realized that he had a special calling that would make marriage quite difficult, then he could surely have remained single. It's true that such a decision would have been perceived as an unusual, even a countercultural choice. But Jesus never shied away from the unusual or countercultural, especially when it came to his relationships with women.

Unlike other Jewish teachers of his day, Jesus had close relationships with women, many of whom were his followers[5] and who learned from him.[6] Several of these women are mentioned by name in the New Testament Gospels, including Mary Magdalene, Joanna, and Susanna, who together helped to financially support Jesus and his other disciples.[7] But nothing in the New Testament suggests that Jesus was ever married to any of these women, or to any other woman, for that matter.

But, you might wonder, what about Mary Magdalene? Isn't there evidence that suggests she was in fact married to Jesus? To answer that question we must examine the evidence, looking both at the New Testament and at the nonbiblical gospels that are touted to contain evidence of Jesus' marriage to Mary Magdalene.

For now, we must acknowledge that the main argument in favor of Jesus' marriage is at best weakly circumstantial. It fails to reckon with Jesus' unique calling and his tendency to flaunt certain cultural conventions. Moreover, it forces us to believe that the most reliable written accounts of Jesus' life failed to mention one of the most salient aspects of that life. How unlikely!

Who Was Mary Magdalene?

The question of Jesus' marriage generally focuses on his supposed wife: Mary Magdalene. We can learn a number of things about this woman, both from the New Testament and from other ancient documents. The New Testament Gospels represent the oldest evidence we have, since they were written within thirty to fifty years after Jesus' death. Moreover, these Gospels are based upon older oral and written sources.

Several women named Mary are mentioned in the biblical Gospels, including Jesus' mother and Mary from Bethany—the sister of Martha and Lazarus, the woman whom Jesus praised for learning from him.[8] One of the Marys mentioned in the Gospels is referred to as Magdalene, which means "from the village of Magdala."

Mary Magdalene is first mentioned as one of the women who accompanied Jesus on his preaching mission, as well as being a woman who helped to support him financially.[9] The gospel writer Luke adds that seven demons had been cast out of her, presumably by Jesus.[10] Nothing in this passage suggests that there was anything unusual about Mary's relationship with Jesus, other than the *very* unusual fact that she was included among Jesus' retinue. Jewish teachers in Jesus' day usually didn't teach women or include them as followers. In his inclusive practice, Jesus was virtually unique. His relationship with Mary and her female counterparts was quite countercultural.

The next time we run into Mary Magdalene she is among the women who observe Jesus being crucified.[11] Then, on Easter morning, she and a couple of female companions go to Jesus' tomb to find it empty. Mary encounters Jesus near the tomb and then goes to announce his resurrection to the other disciples.[12] In a sense, she is the first Christian evangelist, the first person to pass on the good news of Easter.

This is all we know about Mary Magdalene from the biblical Gospels. Several centuries after these texts were written, Mary became associated with the prostitute who bathed and anointed Jesus' feet.[13] But there is nothing in Scripture that makes this connection.

There's also nothing in the biblical material to propose that Mary was Jesus' wife, or, as some have suggested, that he had a sexual relationship with her outside of marriage. What is exceptional about Mary, when understood in her cultural setting, is that she was one of Jesus' closest followers. Moreover, she was the first witness to the risen Christ, a role of exceptional honor and privilege. Surely Jesus held Mary in the highest regard, though not as his wife. Ironically, the efforts to turn Mary the disciple of Jesus into Mary the wife of Jesus actually minimize how truly extraordinary she was as a central follower, supporter, and witness of Jesus.

Because nothing in the New Testament suggests that Jesus and Mary were married, those who advocate this position claim there is evidence in the noncanonical "gospels." Do these extra-biblical writings in fact reveal a secret marriage between Jesus and Mary? The only way to tell is to analyze every passage in the extra-biblical gospels that mentions Mary Magdalene.

MARY MAGDALENE IN THE NONCANONICAL GOSPELS

Most people are not familiar with the noncanonical gospels. Thus, when they hear that these writings reveal Jesus' marriage to Mary Magdalene, they are at a loss to evaluate the claim—often accepting it at face value.

In spite of the fascination many have with such purported evidence, accounts from the noncanonical gospels provide nothing more than weak and scanty information that ultimately provides no sure answers.[14] As we look at the noncanonical texts, bear in mind that dating the nonbiblical gospels is perilous because we have so little solid evidence. Those who want to see these gospels as reliable historical sources often push their authorship as early as possible, sometimes into the first century A.D. For reasons I can't pursue here, this dating is unlikely in almost every case. Most credible scholars date the writing of the noncanonical gospels in the second or third century A.D. These texts are, at any rate, later than the biblical Gospels by a long shot (with the *possible* exception of *The Gospel of Thomas,* which *may* have been written in the first century).

Several of the noncanonical gospels are named after one of the original disciples of Jesus, including Mary, but these disciples had nothing to do with the writing of these extra-biblical works. (For each of the gospels I'll suggest when they might have been written, choosing a date that reflects scholarly consensus, where such is available.)

Mary Magdalene in *The Gospel of Thomas*. Probably the earliest and best known of the noncanonical gospels is *The Gospel of Thomas,* which includes scant information about Mary Magdalene.[15] She plays a tiny role, asking Jesus a question about the disciples: "Whom are your disciples like?" (section 21).[16] This is the only place she speaks. She is mentioned at the end of this gospel in a most curious passage, which reads:

> Simon Peter said to them, "Let Mary leave us, for women are
> not worthy of Life." Jesus said, "I myself shall lead her in order
> to make her male, so that she too may become a living spirit
> resembling you males. For every woman who will make herself
> male will enter the Kingdom of Heaven." (section 114)

One would be hard pressed to see in this passage much hope for women, let alone for the thesis that Mary was Jesus' wife. This passage, in its own strange way, does affirm what we know from the canonical gospels: that Mary was included among Jesus' followers and that he intentionally included women in the circle of his close followers. Of course in the biblical record he valued them as women, not as beings that had eternal value if they became male. Maleness, in this text, should not be understood literally, but as a symbol of one's spiritual or divine nature.

So, one who is looking for evidence of a secret marriage between Jesus and Mary will be disappointed by the earliest of the noncanonical gospels. *The Gospel of Thomas,* in its peculiar way, simply underscores what we already know of Mary from the biblical Gospels.

Mary Magdalene in *The Gospel of Peter*. Written in the second century A.D., *The Gospel of Peter* focuses on the last hours in the life of Jesus.[17] It is noteworthy for its view that Jesus felt no pain when he was crucified (section 10), and for its exoneration of Pontius Pilate for the death of Jesus (sections 1, 45-46). Mary Magdalene appears only on Easter morning, when she and her women friends come to the tomb of Jesus to weep for him. She is described as "a female disciple [Greek *mathetria*] of the Lord" (section 50). At the tomb, Mary and her friends see an angel who announces the resurrection of Jesus, and they run away frightened (section 56-57).

In *The Gospel of Peter* we find no evidence of a marriage between Mary and Jesus. But, once again, Mary is portrayed as a female disciple of Jesus.

Mary Magdalene in *The Dialogue of the Savior*. Also written in the second century A.D., *The Dialogue of the Savior* is a dialogue between the Savior (never called Jesus or Christ) and some of his disciples, including Mary.[18] The disciples ask questions about esoteric religious matters, and Jesus gives equally esoteric answers. Although Mary is one of the frequent interrogators, at one point she makes an observation. The text explains: "This word she spoke as a woman who knew the All" (section 139).[19] In other words, Mary has special knowledge of spiritual reality.

There is no hint in *The Dialogue of the Savior* of a marriage between Jesus and Mary (or the Savior and Mary). She is seen, once again, as central among the disciples and as a person with special insight.

Mary Magdalene in *The Sophia of Jesus Christ*. This is a post-resurrection dialogue between the risen Christ and some of his followers, including Mary.[20] It may have been written as early as the middle of the second century A.D. Twice in this gospel, Mary asks questions of Christ, such as, "Holy Lord, where did your disciples come from, and where are they going, and [what] should they do here?" (section 114).[21] Mary is not singled out further, nor is there a suggestion of a marriage to Jesus.

Mary Magdalene in *The Pistis Sophia*. This Gnostic gospel, written during the third century A.D.,[22] is a revelation of Christ in which Mary plays a prominent role, asking the majority of the questions about a great variety of esoteric matters.

Mary is praised in *The Pistis Sophia* as one "whose heart is more directed to the Kingdom of Heaven than all [her] brothers" (chapter 17).[23] Jesus says that she is "blessed beyond all women upon the earth, because [she shall be] the pleroma of all Pleromas and the completion of all completions" (section 19). In other words, Mary will have the fullness of knowledge and therefore spiritual life within her. So impressed is Jesus with Mary's spiritual excellence that he promises not to conceal anything from her, but to reveal everything to her "with certainty and openly" (section 25). She is the blessed one who will "inherit the whole Kingdom of the Light" (section 61).

From *The Pistis Sophia* we see the growing interest in Mary among the Gnostics, who valued knowledge (*gnosis* in Greek) above all. She came to be regarded as a source of hidden revelation because of her intimate relationship with Jesus. However, nothing in this gospel suggests a marriage between them.

Mary Magdalene in *The Gospel of Mary*. Written in the second century, *The Gospel of Mary* goes even further than *The Pistis Sophia* in portraying Mary as a source of secret revelation because of her close relationship to the Savior.[24] At one point Peter asks, "Sister, we know that the Savior loved you more than the rest of women. Tell us the words of the Savior which you remember—which you know but we do not nor have we heard them" (section 10). So, Mary reveals what the Lord made known to her in a vision, the content of which seems like mumbo jumbo to anyone other than a second-century Gnostic.

The Gospel of Mary reports that several of the disciples were none too impressed by Mary's purported insights. Andrew responded to her revelation by saying "I at least do not believe that the Savior said this. For certainly these teachings are strange ideas" (section 17). Then Peter asked, "Did he really speak privately with a woman and not openly to us? Are we to turn about and all listen to her? Did he prefer her to us?" But Levi speaks up for Mary, saying, "Peter, you have always been hot-tempered. Now I see you contending against the woman like the adversaries. But if the Savior made her worthy, who are you indeed to reject her? Surely the Savior knows her very well. That is why he loved her more than us" (section 18).

At last, here's fuel for the fire of a secret marriage between Mary and Jesus. She is the recipient of his secret revelations and private speeches. The Savior, who is not called Jesus in *The Gospel of Mary*, even preferred Mary to the other disciples, loving her more than them. Mary's relationship with Jesus has clearly entered a new dimension we have not seen before.

But there is nothing here to suggest that Jesus and Mary were married. Jesus' love for Mary leads him to reveal special truths to her, not to take her as his wife. Nothing in *The Gospel of Mary* points to a sexual or spousal relationship between Jesus and Mary.

Mary Magdalene in *The Gospel of Philip*. Finally we come to *The Gospel of Philip*, the last of the extra-biblical gospels to mention Mary Magdalene, and the one that excites proponents of her marriage to Jesus more than any other ancient document.[25]

The Gospel of Philip is one of the latest of the noncanonical gospels, written well into the third century. It is not a gospel in any ordinary sense, but rather a collection of theological observations written from a gnostic point of view. Two passages refer to Mary Magdalene, who plays a tiny role in this gospel.

The first of these passages reads, "There were three who always walked with the Lord: Mary his mother and her sister and Magdalene, the one who was called his companion" (section 59). Much has been insinuated about the word *companion*, which, in the Greek original is *koinonos*. But contrary to the wishful thinking of some, this word doesn't mean spouse or sexual consort. It means "partner" and is used several times in the New

Testament with this ordinary meaning. For example, Paul refers to himself as Philemon's *koinonos*.[26]

The second passage in *The Gospel of Philip* that concerns Mary is the most suggestive:

> And the companion of the Savior is Mary Magdalene. But
> Christ loved her more than all the disciples and used to kiss her
> often on her mouth. The rest of the disciples were offended by
> it and expressed disapproval. They said to him, "Why do you
> love her more than all of us?" The Savior answered and said to
> them, "Why do I not love you like her? When a blind man and
> one who sees are both together in darkness, they are no differ-
> ent from one another. Then the light comes, then he who sees
> will see the light, and he who is blind will remain in darkness."
> (sections 63-63)

Even if we suppose that this passage, which appears in no other document and which was written two centuries after the biblical Gospels, con-
veys historically accurate information, the passage itself seems to *disprove*
Jesus' marriage to Mary. Surely if Jesus had been married to Mary then his
special affection for her wouldn't have been an offense. And surely Jesus
could have satisfied the disciples' question by explaining that Mary was his
wife. But he doesn't do this. Instead he explains his special affection for
Mary by pointing to her ability to see the light, that is, to have knowledge.
Nothing in this passage suggests that Jesus and Mary were married, even if
we read it literally. Moreover, given what is said elsewhere in *The Gospel of
Philip* about kissing (sections 58-59), it's possible that this passage isn't even
meant to be taken literally. The text may use *kissing* as a metaphor to say
that Jesus revealed truth to Mary. If this is true, *The Gospel of Mary* is consistent with what we have seen elsewhere in the Gnostic gospels.

And that's it—the best noncanonical evidence for the marriage of Jesus and Mary. And even if this "evidence" is taken at face value as a historically accurate account, which one would be silly to do, it seems to contradict the hypothetical marriage. The only way to find this marriage in the non-canonical gospels is to interject it there yourself. The texts simply do not support the theory that Jesus and Mary were married.

WHAT ARE WE TO BELIEVE?

One who accepts as fact the fictional history in *The Da Vinci Code* will no doubt object at this point: But you don't understand. Jesus' marriage to Mary was *a secret*. These texts only give tiny clues. The real truth of Jesus' marriage was hidden, and that's why the noncanonical gospels say so little about it.

Theoretically speaking, this could be true. But I'd argue that we have much more evidence for Jesus having been a space alien than the husband of Mary Magdalene. After all, he is transfigured on a mountain as he stands with glowing beings[27] and he ascends to heaven in a cloud.[28] One can make up all sorts of crazy theories about Jesus, but the only way to evaluate these theories is with the facts of the ancient texts. And these texts do not support the theory that Jesus was married—or that he was a space alien, for that matter.

You may wonder why I bother to carefully analyze the biblical and nonbiblical evidence for the alleged marriage of Jesus. I could have just pooh-poohed the whole thing as fictional nonsense. But that wouldn't help you when your friend, having just read *The Da Vinci Code,* is convinced that the noncanonical gospels are filled with evidence about Jesus' marriage to Mary Magdalene. Given the sustained popularity of Dan Brown's novel, the question of Jesus' marriage to Mary will continue to attract widespread interest.

A second reason that I have examined the noncanonical material in detail is because most people (both Christian and non-Christian) are unfamiliar with these texts. When somebody says the noncanonical gospels really show that Jesus was married, most people don't know how to respond. Now you have seen the evidence. So, when someone states confidently that the noncanonical gospels reveal Jesus' marriage to Mary, you can respond: "Have you ever studied what the noncanonical gospels actually say about Jesus and Mary? You know, I've looked at this evidence and there is nothing there. Mary appears rarely in the noncanonical gospels, and when she does appear, it's usually as a close disciple of Jesus, and sometimes as one who reveals special knowledge that Jesus revealed first to her. And that's it!"

A third reason I have devoted so much effort to this issue is that most proponents of the marriage-of-Jesus thesis have an agenda. They are trying to strip Jesus of his uniqueness and especially his deity. They prefer a Jesus who was a mere human being, one with spiritual insight but otherwise ordinary. The supposed marriage of Jesus is taken by many to be proof that he really wasn't God in the flesh.

Along with Christians throughout the ages, I believe that Jesus was fully God and fully human. Ironically, my faith in the unique nature of Jesus doesn't demand that he was single. Jesus could have married and maintained his sinless, human-divine nature. But the fact is he didn't do this. We can speculate about the reasons. I imagine Jesus realized his unique calling was incompatible with marriage and family life. Moreover, if Jesus had married and fathered children, their mix of divine-sinless nature and human-sinful nature would have been extremely confusing, something I expect Jesus would have wanted to avoid by remaining unmarried. But I don't know for sure why Jesus didn't marry because the facts of the biblical texts don't tell me.

And I do care about facts. Yes, I'm aware of my inadequacy when it comes to discerning truth and falsehood.[29] But Christianity isn't a figment of the imagination or mere wishful thinking. It's based upon what God has done in history, most of all through Jesus Christ. Thus we should make every effort to find out what really happened. Wild theories that depend on unreliable evidence produced centuries after an event might make for entertaining fiction, but they aren't the stuff of genuine faith.

The *Real* Jesus-Mary Relationship

Perhaps the most amazing facts concerning the relationship of Mary Magdalene and Jesus are those that emerge from the pages of Scripture and which, ironically, are also supported in much of the noncanonical literature. Mary was a close follower of Jesus. She accompanied him on his journeys, helped to support him financially, learned from him, remained faithful to him in his darkest hour when his male disciples fell away, was the first to see him after the Resurrection, and was the first person in history to announce to others the good news that Jesus is risen. Jesus' intentional inclusion of Mary, in a day when Jewish teachers almost never taught women or had female disciples, is a striking symbol of the inclusiveness of the kingdom of God. Women living under God's reign will not be defined *primarily* by their roles in the family, but by their relationships to Jesus as his disciples. This was true of Mary Magdalene in the first century, and it's true of every female Christian today.

Once when Jesus was preaching, he was approached by his natural family. The crowd told him that they were there to see him. "Jesus replied, 'Who is my mother? Who are my brothers?' Then he looked at those around him [his disciples] and said, 'These are my mother and brothers. Anyone who does God's will is my brother and sister and mother.'"[30]

Ironically, Jesus is more inclusive and countercultural than those who would tie Mary Magdalene's significance primarily to her filling the traditional role of wife. Though much in Scripture supports the importance of natural family, the relationship that matters most of all is our relationship with Jesus as his disciples. Together, we disciples are the church of Jesus Christ, his only true bride.[31]

NOTES

Preface

1. N. T. Wright and Ben Witherington III are New Testament scholars whose principal works on Jesus are intended primarily for the academic community. Wright's major writings are *The New Testament and the People of God* (Minneapolis: Augsburg Fortress, 1992) and *Jesus and the Victory of God* (Minneapolis: Augsburg Fortress, 1996). He has presented his insights in a more accessible form in *The Challenge of Jesus: Rediscovering Who Jesus Was and Is* (Downers Grove, Ill.: InterVarsity, 1999) and *Who Was Jesus?* (Grand Rapids: Eerdmans, 1992). Witherington's main writings on Jesus are for scholars, namely *The Christology of Jesus* (Philadelphia: Fortress, 1990); *Jesus the Sage: The Pilgrimage of Wisdom* (Minneapolis: Augsburg Fortress, 1994); and *The Jesus Quest: The Third Search for the Jew of Nazareth,* 2nd edition (Downers Grove, Ill.: InterVarsity, 1997). For those seeking a less academic approach, I would recommend a helpful volume that summarizes the major academic issues in a more accessible form: *Dictionary of Jesus and the Gospels,* edited by Joel B. Green and Scot McKnight (Downers Grove, Ill.: InterVarsity, 1992).

Chapter 1

1. Copyright © Ananova. Retrieved from the Internet at http://www.lineone.net/newswire/cgi-bin/newswire.cgi/new_wire/pa_world/story/2001/1/c—2001-1-16-1n28.html.
2. "Pizza Hut's Lunch Special: It's Heavenly," *Chicago Tribune,* North Sports Final, C Edition (23 May 1991): 44.
3. "The Miraculous Tortilla," *Newsweek* (14 August 1978): 58.
4. Quotation from Robert Funk, founder of the Jesus Seminar, in "The Coming Radical Reformation: Twenty-One Theses," *The Fourth R* (July/August 1998): 11:4.

Available electronically at http://www.westarinstitute.org/Periodicals/
4R_Articles/Funk_Theses/funk_theses.html.

5. For a trenchant critique of the Jesus Seminar, see Luke Timothy Johnson, *The Real Jesus* (San Francisco: HarperSanFrancisco, 1996), and Michael J. Wilkins and J. P. Moreland, *Jesus Under Fire* (Grand Rapids: Zondervan, 1995).

6. This book is not meant to be a scholarly defense of orthodox Christian beliefs about Jesus. Though I draw generously from contemporary scholarship about Jesus, I am writing for the typical Christian who wants to know Jesus better. If you are looking for a more scholarly approach, I would recommend the marvelous works of N. T. Wright and Ben Witherington (see note 1 of the preface).

7. Rev. Dirk Ficca, presentation to The 2000 Peacemaking Conference at Chapman University, Orange, Calif., 29 July 2000. His full message is available on-line at http://www.presbyweb.com/FiccaText082600.htm.

8. Rev. Norman Vincent Peale, quoted in *The American Mercury*, December 1935. Cited in Christopher Cerf and Victor Navasky, *The Experts Speak* (New York: Pantheon, 1984), 307.

9. From the *Daily Telegraph* (London) (16 June 1992). Cited in *The Columbia Dictionary of Quotations* (New York: Columbia University Press, 1993). Retrieved through Microsoft Bookshelf, Copyright © 1987–1994 Microsoft Corporation.

10. From the Helmet Law Defense League Web site: http://www.usff.com/hldl/archives/buseymail.html.

11. Quotation from "Brother Coffee," on The Christian Metal Network, http://www.radiojc.net/cmn/cmngb/guestbook.html, now moved to http://www.christianmetal.com/cmn/cmngb/pitarchive1.html.

12. From a sermon delivered at Marble Collegiate Church, New York, New York. Quoted in *U.S. News & World Report* (27 December 1999): 64.

13. If you are interested in such a book, I would recommend Philip Yancey, *The Jesus I Never Knew* (Grand Rapids: Zondervan, 1995).

Chapter 2

1. According to records maintained by the Social Security Administration.

2. See Matthew 1:20-21.

3. This data comes from the Jewish historian Josephus. See especially note 4 to *Jewish Antiquities* 20.8.5 in William Whiston, ed. and trans., *The Works of Josephus,* New Updated Edition (Peabody, Mass.: Hendrickson, 1987). Electronic text prepared by OakTree Software Specialists.

4. For the text of the Kaddish prayer, see "Kingdom of God, Kingdom of Heaven: OT, Early Judaism, and Hellenistic Usage," *Anchor Bible Dictionary,* vol. 4 (New York: Doubleday, 1992).

5. These stories and more like them are found in "The Infancy Gospel of Thomas," a document that was probably written in the late second century A.D. See *The Infancy Story of Thomas,* in Edgar Hennecke and Wilhelm Schneemelcher, eds., *New Testament Apocrypha,* vol. 1, trans. R. McL. Wilson (Philadelphia: Westminster, 1963), 388-400.

6. See Mark 6:30-44.

7. See Exodus 16:1-35.

8. See Deuteronomy 18:15-18; 34:10-12. The connection between Jesus' miraculous provision of food and his being the prophet like Moses is especially clear in John 6:1-15. For further discussion, see chapter 4 of this book on Jesus the Prophet.

9. See Isaiah 40:10-11.

10. See Ezekiel 34:11-23.

11. See Isaiah 25:6-10; Matthew 22:1-10.

12. The English term *docetism* comes from the Greek verb *dokein,* which means "to seem." Docetists believe that Jesus only *seemed* to be human.

13. *The Apocalypse of Peter* 81:3-25. In James M. Robinson, ed., *The Nag Hammadi Library* (San Francisco: Harper and Row, 1977).

14. See John 1:14. For further discussion, see chapter 11 of this book on Jesus the Word of God.

15. See Hebrews 4:15.

16. See John 19:28; Isaiah 53:4-12.

17. From the "Symbol of Chalcedon." This creed was the product of a worldwide church council held in Asia Minor in A.D. 451. The council reaffirmed the full humanity and deity of Christ. For the text of the Symbol, see Philip Schaff, ed.,

David Schaff, rev., *The Creeds of Christendom*, vol. 2 (Grand Rapids: Baker, reprint 1983), 62-5.

18. Jesus wept (John 11:35); Jesus felt anger (Mark 3:5); Jesus struggled with God's will (Mark 14:32-42).

19. See John 1:14.

20. Joseph Scriven, "What a Friend We Have in Jesus," public domain.

21. The Aramaic word *mammon* means "wealth" (see Matthew 6:24). The phrase *talitha coum* means "Little girl, get up!" (see Mark 5:41). *Abba* means "father/daddy" (see Mark 14:36).

22. It is likely that Jesus could read Hebrew and use it in theological discussions. He probably knew at least some Greek as well. A craftsman in first-century Galilee had to know enough Greek to do business with wealthy Gentiles in the region who did not speak Aramaic. Moreover, when Jesus and Pilate conversed prior to the Crucifixion, they probably spoke in Greek rather than in Jesus' Aramaic or Pilate's Latin.

23. In his various writings, N. T. Wright demonstrates that first-century Palestinian Jews would have thought of themselves as still in exile, even though they lived within the boundaries of the Promised Land.

24. See Exodus 34:6-7.

25. See Deuteronomy 28:15-68.

26. For the sake of clarity in this scripture quotation, I have translated the Hebrew name of God, YHWH, as "Yahweh" rather than "the LORD."

27. See Isaiah 49:15.

28. The personal dimensions and benefits of salvation will be explored more thoroughly in chapter 8 of this book on Jesus the Savior.

29. This understanding of salvation is evaluated extensively in the scholarship of N. T. Wright. For references to his books, see note 1 of the preface.

30. See Isaiah 12:1-6; 51:3; Zechariah 9:14-17; 1 Thessalonians 4:16.

31. The prophecy found in Jeremiah 31 begins to be fulfilled in Jesus and his ministry, especially in his death and resurrection. It will not be completely fulfilled, however, until the kingdom has fully come. For a detailed discussion, see chapter 4 of this book on Jesus the Prophet.

32. See Romans 5:1-10.

Chapter 3

1. Thomas S. Kuhn, *The Structure of Scientific Revolutions,* 3rd ed. (Chicago: University of Chicago Press, 1996).

2. See Mark 9:5, for example.

3. Mishnah, *'Abot* 1.1. The Mishnah is a written collection of rabbinic oral traditions. Though it was written down late in the second century A.D., it incorporates sayings of earlier rabbis, including those in the time of Jesus (and before). Though it is difficult to determine exactly which rabbinic teachings and practices thrived in the time of Jesus, it is likely that many specific sayings and the general worldview of the Mishnah were present in his era, especially among the Pharisees. I am using a version of the Mishnah published by Judaica Press (New York, 1964).

4. Author's paraphrase of Mishnah, *'Abot* 1.6.

5. Author's paraphrase of Mishnah, *Yadayim* 2.1.

6. Author's paraphrase of Mishnah, *'Abot* 1.16. According to Acts 22:3, Paul was educated by Rabbi Gamaliel.

7. See Matthew 8:20; Mark 3:14.

8. See Matthew 8:21-22; 19:21-22.

9. Justin Pritchard, "Kids with Pets Have Fewer Allergies," *AP Online* (8 June 2001).

10. Wade Clark Roof, *A Generation of Seekers: The Spiritual Journeys of the Baby Boom Generation* (San Francisco: HarperSanFrancisco, 1993), 256.

11. See Mark 1:14-15.

12. See Matthew 19:1-9.

13. See John 10:10.

14. See John 15:11; 17:13.

Chapter 4

1. Josephus, *The Jewish War,* in William Whiston, ed. and trans., *The Works of Josephus,* New Updated Edition (Peabody, Mass.: Hendrickson, 1987), 6:300-9. Electronic text prepared by OakTree Software Specialists.

2. See Deuteronomy 18:20-22; Jeremiah 28:9.

3. See Mark 8:28.

4. See Malachi 4:1-6; Mark 6:15. The hope for Elijah's return is also found in the Jewish writing called "The Wisdom of Jesus Son of Sirach." See Sirach 48:1-10.

5. See Deuteronomy 18:15-18; 34:10-12; John 6:1-15; Acts 3:22.

6. See John 6:15.

7. See Mark 6:4; Luke 4:24; 13:33.

8. See Luke 24:19.

9. Unlike the prophets, however, Jesus did not quote God: "Thus says the LORD." Rather, he spoke authoritatively in his own voice. This is parallel to what we observed about the contrast between the teaching styles of Jesus and other rabbis. Even as Jesus did not quote human authorities to bolster his message, he didn't quote the Lord either. He spoke in his own authority as Lord of the universe.

10. See Isaiah 20:1-6; Jeremiah 13:1-11; Mark 11:12-21.

11. Here are the apt comparisons: controlling weather, Jesus in Mark 4:35-39 and Elijah in 1 Kings 17:1-16; healing, Jesus in Mark 6:56, for example, and Elisha in 2 Kings 5:1-14; raising the dead, Jesus in Mark 5:35-42 and Elisha in 2 Kings 4:32-37.

12. See Matthew 5:17.

13. See Mark 13, for example.

14. See Ezekiel 14:6; Matthew 6:33; Mark 1:15. For the priority of God's righteousness in the Old Testament prophets, see, for example, Isaiah 51:1; 61:3,11; Jeremiah 22:3; Hosea 10:12; Zephaniah 2:3; Zechariah 8:8; Malachi 3:3.

15. The exact phrase "the kingdom of God" does not appear among the Old Testament prophets, but the theme of God's kingdom or reign pervades their message. See, for example, Isaiah 9:7; 33:22; 52:7-10; Ezekiel 20:33; Daniel 7:13-14; Micah 4:6-7.

16. See Deuteronomy 28:15-61; Ezekiel 5:1-17; Daniel 9:1-19.

17. See Psalm 47:1-9.

18. For other prophetic passages about God's kingdom, see Isaiah 9:6-7; Ezekiel 20:33-34; 34:1-31; Daniel 7:13-18.

19. Josephus, *Jewish Antiquities,* 20.169-72; *Jewish War,* 2.261-3; in William Whiston, ed. and trans., *The Works of Josephus,* New Updated Edition (Peabody, Mass.: Hendrickson, 1987). Electronic text prepared by OakTree Software Specialists.

20. The Kaddish prayer is commonly used in synagogue worship to this day.

21. Benedictions 10 and 11. This translation from Everett Ferguson, *Backgrounds of Early Christianity,* second edition (Grand Rapids: Eerdmans, 1993), 543.

22. Gordon Fee, "Jesus: Early Ministry/Kingdom of God," lecture delivered at Regent College. Tape Series 2235E, Pt. 1. Copyright © Regent College, Vancouver, B.C., Canada.

23. See Psalm 47:1-7.

24. See Jeremiah 31:31-34.

25. The verse is translated this way in the *New Living Translation* and in the *New Revised Standard Version.*

26. See Matthew 6:10; Revelation 11:15.

27. See Psalm 11:4; 103:19; Isaiah 37:16.

28. This phraseology is found in the gospel of Matthew. See, for example, Matthew 3:2; 4:17.

29. See John 18:36.

30. See also Matthew 16:27-28.

31. See Mark 1:15.

32. Once again Jesus employs an Old Testament prophetic image for the coming of God's kingdom. See Ezekiel 17:22-24.

33. See also Ezekiel 34:15-16.

34. See John 6:15.

35. See Isaiah 60:1-3.

36. See Mark 12:13-17.

37. See Matthew 5:39-44.

38. See Matthew 26:52.

39. See Matthew 5:39.

40. See Hebrews 2:14; 1 John 3:8.

41. See Luke 11:15.

42. See Luke 10:19.

43. In his call to repentance, Jesus echoed the Old Testament prophets who urged Israel to lay aside their sin and to return to the Lord. This U-turn in heart and in lifestyle would lead to mercy, pardon, healing, and a renewed relationship with God himself. See Isaiah 55:7; Hosea 6:1-3; 14:1-2; Zechariah 1:3.

44. Charles Colson's story is told in his autobiographical book *Born Again* (Old Tappan, New Jersey: Chosen, 1976).

Chapter 5

1. See Hebrews 2:14; 1 John 3:8.
2. See John 6:69; Acts 2:27. See also Revelation 3:7. The title "Holy One of God" was rarely used among early Christians, probably because they didn't want to confuse Jesus as the Holy One with the Holy Spirit.
3. See 2 Kings 4:9.
4. See Wisdom of Sirach 45:6; 4 Maccabees 6:30; 7:4.
5. See Mark 6:20.
6. See Mark 2:15.
7. See Luke 18:9-14.
8. See Luke 7:36; 14:1.
9. See John 3:1-21.
10. See Romans 5:8.
11. J. Wilbur Chapman, "Jesus! What a Friend for Sinners," also known as "Our Great Savior," public domain.
12. See Mark 7:21.
13. For a thorough investigation of biblical teaching on homosexuality, see Thomas E. Schmidt, *Straight and Narrow? Compassion & Clarity in the Homosexuality Debate* (Downers Grove, Ill.: InterVarsity, 1995); Robert A. J. Gagnon, *The Bible and Homosexual Practice: Texts and Hermeneutics* (Nashville: Abingdon, 2001); and Richard B. Hayes, *The Moral Vision of the New Testament* (San Francisco: HarperSanFrancisco, 1996).
14. See Mark 2:16.

Chapter 6

1. The expression and title *Son of God* flowed from the lips of Jesus in John 5:25; 11:4. He used the word *Messiah* or *Christ* only once, in an oblique reference to himself (see Matthew 23:10). In Mark 14:61-62, Jesus admitted to being the Messiah but did not use the title for himself.

2. See Mark 8:29-31; 14:61-62.

3. See Mark 8:27-33; 10:35-45.

4. See Ezekiel 2:1-8, for example. A similar sense is found in the Psalms, "[W]hat is man that you are mindful of him, the son of man that you care for him?" (Psalm 8:4, NIV).

5. See Daniel 7:1-28.

6. See 1 *Enoch* 46:4-6. Translation by E. Isaac in James H. Charlesworth, ed., *The Old Testament Pseudepigrapha,* vol. 1 (Garden City, N.Y.: Doubleday & Co., 1983).

7. See 1 *Enoch* 47–48.

8. See 4 *Ezra* 13:1-4. Translation by B. M. Metzger in Charlesworth, *Old Testament Pseudepigrapha,* vol. 1.

9. See 4 *Ezra* 13:5-57.

10. One of the occasions in which Jesus referred to himself as the Son of Man reveals a significant difference between Jesus' conception of the Son of Man and that of his Jewish contemporaries. When a paralyzed man was presented before him for healing, Jesus stunned his audience by saying, "My son, your sins are forgiven" (Mark 2:5). His assumption of the authority to forgive sins upset the religious officials in the crowd, who accused Jesus of blasphemy. He responded by asking, "Why do you raise such questions in your hearts? Which is easier, to say to the paralytic, 'Your sins are forgiven,' or to say, 'Stand up and take your mat and walk'? But so that you may know that the Son of Man has authority on earth to forgive sins"—he said to the paralytic—"I say to you, stand up, take your mat and go to your home" (Mark 2:8-11, NRSV). In this case, Jesus not only referred to himself as the Son of Man but also claimed to be able to forgive sins, an action reserved for God alone. Like the Son of Man the Jews expected, Jesus rendered judgment with divine authority. But, unlike his Jewish antecedent, Jesus the Son of Man used his authority not to condemn, but to forgive. He came to fulfill Jewish hopes for the Son of Man, but in unexpected ways.

11. Peter wasn't the only one to be confused by Jesus' talk of the suffering Son of Man. In the hours before his death, Jesus said, "The hour has come for the Son of Man to be glorified" (John 12:23, NRSV). But, Jesus explained, he will be glorified, not at first by assuming his position in the heavenly court, but by being lifted up on the

cross, thus drawing all people to himself through his death. The crowd was understandably perplexed. They asked, "How can you say that the Son of Man must be lifted up? Who is this Son of Man?" (John 12:34, NRSV).

12. See Isaiah 53:2-3.

13. Other passages in the Gospels that associate the Son of Man with death include Matthew 12:40; 17:12; Mark 10:33.

14. See John 12:32-33.

15. See Matthew 25:31, for example.

16. See Matthew 24:36.

17. See Matthew 26:52: "Those who use the sword will be killed by the sword."

18. Charles Wesley, "And Can It Be That I Should Gain?" public domain.

Chapter 7

1. See Luke 4:16-30.

2. See 2 Samuel 2:4.

3. See Exodus 29:1-7; 1 Kings 19:16; 1 Chronicles 16:22; 29:22.

4. See Psalm 2:1-8.

5. See Jeremiah 31, for example.

6. See Ezekiel 34:23-24; 37:24-25. He is also described as a "righteous Branch" (Jeremiah 23:5), an offshoot from the stump of David.

7. See Isaiah 61:4-6.

8. This belief is found in the *Rule of the Community,* a manual describing life among the Jews who lived at Qumran (1QS 9:11-12).

9. *Psalms of Solomon* 17:21-22,26,32. Translation by R. B. Wright, in *The Old Testament Pseudepigrapha,* vol. 2, ed. James H. Charlesworth (Garden City, N.Y.: Doubleday, 1985).

10. Josephus, *Jewish Antiquities,* in William Whiston, ed. and trans., *The Works of Josephus,* New Updated Edition (Peabody, Mass.: Hendrickson, 1987), 17.10.5-10. Electronic text prepared by OakTree Software Specialists.

11. Josephus, *Jewish Antiquities,* 17.10.10.

12. See Luke 4:22-30.

13. See Mark 14:61-62, for example.

14. See Matthew 16:20.

15. See Luke 24:26,46. The phrase "Jesus Christ" also appears in Jesus' prayer in John 17.

16. See Matthew 5:39. See also his statement that "those who use the sword will be killed by the sword" (Matthew 26:52).

17. See Mark 11:15-17; 13:2.

18. See Matthew 24:14; Mark 13:10. Jesus even predicted that the Gentiles would receive the kingdom of God more positively than would the Jewish people (Matthew 21:33-43).

19. See Luke 4:18.

20. For a further discussion of the political implications of Jesus' ministry, see John Howard Yoder, *The Politics of Jesus*, 2nd ed. (Grand Rapids: Eerdmans, 1994).

21. Text from Handel's *Messiah*. See Revelation 11:15.

22. Elie G. Kaunfer, "Rabbi's Death Throws Some into Confusion," *Boston Globe* (13 June 1994): 4. Allan Nadler, "The Lubavitchers' Power and Presposterous Messianism," *The New Republic* (4 May 1992).

23. See especially Isaiah 52:7-10 and 53:4-10.

24. See 2 Corinthians 5:16-21.

25. See Romans 6:10,23; Galatians 3:28; Colossians 1:20.

26. See 1 Corinthians 15:6.

27. See Luke 24:44-46.

28. See Isaiah 53:10-12.

29. See 1 Corinthians 15:20-23.

30. See 1 Corinthians 15:24-26.

31. See Acts 2:14-36.

32. See John 14:27.

33. Matthew Bridges and Godfrey Thring, "Crown Him with Many Crowns," public domain.

34. Joseph Scriven, "What a Friend We Have in Jesus," public domain.

Chapter 8

1. The moving story of Beck Weathers can be found in a number of sources. Two of the best are Jon Krakauer, *Into Thin Air* (New York: Villard, 1998); and Beck Weathers, *Left for Dead: My Journey Home from Everest* (New York: Villard, 2000).

2. See Ephesians 2:1-10.

3. When God protected David from being killed by King Saul, for example, David celebrated by singing, "I will call on the LORD, who is worthy of praise, for he saves me from my enemies" (2 Samuel 22:4). The chief paradigm of salvation in the Old Testament is the Exodus from Egypt. After God finally set his people free from the Egyptians, they praised him with a song: "The LORD is my strength and my might, and he has become my salvation" (Exodus 15:2, NRSV).

4. See Isaiah 52:7-10.

5. See Isaiah 38:16-20; Jeremiah 17:14; Psalm 91:16.

6. See Psalm 6:4-5.

7. See Isaiah 52:7-10.

8. See Judges 2:16; 3:9; 2 Kings 13:5; Psalm 72:4.

9. See Isaiah 49:6, 56:6-7; Jeremiah 3:17; Daniel 7:14.

10. See Genesis 3, also Psalm 8 and Romans 8.

11. See Genesis 2:15-17.

12. See Colossians 2:14.

13. See Hebrews 2:17; 4:14-15; 9:7. According to Jesus, one seeking forgiveness of sins did not need to journey to Jerusalem to make atoning sacrifices because Jesus himself could forgive sins with divine authority (Mark 2:1-12).

14. Quotation from the *San Francisco Chronicle,* final ed., News (17 December 1985): 8.

15. See Weathers, *Left for Dead,* 57-61.

16. If you are looking for evidence that the resurrection of Jesus did in fact happen, you might begin with the fine book by Lee Strobel, *The Case for Christ* (Grand Rapids: Zondervan, 1998).

17. See Weathers, *Left for Dead,* 61-7.

18. These citations from ancient inscriptions are found in *"sozo, soter, soteria, soterios,"* by Ceslas Spicq, O.P., *Theological Lexicon of the New Testament,* translated by James D.

Ernest (Peabody, Mass.: Hendrickson Publishers, 1994). Electronic text by OakTree Software, Inc., version 1.2.

19. It's possible, as we saw in chapter 6, that the Son of Man began to take on some divine characteristics in Jewish speculation. But it would go beyond the evidence to say that Jews considered the Son of Man to be divine in any strong sense.

20. The following chapters on Jesus as Lord (chapter 9) and Jesus as the Word Incarnate (chapter 11) will explore the divinity of Jesus in greater depth.

21. See Weathers, *Left for Dead,* 290-1.

22. "Heidelberg Catechism," Question 32, in Philip Schaff, ed., David Schaff, rev., *The Creeds of Christendom,* vol. 3 (Grand Rapids: Baker, reprint 1983), 318.

23. Bernard de Clairvaux (1001–1153), "O Sacred Head, Now Wounded," translation by James Waddell Alexander, public domain.

Chapter 9

1. See Ephesians 2:8.

2. 2 Peter 3:18 (NRSV), emphasis added.

3. See Mark 7:28, for example.

4. See Matthew 18:21.

5. See Mark 11:3, for example. At one point in his ministry Jesus does imply that his lordship is more than human. "Later, as Jesus was teaching the people in the Temple, he asked, 'Why do the teachers of religious law claim that the Messiah will be the son of David? For David himself, speaking under the inspiration of the Holy Spirit, said, "The LORD said to my Lord, Sit in honor at my right hand until I humble your enemies beneath your feet." Since David himself called him Lord, how can he be his son at the same time?' " (Mark 12:35-37). This passage may have encouraged early Christians to see Jesus as Lord in a divine sense. But it is the exception to the rule found elsewhere throughout the Gospels. See I. Howard Marshall, "Jesus as Lord: The Development of the Concept," in I. Howard Marshall, *Jesus the Savior* (Downers Grove, Ill.: InterVarsity, 1990), 204-6.

6. Since Jews in the time of Jesus would not say God's name, *Yahweh,* wherever this word appeared in the Hebrew Scriptures, they would say *adonai,* or the Hebrew word for *Lord,* instead. The same would be true of the Aramaic word *mar.*

7. See the discussion of C. F. D. Moule, *The Origin of Christology* (London: Cambridge University Press, 1977), 41.

8. For God as healer, see Isaiah 35:5-6; 42:6-7. For God as the one who alone has the right to forgive, see Jeremiah 31:34; Mark 2:6-7.

9. N. T. Wright makes this point throughout his writings.

10. John Train, "Crazy Salad," *Harvard Magazine* (March–April 1994): 22.

11. "Letter from Apion to Epimachos," in John L. White, *Light from Ancient Letters* (Philadelphia: Fortress, 1986), 159-160.

12. The references in this paragraph can be found in "Roman Imperial Cult," by Donald L. Jones, in *Anchor Bible Dictionary* (New York: Doubleday, 1992).

13. *Martyrdom of Polycarp* 8:2. In Kirsopp Lake, ed. and trans., *The Apostolic Fathers*, vol. 2 (Cambridge: Harvard, 1976).

14. See Exodus 34:14.

15. See 2 Thessalonians 1:11.

16. See Hebrews 4:15-16.

17. See Romans 12:1-2.

Chapter 10

1. See the Nicene Creed (A.D. 381) and the Symbol of Chalcedon (A.D. 451) in Philip Schaff, ed., David Schaff, rev., *The Creeds of Christendom*, vol. 2 (Grand Rapids: Baker, reprint 1983), 57-65.

2. See Isaiah 43:6.

3. See the Wisdom of Solomon 2:13,16, NRSV.

4. See the Wisdom of Solomon 2:17-18, NRSV.

5. See also Isaiah 61:1.

6. See Isaiah 49:1-6; 53:1-12.

7. See Mark 1:11.

8. In the Lord's Prayer, the English phrase "Our Father" is rendered as *abba* in Aramaic.

9. See Romans 8:15; Galatians 4:6. Paul's use of *abba* in these Greek letters suggests not only Paul's knowledge that Jesus encouraged his followers to address God in this way but also his familiarity with this practice in the Greek-speaking Galatian and Roman churches.

10. See Hebrews 4:15.

11. See Isaiah 52–53.

12. See Isaiah 42:1. See also the discussion in chapter 6 of this book, Jesus as the Son of Man.

13. See Luke 15:11-32.

14. The idea of the "prodigal father" was first suggested to me through the writing of Helmut Thielicke, *The Waiting Father: Sermons on the Parables of Jesus,* trans. John Doberstein (New York: Harper, 1959).

Chapter 11

1. See 2 Samuel 24:11, for example.

2. Wisdom of Solomon 7:24-26, NRSV.

3. Wisdom of Solomon 9:1-2, NRSV.

4. Sirach 24:6-8, NRSV.

5. See Sirach 24:10, NRSV.

6. See Exodus 26.

7. Baruch 3:35-37, NRSV.

8. Baruch 4:1-2, NRSV.

9. See Proverbs 8:22-30.

10. See Wisdom of Solomon 7:26; Proverbs 16:22, NRSV.

11. See John 1:9-12.

12. Sirach 24:8,10, NRSV.

13. Similar language is found in the epistle to the Hebrews, where God has created the universe "through the Son," the one who "reflects God's own glory" (Hebrews 1:2-3).

14. This suggestion has also been made by other scholars, especially Ben Witherington III in *Jesus the Sage: The Pilgrimage of Wisdom* (Minneapolis: Fortress, 1994). Witherington briefly summarizes his own results in *The Jesus Quest,* 2nd ed. (Downers Grove, Ill.: InterVarsity, 1997), 185-94.

15. Sirach 6:18-19,24-26,28,30, NRSV.

16. Sirach 24:19-20, NRSV.

17. See John 15:11; 14:27.

18. See John 1:18.
19. See Genesis 12–25.
20. See Exodus 3.
21. See John 1:14-17.
22. Lyrics by John Francis Wade, verse 3 and chorus of "O Come All Ye Faithful," public domain.

Chapter 12

1. See Luke 2:25-26.
2. See Psalm 26:8; Isaiah 60:1-20.
3. See Genesis 1:1-3.
4. See Genesis 1:14-15.
5. See Exodus 3:1-2; 13:21.
6. See Numbers 6:25, NIV; Psalm 67:1.
7. See Psalm 27:1.
8. See John 1:5.
9. See Matthew 6:1-6.
10. This quotation comes from a helpful overview of Elizabeth Fry's life: Danny Day, "Brutality Behind Bars," *Christian History*, 53 (1997), 39-40.
11. See 2 Corinthians 5:21.
12. See Matthew 28:20; John 14:12-14.
13. See 1 Corinthians 13:12.

Appendix

1. Dan Brown, *The Da Vinci Code* (New York: Doubleday, 2003). See my review of this novel at www.markdroberts.com/htmfiles/archives/ 12.21.0312.27.03.htm#davinci.
2. Found at www.beliefnet.com.
3. William E. Phipps, *Was Jesus Married? The Distortion of Sexuality in the Christian Tradition* (New York: Harper & Row, 1970).
4. For more on this idea, see chapter 2 of this book.

5. See Luke 8:2-3.

6. See Luke 10:38-42.

7. See Luke 8:2-3.

8. See Luke 10:38-42.

9. See Luke 8:1-3.

10. See Luke 8:2.

11. See Mark 15:40.

12. See John 20:1-18.

13. See Luke 7:36-50.

14. The nonbiblical writings that mention Mary Magdalene can be found in several published sources. Many of the noncanonical gospels are part of the collection of documents found at Nag Hammadi in Egypt. Translations of these texts can be found in James M. Robinson, ed., *The Nag Hammadi Library in English: Revised Edition* (San Francisco, Calif.: HarperSanFrancisco, 1990). Other noncanonical gospels can be found in *New Testament Apocrypha: Vol 1: Gospels and Related Writings,* ed. Wilhelm Schneemelcher, trans. R. McL. Wilson, rev. ed. (John Knox Press, 2003). These documents also can be accessed online. Peter Kirby has provided links to the noncanonical gospels at his helpful Early Christian Writings Web site. See www.earlychristianwritings.com/.

15. *The Gospel of Thomas* appears in *The Nag Hammadi Library;* and online at www.earlychristianwritings.com/thomas.html.

16. All translations of *The Gospel of Thomas* by T. O. Lambdin in *The Nag Hammadi Library.*

17. This gospel can be found in *New Testament Apocrypha;* and online at www.earlychristianwritings.com/gospelpeter.html.

18. This gospel appears in the *The Nag Hammadi Library;* and online at www.earlychristianwritings.com/dialoguesavior.html.

19. Trans. Harold W. Attridge in *The Nag Hammadi Library.*

20. This gospel can be found in *The Nag Hammadi Library;* and online at www.earlychristianwritings.com/sophia.html.

21. Trans. Douglas M. Parrott, *The Nag Hammadi Library.*

22. Found in *New Testament Apocrypha;* and online at www.earlychristianwritings.com/pistis.html.

23. This and other quotations of *The Pistis Sophia* translated by Carl Schmidt and Violet MacDermott, found at www.earlychristianwritings.com/pistis.html.

24. *The Gospel of Mary* is in the *The Nag Hammadi Library;* online at www.earlychristian-writings.com/gospelmary.html. I quote here from the translation of George W. MacRae and R. McL. Wilson in the *The Nag Hammadi Library.*

25. *The Gospel of Philip* appears in the *The Nag Hammadi Library;* online at www.earlychristianwritings.com/gospelphilip.html. All quotations are translated by Wesley W. Isenberg in the *The Nag Hammadi Library.*

26. See Philemon 1:17.

27. See Mark 9:2-8.

28. See Acts 1:9.

29. I have written about these very things in my book *Dare to Be True.* See Mark D. Roberts, *Dare to Be True: Living in the Freedom of Complete Honesty* (Colorado Springs, Colo.: WaterBrook Press, 2003).

30. Mark 3:33-35.

31. See Ephesians 5:21-33.

For more information about the author and his books, visit www.markdroberts.com.